MW00514016

THE BENCH GUIDE TO

LANDLORD & TENANT DISPUTES

IN

NEW YORK

THIRD EDITION

Hon. Stephen L. Ukeiley

Suffolk County
District Court Judge

EMMA S. CLARK MEMORIAL LIBRARY
Setauket, L.I., New York 11733

© 2017 Stephen L. Ukeiley
All rights reserved
ISBN: 978-0-9840432-3-1

For authorization to photocopy, contact Thomas A. O'Rourke, Esq., at Bodner & O'Rourke, 425 Broadhollow Road, Melville, New York 11747, or by telephone at (631) 249-7500. Please outline the specific material requested, the purpose and format of the requested usage and the number of copies you wish to distribute.

This publication is designed to provide accurate information regarding the subject matter contained herein. This publication is not a solicitation of legal advice nor should it be construed by the user in any manner as providing legal, accounting or other professional advice or service. This publication is not a substitute for the advice of an attorney or other professional. If you require legal or other expert advice, you should seek the service of a competent attorney and/or other professional.

If you would like to inquire about this publication or place an order, please visit www.benchguideny.com.

"You never really understand a person until you consider things from his point of view ..."

Atticus Finch in *To Kill a Mockingbird*
by Harper Lee

INTRODUCTION

The bedrock of our legal system is the pursuit of justice in a neutral forum where the laws are applied indiscriminately and without favor. This pursuit, in conjunction with the fair-minded goal of thoughtful yet expedient resolutions to housing disputes, is on display everyday in courthouses throughout the State of New York. Notwithstanding these guiding principles, one of the more difficult tasks asked of the Court is to authorize the eviction of an individual or longstanding community business.

With more than 340,000 Landlord and Tenant proceedings commenced each year in New York, the Courts are inundated with Landlords and Tenants—the majority of whom are unfamiliar with the Courts' procedures and protocols. *The Bench Guide to Landlord & Tenant Disputes in New York (Third Edition)*© ("Bench Guide" or "Third Edition") continues to be part of the effort to inform and educate those who find themselves embroiled in this highly specific and technical area of law. The Third Edition is a complete reprint with hundreds of new citations, additional affirmative defenses, an expanded discussion on predicate notices and updated Appendices, to name just a few of the additions.

The Third Edition takes the reader through each stage of a Landlord and Tenant summary proceeding from inception to post-judgment applications and emergency stays. Significant time is spent identifying and analyzing the routine, and not so routine, issues that arise in the Housing Parts, both procedurally and substantively. Possible resolutions and remedies to common issues are addressed, with a focus on practical experience. Actual cases and fact patterns are utilized both for their informational and anecdotal effect.

Whether a practitioner, member of the Judiciary, law student or a litigant, the Bench Guide is a practical, informative and useful resource. The idea for the Bench Guide originated with my creation of an outline for quick reference while on the Bench. The outline has been transformed into this portable, user-friendly Bench Guide that I continue to use today.

An undertaking such as this cannot be performed by one person alone. I have and continue to receive input from my colleagues, practitioners and Court personnel which makes for lively debate and discussion. In addition, my Landlord and Tenant Law students, the next generation of attorneys, continue to provide tremendous inspiration.

I express my unequivocal appreciation and respect for my colleagues and friends, the Honorable C. Randall Hinrichs, Suffolk County District Administrative Judge, the Honorable Richard I. Horowitz, Court of Claims Judge and Acting Suffolk County Supreme Court Justice, and the Honorable Karen Kerr, Supervising Judge of the Suffolk County District Court, who have always offered encouragement and support. Special thanks to Patrick McCormick, Esq. and Jeffrey Fried, Esq., Associate Court Attorney, Trial Part, for their friendship, extraordinary efforts and the invaluable wealth of knowledge they possess regarding Landlord and Tenant Law. My gratitude and appreciation to my friend and colleague Phil Gallo, Esq., Associate Court Attorney, who is an instrumental resource in the courtroom. My gratitude and special thanks to Touro Law Center's Associate Deans Rodger Citron (Academic Affairs) and Myra Berman (Experiential Learning), who have always been supportive and gracious in sharing their vast experiences in the law. Further appreciation to Nicole Berkman, Esq., Marissa Luchs Kindler, Esq., Michele Rosenblatt, Esq., and Matthew Walker, Esq. for their dedicated efforts and thoughtful contributions. Finally, my appreciation to all of the dedicated clerks, Court office personnel and Court Officers whose commitment and professionalism truly make the courtroom a functioning forum for the resolution of legal disputes.

This book is dedicated to my beautiful wife and best friend Cynthia and our two wonderful children. I also thank my parents, Richard and Dorothy, my brother Scott, and my entire family who are always supportive of all of my endeavors.

Respectfully,
Hon. Stephen L. Ukeiley
Suffolk County District Court Judge

FOREWORD

The stakes in landlord-tenant disputes are extraordinarily high. On one side, you may have a landlord, dependent on rents to feed her family, and whose property is her sole asset. On the other, you may have a tenant, literally fighting to maintain the roof over his head.

Landlord-tenant law is complex, nuanced, often fact-specific, and ever changing due to new legislation, regulations or appellate court rulings. Those variables are compounded by the fact that a great many of the litigants appear without benefit of an attorney, which deprives the litigants of legal representation and the court the opportunity to hear from learned counsel. There is very little margin for error—and the consequences of error are potentially life-altering.

Since the very first edition, *The Bench Guide to Landlord & Tenant Disputes in New York* has been the bible for those presiding over and practicing in Landlord-Tenant Court—an everything-you-need-to-know-but-didn't-immediately-know-where-to-look-guide for our busy judges, practitioners, law students and litigants. Dog-eared copies reside in every single town and village Justice Court in the state, as well as countless judicial chambers, law offices and legal libraries.

The key to its success—and the fact that this is the third edition is testament to its success—is, I believe, not only in its completeness, but its readability. This is a *practical* resource designed and written for busy people who need an answer and need it now.

Judge Ukeiley tells us in one volume what we need to know about the sometimes arcane mechanics of rent control and stabilization, the gradation between possession and title, the dollars and cents of money judgments and how and when attorney fees come into play. It covers claims and counterclaims, discovery and defenses, procedures and protocol—and the interplay of Social Service Law and New York's Real

Property Actions and Proceedings Law.

Landlord-Tenant Law can be a legal minefield. Judge Ukeiley's guidebook helps us navigate the obstacles and hazards, with the ultimate goal of ensuring fairness for the hundreds of thousands of property owners and occupants who seek justice in New York's courts each year.

Hon. A. Gail Prudenti
Interim Dean, Maurice A. Deane School of Law
at Hofstra University
and former Chief Administrative Judge of the Courts
of the State of New York

ABOUT THE AUTHOR

The Honorable Stephen L. Ukeiley is in his second term as a duly elected Suffolk County District Court Judge. Judge Ukeiley has sat in every Part of the District Court, and has presided over in excess of 75,000 civil and criminal matters to completion, including more than 16,000 Landlord and Tenant summary proceedings. In 2014, he was appointed by the Chief Administrative Judge of the State of New York, the Honorable A. Gail Prudenti (retired), to Acting County Court Judge, and, in that capacity, served as the Presiding Judge of Suffolk County's Human Trafficking Court.

Judge Ukeiley is an adjunct professor of law at both the Touro College Jacob D. Fuchsberg Law Center and the New York Institute of Technology. He frequently lectures before judges and attorneys throughout the State, and has had the honor of lecturing on numerous occasions at the New York State Judicial Institute in White Plains, and the New York State Magistrate Association's conferences in Albany, Lake Placid, New York City, Niagara Falls and Syracuse. Judge Ukeiley is an active member of multiple Bar Associations, including his hometown Suffolk County Bar Association, where he co-Chairs the Landlord and Tenant Law Committee and authors a regular column in *The Suffolk Lawyer*. In 2014, *The Bench Guide to Landlord & Tenant Disputes in New York (Second Edition)©* was distributed to every Town and Village Justice Court in New York.

Judge Ukeiley is the former Principal Law Clerk to the Honorable E. Thomas Boyle, United States Magistrate Judge for the Eastern District of New York (retired), and the Honorable Richard I. Horowitz, New York State Court of Claims Judge and Acting Suffolk County Supreme Court Justice. Judge Ukeiley also served on the Board of Directors of the Suffolk County Women's Bar Association, and has been honored with numerous

Recognition Awards for exemplary service and commitment to continuing legal education programs.

Prior to taking the Bench, Judge Ukeiley was a partner at a Long Island law firm and a Court-appointed arbitrator. Judge Ukeiley earned his Juris Doctor from Hofstra Law School, where he was the Editor-in-Chief of the Hofstra Labor Law Journal, and his Bachelor of Arts from Rutgers University.

TABLE OF CONTENTS

JURISDICTION
OF THE COURT

The Housing Parts that hear Landlord and Tenant cases throughout New York State are highly specialized Courts.[1] The scope of jurisdiction in these proceedings is limited and non-expandable even with the consent of the parties.

The authority to preside over residential and commercial Landlord and Tenant disputes is set forth in the Uniform District Court Act,[2] Uniform City Court Act,[3] New York City Civil Court Act[4] and Uniform

---

1 JACK B. WEINSTEIN, HAROLD L. KORN & ARTHUR R. MILLER, CPLR Manual § 1.04(q) (David L. Ferstendig ed. 2010). Throughout this Bench Guide, the terms "Housing Part" and "Court" are used interchangeably in reference to the designated parts within the State Courts that have jurisdiction over Landlord and Tenant matters. The term "Housing Court", although perhaps more readily recognized, is actually a misnomer because there are "no separately designated" Courts called "Housing Courts" within the State of New York. *See id.* However, in New York City, the judges presiding within the Housing Parts are referred to as Housing Court Judges. N.Y. CITY CIV. CT. ACT § 110(e) (McKinney 2009). Although most New York judges presiding over Landlord and Tenant disputes are elected to the Bench, Housing Court Judges are appointed by the State's Chief Administrative Judge for a renewable term of five (5) years from a list of candidates recommended by the Housing Court Advisory Council.

2 N.Y. UNIFORM DIST. CT. ACT § 204 (McKinney 2009).

3 N.Y. UNIFORM CITY CT. ACT § 204 (McKinney 2009).

4 N.Y. CITY CIV. CT. ACT § 204. In the New York City Civil Courts, residential and commercial Landlord and Tenant disputes are heard in separate courtrooms. *See* 32-05 Newtown Ave. Assocs., LLC v. Caguana, 22 N.Y.S.3d 139 (App. Term, 2d, 11ᵗʰ & 13ᵗʰ Jud. Dists. 2015) (dismissing residential eviction proceeding commenced in commercial Housing Part); Artykova v. Avramenko, 953 N.Y.S.2d 811 (App. Term, 2d, 11ᵗʰ & 13ᵗʰ Jud. Dists. 2012) (dismissing proceeding brought in commercial Housing Part to recover residential property).

Justice Court Act.[5] Although the Supreme Court and County Court have concurrent jurisdiction over these proceedings,[6] the majority of cases are commenced in the local Courts specifically created to resolve Landlord and Tenant disputes in an expeditious and efficient manner.[7]

Where there are multiple litigations pending, there is a presumption against staying the Housing Part proceeding because the Landlord is "entitled by statute to an expeditious determination of its claim that it is wrongfully being denied possession".[8] This is particularly the case where the claims asserted in the Supreme Court could have been adjudicated in the Housing Part.[9] The Supreme Court may remove a summary proceeding from the Housing Part to join an existing Supreme Court action where common issues of law and/or fact are raised and there is no resulting prejudice.[10]

The District Courts are similar to many local Courts having both criminal and civil jurisdiction. The District Courts are exclusively

---

5 N.Y. UNIFORM JUST. CT. ACT § 204 (McKinney 2009). *See, e.g.*, Burke v. Aspland, 56 A.D.3d 1001, 867 N.Y.S.2d 759 (App. Div., 3d Dep't 2008); MTC Commons, LLC v. Millbrook Training Ctr. & Spa, Ltd., 31 N.Y.S.3d 922 (App. Term, 9th & 10th Jud. Dists. 2016).

6 Extell Belnord LLC v. Uppman, 113 A.D.3d 1, 976 N.Y.S.2d 22 (App. Div., 1st Dep't 2013); Chelsea 18 Partners, LP v. Mak, 90 A.D.3d 38, 933 N.Y.S.2d 204 (App. Div., 1st Dep't 2011); Carter v. Levian, Index No. 15757-10, 2010 WL 4809274, at *3, 2010 N.Y. Misc. LEXIS 5660, at *4 (Nassau Cnty. Sup. Ct. Nov. 12, 2010).

7 N.Y. JUD. CT. ACTS LAW vol. 29, pts. 2-3 (McKinney 2009). The local Courts were created by the State Legislature with a series of laws passed during a four (4) year period. The New York City Civil Court Act was enacted in 1962, and took effect in 1963; the Uniform District Court Act became law in 1963; the Uniform City Court Act became law in 1964, and took effect in 1965; and the Uniform Justice Court Act became law in 1966, and took effect in 1967. All four (4) statutes were amended in 1989. *See id.*

8 2094-2096 Boston Post Rd., LLC v. Mackies Am. Grill, Inc., Index No. 2023-15, 2016 WL 3083340, 2016 N.Y. Misc. LEXIS 1975 (App. Term, 9th & 10th Jud. Dists. May 25, 2016); DiStasio v. Macaluso, 16 N.Y.S.3d 791 (App. Term, 9th & 10th Jud. Dists. 2015) (error to stay summary proceeding pending the conclusion of Respondent's matrimonial action).

9 *2094-2096 Boston Post Rd., LLC*, 2016 WL at 3083340, 2016 N.Y. Misc. LEXIS at 1975; *DiStasio*, 16 N.Y.S.3d at 791.

10 *See* Rogin v. Rogin, 90 A.D.3d 507, 936 N.Y.S.2d 109 (App. Div., 1st Dep't 2011) (granting removal to join Supreme Court action, in part, because the Plaintiff-Tenant "[s]eeks an equitable remedy, an injunction, which the [Housing Part] cannot grant"). *Cf.* Winters v. Rokoszak, 94 A.D.3d 1009, 943 N.Y.S.2d 122 (App. Div., 2d Dep't 2012) (denying removal application made on the eve of the hearing because the Housing Part is "[t]he preferred forum for the resolution of landlord-tenant disputes").

situated on Long Island, and more specifically, in Nassau County, and in each of the five (5) western Towns of Suffolk County—Babylon, Brookhaven, Huntington, Islip and Smithtown. As a result of having multiple District Court courthouses within the five (5) western Towns of Suffolk County, proceedings to regain possession of real property must be commenced in the District Court located within the Town where the property is located.[11]

A proceeding to regain possession of property in New York City must be commenced in the New York City Civil Court within the same county where the property is located.[12] Proceedings regarding properties situated in cities outside New York City must be commenced within the designated City Court,[13] and the Justice Courts may hear cases regarding properties situated within their particular municipalities.[14]

A. RENT CONTROL AND RENT STABILIZATION

The reader should be mindful that certain residential properties, both within and outside New York City, are governed by rent control and stabilization laws.[15] Rent regulation was the government's response to a "[s]evere housing shortage following World War II"[16] and was intended "to prevent speculative, unwarranted and abnormal increases in rents".[17] Historically, rent control laws were originally enacted, and rent

---

11   N.Y. UNIFORM DIST. CT. ACT § 303 (McKinney 2009).

12   N.Y. CITY CIV. CT. ACT § 303.

13   N.Y. UNIFORM CITY CT. ACT § 204 (McKinney 2009).

14   N.Y. UNIFORM JUST. CT. ACT § 204 (McKinney 2009).

15   The New York State Division of Homes and Community Renewal ("DHCR") has authority, *inter alia*, to regulate the rents of rent controlled and stabilized apartments and resolve disputes in an administrative proceeding independent of the Courts.

16   Rent Stabilization Ass'n of N.Y.C., Inc. v. New York State Div. of Hous. and Cmty. Renewal, 83 N.Y.2d 156, at 164, 608 N.Y.S.2d 930, 932 (1993). The New York City Rent Stabilization Law has been held constitutional under the Takings, Contracts, Due Process and Equal Protection Clauses of the United States Constitution. *See* Harmon v. Markus, Index No. 1126-10, 2011 WL 782233, 2011 U.S. App. LEXIS 4629 (2d Cir. March 8, 2011), *cert. denied*, Harmon v. Kimmel, 132 S.Ct. 1991 (2012).

17   Georgetown Unsold Shares, LLC v. Ledet, 130 A.D.3d 99, 12 N.Y.S.3d 160 (App. Div., 2d

stabilization laws thereafter followed within and outside New York City in 1969 and 1974, respectively.[18]

Rent control laws limit the amount of rent that may be charged and impose restrictions on evictions.[19] These laws apply to residential dwellings built prior to February 1947 in locations that have adopted such provisions, including New York City and sections of Albany, Erie, Nassau and Westchester counties.[20] On the other hand, rent stabilization laws generally impact residential buildings with six (6) or more apartments either built between February 1, 1947 and December 31, 1973, or for buildings constructed prior to February 1, 1947, where the Tenant took possession after June 30, 1971.[21] Outside New York City, rent stabilization is authorized by the Emergency Tenant Protection Act ("ETPA") and is applicable within sections of Nassau, Rockland and Westchester counties.[22]

Dep't 2015).

18 *Id.*

19 In denying Landlord's application to deregulate a New York City rent-controlled apartment based on the occupants' income surpassing the $175,000 minimum threshold for two (2) consecutive years (*see* Rent Regulation Reform Act of 1993, § 5), the Appellate Division, First Department held that the income of any individual occupant, in this particular case the Respondent's husband, may <u>not</u> be included in the income computation where that individual vacated the premises prior to the Landlord's service of an Income Certification Form. *See* Brookford, LLC v. New York State Div. of Hous. and Comm. Renewal, 142 A.D.3d 433, 36 N.Y.S.3d 39 (App. Div., 1st Dep't 2016).

20 *See* CITY RENT AND REHABILITATION LAW, N.Y. UNCONSOL. LAW §§ 26-401 to 26-415 (McKinney 2000) (rent control within New York City); EMERGENCY HOUSING RENT CONTROL LAW, N.Y. UNCONSOL. LAW §§ 8581 to 8597 (McKinney 2002) (rent control outside New York City).

21 RENT STABILIZATION LAW, N.Y. UNCONSOL. LAW §§ 26-501 to 26-520 (McKinney 2000) (rent stabilization within New York City). *See generally* Robrish v. Watson, 26 N.Y.S.3d 216 (App. Term, 2d, 11th & 13th Jud. Dists. 2015) (housing accommodation for 10 rooms in a residence built prior to 1974 is subject to rent stabilization). A "housing accommodation" is defined as the "part of any building or structure, occupied or intended to be occupied by one or more individuals as a residence, home, dwelling unit or apartment". *See* RENT STABILIZATION CODE ("RSC") [9 N.Y.C.R.R.] § 2520.6(a).

22 Emergency Tenant Protection Act, N.Y. Unconsol. Law §§ 8621 to 8634 (McKinney 2007) (rent stabilization outside New York City). *See generally* New York State Homes and Community Renewal website, at http://www.nyshcr.org/rent/about.htm for a discussion regarding the application and enforcement of rent control and stabilization laws in New York.

In New York City, the Rent Guidelines Board ("NYCRGB") determines rent increases for rent stabilized apartments, lofts, hotels and single room occupancies. For rent stabilized apartments and lofts, during the most recent year of this publication, the NYCRGB imposed a zero percent (0%) increase for one-year and a two percent (2%) increase for two-year lease renewals between October 1, 2016 and September 30, 2017.[23]

The Appellate Courts have routinely upheld the forfeiture of rent decontrol provisions and the deregulation of rent-stabilized apartments in New York City.[24] Moreover, the Court of Appeals has permitted class actions for rent overcharge claims where the Tenants waived the right to recover nonmandatory statutory penalties (i.e., treble damages).[25]

B. SUMMARY PROCEEDINGS

The Housing Parts conduct summary proceedings which are "special proceeding[s] governed entirely by statute and it is well established that there must be strict compliance with the statutory requirements to give the court jurisdiction".[26] Two (2) types of cases comprise the overwhelming majority of Landlord and Tenant summary proceedings: non-payment and holdover proceedings. It is incumbent upon the Landlord, referred to as the Petitioner in a summary proceeding,

---

23   See NYCRGB Order No. 48, June 27, 2016. A copy of the Order may be obtained at the New York City Rent Guidelines Board website, www.nycrgb.org.

24   See, e.g., Roberts v. Tishman Speyer Props., L.P., 13 N.Y.3d 270, 890 N.Y.S.2d 388 (2009); 73 Warren St., LLC v. New York Div. of Hous. and Cmty. Renewal, 96 A.D.3d 524, 948 N.Y.S.2d 2 (App. Div., 1st Dep't 2012). Cf. Todres v. W7879, LLC, 137 A.D.3d 597, 26 N.Y.S.3d 698 (App. Div., 1st Dep't 2016) (holding that the property owners did not fraudulently scheme to deregulate the premises).

25   See Borden v. 400 E. 55th St. Assocs., L.P., 24 N.Y.3d 382, 998 N.Y.S.2d 729 (2014). The factors to consider in certifying a class are (1) the class size and if joining all of the members is practical; (2) whether there are common questions of law or fact pertaining to the class that exceed questions that impact only individual class members; (3) are the claims or defenses typical of the class; (4) are the representative parties capable of adequately protecting the interest of the class; and (5) whether a class action is the preferred method to achieving a just result. Id.; see CPLR § 901(a).

26   Riverside Syndicate, Inc. v. Saltzman, 49 A.D.3d 402, 852 N.Y.S.2d 840 (App. Div., 1st Dep't 2008) (citations omitted).

to commence the proper type of proceeding.[27] It should be noted that strict adherence to procedure is required.

Petitioners in both non-payment and holdover proceedings seek to regain "possession" of the subject premises.[28] As a result, the occupant must be in physical possession of the premises when the summary proceeding is commenced. Otherwise, the Court is without subject matter jurisdiction.[29]

A significant distinction between non-payment and holdover proceedings is that the former presupposes the parties have a valid Landlord and Tenant relationship, and the latter presupposes that a valid Landlord and Tenant relationship does not exist when the summary proceeding is commenced.[30] There are various subcategories of holdover proceedings, but the common element is that notwithstanding whether there once was a Landlord and Tenant relationship, the parties do not have such a relationship when the holdover proceeding is commenced.

C. THE HOUSING PART DETERMINES "POSSESSION" AS OPPOSED TO "TITLE"

In a Landlord and Tenant summary proceeding, the Court has jurisdiction to determine who is entitled to "possession". The Court further has the authority to terminate a Landlord and Tenant relationship by issuing a judgment of possession and a warrant of eviction.[31] The warrant of eviction is the instrument that authorizes the eviction.

The Housing Parts may not grant declaratory and/or injunctive relief, other than staying enforcement of the judgment and warrant of

---

27 *See, e.g.,* Whalen v. Veltre, Index No. 1679-00, 2002 WL 655293, 2002 N.Y. Misc. LEXIS 278 (App. Term, 9th & 10th Jud. Dists. Jan. 31, 2002).

28 *See* 36 Main Realty Corp. v. Wang Law Office, PLLC, 19 N.Y.S.3d 654 (App. Term, 2d, 11th & 13th Jud. Dists. 2015) (non-payment proceeding).

29 Jah Jeh Realty Corp. v. Staten Is. Univ. Hosp.-EAP, 839 N.Y.S.2d 433 (App. Term, 2d & 11th Jud. Dists. 2007).

30 *See* Predicate Notices *infra*, Chapter 3.

31 *See* N.Y. REAL PROPERTY ACTIONS AND PROCEEDINGS LAW ("RPAPL") § 749(3) (McKinney 2008).

eviction.[32] The Court's limited authority to determine "possession", as opposed to "title" or "ownership", is significant because there have been occasions where the parties have a legitimate dispute over the identity of the rightful owner. As a general matter, the parties retain the right to litigate "ownership" in the Supreme Court notwithstanding the outcome of the summary proceeding.[33] As with many rules, there is a notable exception that will be addressed later.[34]

D. MONEY JUDGMENTS

In addition to a judgment of possession and a warrant of eviction, a prevailing Landlord may be awarded a money judgment without regard to amount because the Court's maximum dollar jurisdictional limit does not apply to summary proceedings.[35] Although RPAPL § 711(2) authorizes the right to maintain a non-payment proceeding, RPAPL §§ 741(5) and 747(4) allow for the recovery of rent.[36] To enforce the money judgment, the Landlord must obtain a transcript of judgment which may be filed with the County Clerk's Office. Article 52 of the CPLR sets forth the appropriate mechanisms for enforcing the money judgment.[37]

Under common law, rent was not earned "until the end of the rental period".[38] However, as a practical matter, the parties typically

---

32 *See* London Paint & Wallpaper Co., Inc. v. Kesselan, 138 A.D.3d 632, 30 N.Y.S.3d 90 (App. Div., 1st Dep't 2016).

33 *See generally* Barsyl Supermarkets, Inc. v. Avenue P Assocs., LLP, 86 A.D.3d 545, at 548, 928 N.Y.S.2d 45, 48 (App. Div., 2d Dep't 2011) (action seeking declaratory judgment may not be decided by the Housing Part).

34 *See* Affirmative Defenses *infra*, Chapter 8 subdiv. H.

35 N.Y. CITY CIV. CT. ACT § 204 (McKinney 2009); N.Y. UNIFORM CITY CT. ACT § 204 (McKinney 2009); N.Y. UNIFORM DIST. CT. ACT § 204 (McKinney 2009); N.Y. UNIFORM JUST. CT. ACT § 204 (McKinney 2009). *See, e.g.*, MTC Commons, LLC v. Millbrook Training Ctr. & Spa, Ltd., 31 N.Y.S.3d 922 (App. Term, 9th & 10th Jud. Dists. 2016) (summary proceeding commenced in Justice Court).

36 *36 Main Realty Corp.*, 19 N.Y.S.3d at 654.

37 Cantalupo Constr. Corp. v. 2319 Richmond Terr. Corp., 34 N.Y.S.3d 616 (App. Div., 2d Dep't 2016) (civil contempt generally not available to enforce money judgment obtained in summary proceeding).

38 Eujoy Realty Corp. v. Van Wagner Comms., LLC, 22 N.Y.3d 413, 981 N.Y.S.2d 326 (2013)

negotiate an earlier "earned" date by agreeing that the rent is to be paid on a date certain prior to the last day of the term, typically the 1st day of each month. In other words, the Tenant's debt accrues when the rent is due.[39]

A Tenant may <u>not</u> recover rent paid "in advance" where the lease is terminated early unless otherwise agreed.[40] Moreover, the obligation to pay previously accrued rent is <u>not</u> impacted by the early termination.[41]

1. RENT AND USE AND OCCUPANCY

The term "rent" refers to the agreed dollar amount to occupy property pursuant to a rental agreement. The term "use and occupancy" refers to the fair and reasonable value to occupy the property in the absence of a rental agreement.[42] Even though "rent" and "use and occupancy" may be identical, the terms are <u>not</u> interchangeable.[43]

Unless waived by agreement, the Landlord may pursue use and occupancy in a plenary action for the days the Tenant remained in possession following entry of the judgment and warrant of eviction.[44] Where the lease expired and the Tenant remains in possession without entering into a new agreement, use and occupancy need <u>not</u> be demonstrated

---

(citations omitted).

39 *Id.*

40 1251 Ams. Assoc. II, L.P. v. Rock 49th Rest. Corp., 831 N.Y.S.2d 360 (App. Term, 1st Dep't 2006).

41 *Eujoy Realty Corp.*, 22 N.Y.3d at 413, 981 N.Y.S.2d at 326 (where the rental agreement required payment of the annual rent on January 1st, the Tenant's termination of the lease on January 8th did not negate its obligation to pay the full year's rent).

42 *London Paint & Wallpaper Co., Inc.*, 138 A.D.3d at 632, 30 N.Y.S.3d at 90.

43 *See generally* Madden v. Juliet, 13 N.Y.S.3d 850 (App. Term, 9th & 10th Jud. Dists. 2015) (in small claims action, awarding use and occupancy for the 16 days the Tenant remained in possession following lease termination, or 16/30 of the monthly rent); Young v. Carruth, 89 A.D.2d 466, at 466-67, 455 N.Y.S.2d 776, 777 (App. Div., 1st Dep't 1982) (staying enforcement of award pending appeal "on condition that appellant pay to petitioner for use and occupancy an amount equal to the rent stipulated in the lease"); Sap V/Atlas 845 WEA Assocs. NF LLC v. Jannelli, 918 N.Y.S.2d 691 (App. Term, 1st Dep't 2010) (occupants permitted to remain in possession provided they pay use and occupancy "identical to the rent they had been paying").

44 Rustagi v. Sanchez, 999 N.Y.S.2d 798 (App. Term, 2d, 11th & 13th Jud. Dists. 2014).

through the testimony of a licensed realtor or appraiser, but rather may be assessed in an amount equal to the rent set forth in the expired lease.[45]

The distinction between "rent" and "use and occupancy" is further significant in defining the parties' relationship. In a non-payment proceeding, the Landlord seeks, among other relief, unpaid rent. In a holdover proceeding, the Landlord generally will <u>not</u> make a claim for rent (other than prior rent arrears) because the tenancy either ended or a Landlord and Tenant relationship never existed.

2. RULE AGAINST APPORTIONMENT

It is well-established that the "rule against apportionment" applies to rent, but <u>not</u> use and occupancy.[46] This means that the Tenant is liable for the full month's rent when the lease is terminated prior to the end of the month. On the other hand, use and occupancy is "apportioned" by awarding a prorated amount, or other equivalent, for the precise number of days the Tenant remained in possession without a rental agreement.[47] For example, if the monthly rent was $300, equivalent to $10 per day, and the Tenant remained in possession for ten (10) days following the termination of the lease, then the Landlord would be entitled to use and occupancy in the amount of $100. As stated previously, the Landlord may bring a plenary action to recover use and occupancy "[w]hich accrued after entry of a final judgment in a summary proceeding".[48]

3. ADDITIONAL RENT

In addition to unpaid rent and/or use and occupancy, the money judgment may include, without regard to amount, items identified within a written lease as "added" or "additional" rent. These items typically include, but are not limited to, utilities, late fees and reasonable attorney's fees.

---

45 *See* Vanchev v. Mulligan, Index No. 2350-14, 2016 WL 4021103, 2016 N.Y. Misc. LEXIS 2759 (App. Term, 2d, 11th & 13th Jud. Dists. July 13, 2016); Siodlak v. Light, 31 N.Y.S.3d 924 (App. Term, 9th & 10th Jud. Dists. 2016).

46 Priegue v. Paulus, 988 N.Y.S.2d 525 (App. Term, 9th & 10th Jud. Dists. 2014).

47 *See, e.g.*, *Vanchev*, 2016 WL at 4021103, 2016 N.Y. Misc. at LEXIS 2759.

48 *See Rustagi*, 999 N.Y.S.2d at 798.

The requirement that an item is defined within a written lease as "added" or "additional" rent to be awarded in a summary proceeding is strictly enforced.[49] For example, where the rental agreement provides that a prevailing Landlord is entitled to attorney's fees but fails to identify the fees as "additional" or "added" rent, then the fees may <u>not</u> be awarded in a summary proceeding.[50] Instead, the Landlord may seek the attorney's fees in a separate plenary action for damages in the Civil Part of the Court or other court of competent jurisdiction.[51] On the other hand, if attorney's fees are defined as "additional" rent but the Petitioner fails to request them in the summary proceeding, then they may <u>not</u> be obtained in a subsequent plenary action because that "[w]ould constitute an improper splitting of a cause of action".[52]

Expenses identified as "additional" or "added" rent that are not incurred at the time of the hearing are <u>not</u> recoverable.[53] The reader

---

49 *See generally* Fairview Hous., LLC v. Dickens, 972 N.Y.S.2d 143 (App. Term, 9th & 10th Jud. Dists. 2013) (attorney's fees); 33 Fifth Ave. Owners Corp. v. 33 Fifth Endo, LLC, 17 N.Y.S.3d 386 (App. Term, 1st Dep't 2015) (sublet surcharge unrecoverable where it was not listed in lease as "part of the 'rent' "); Saunders St. Owners, Ltd. v. Broudo, 936 N.Y.S.2d 61 (App. Term, 2d, 11th & 13th Jud. Dists. 2011) (sublet fees).

50 RPAPL § 741(5); *see* Henry v. Simon, 890 N.Y.S.2d 369 (App. Term, 9th & 10th Jud. Dists. 2009); Binghamton Hous. Auth. v. Douglas, 217 A.D.2d 897, at 897-98, 630 N.Y.S.2d 144 (App. Div., 3d Dep't 1995); Acierno v. Faldich, 782 N.Y.S.2d 509, 509-10 (App. Term, 9th & 10th Jud. Dists. 2004).

51 If the disputed amount arises from the same transaction that was or could have been adjudicated in the summary proceeding, then the Landlord may be barred from pursuing the claim in a plenary action. *See* See Why Gerard, LLC v. Gramro Entm't Corp., 94 A.D.3d 1205, 941 N.Y.S.2d 350 (App. Div., 3d Dep't 2012); *see generally* Blue Point Townhouse Owners Ass'n, Inc. v. Kapsokefalos, 129 A.D.3d 1267, 11 N.Y.S.3d 341 (App. Div., 3d Dep't 2015) (challenge of homeowners' association dues precluded where the issue could have been raised in prior action).

52 *Acierno*, 782 N.Y.S.2d at 509-10; Diba Family Ltd. P'ship v. Ross, Index No. 14-CV-4337, 606 Fed. Appx. 628, 2015 U.S. App. LEXIS 9274 (2d Cir. June 4, 2015); Landmark Props. v. Olivo, 62 A.D.3d 959, at 961, 881 N.Y.S.2d 110 (App. Div., 2d Dep't 2009).

53 40 Rector Owner LLC v. City of New York, 137 A.D.3d 700, 29 N.Y.S.2d 282 (App. Div., 1st Dep't 2016) ("[n]o indication that plaintiff incurred any attorneys' fees" regarding re-letting the premises); Madden v. Juliet, 13 N.Y.S.3d 850 (App. Term, 9th & 10th Jud. Dists. 2015) (inadequate proof attorney's fees were paid); Inland Diversified Real Estate Serv., LLC v. Keiko New York, Inc., 36 N.Y.S.3d 407 (App. Term, 9th & 10th Jud. Dists. 2016) (Petitioner must demonstrate the utilities were "actually paid"); Walden Ctr. Assocs., L.P. v. Cardenas, 930 N.Y.S.2d 177 (App. Term, 9th & 10th Jud. Dists. 2011) (painting, cleaning and re-letting charges).

should be mindful that a general catch-all lease provision which states "all costs the Tenant is obligated to incur pursuant to the lease are deemed 'additional rent' " has been upheld even where the specific lease provision omits the necessary "added" rent language.[54] The Landlord is generally required to submit a copy of the rental agreement to demonstrate entitlement to "additional" rent items.[55]

a. ATTORNEY'S FEES

The Court maintains limited discretion to deny a prevailing Landlord's request for attorney's fees based on "equitable considerations and fairness".[56] However, this discretion should be exercised only "where bad faith is established on the part of the successful party or where unfairness is manifest".[57]

Any permissible award must be reasonable and just. In determining the reasonableness of a request for attorney's fees, the Court may consider "counsel's testimony and records as to the nature, extent and necessity of the legal services rendered on landlord's behalf in the [summary] proceeding".[58] The Housing Part may only award attorney's fees incurred in the summary proceeding, and not those fees related to a separate action.[59]

A lease provision that provides for the recovery of Landlord's

---

54 *See Inland Diversified Real Estate Serv., LLC*, 36 N.Y.S.3d at 407. The summary proceeding was dismissed for other reasons, namely, the Landlord's failure to introduce the bills, or other proof, demonstrating payment was made. *Id.*

55 Oakwood Terr. Hous. Corp. v. Monk, 36 N.Y.S.3d 48 (App. Term, 9th & 10th Jud. Dists. 2016); *see also* Evans v. Tracy, 951 N.Y.S.2d 85 (App. Term, 9th & 10th Jud. Dists. 2012) (denying award of attorney's fees where Landlord failed to produce the rental agreement); Halpern v. Tunne, 966 N.Y.S.2d 346 (App. Term, 2d, 11th & 13th Jud. Dists. 2012) (same).

56 *See* Greenbrier Garden Apts. v. Eustache, 31 N.Y.S.3d 921 (App. Term, 9th & 10th Jud. Dists. 2016).

57 *Id.* (attorney's fees denied where Landlord misapplied earmarked rent payments and failed to respond to Tenant's request for information).

58 600 Realty Heights, LLC v. Paula-Molina, 26 N.Y.S.3d 216 (App. Term, 1st Dep't 2015); 125-127 Allen St. Assocs. v. Lin, 26 N.Y.S.3d 214 (App. Term, 1st Dep't 2015); APF 286 Mad LLC v. RIS Real Props., Inc., 13 N.Y.S.3d 849 (App. Term, 1st Dep't 2015).

59 Hawthorne Gardens Owners Corp. v. Jacobs, 17 N.Y.S.3d 382 (App. Term, 9th & 10th Jud. Dists. 2015).

attorney's fees merely for maintaining a summary proceeding, regardless of the outcome, is an unenforceable penalty.[60] This is because only a prevailing party is entitled to recover attorney's fees pursuant to a rental agreement.[61] The fact that the Housing Part may have stayed execution of the warrant of eviction does <u>not</u> change the Petitioner's status as the prevailing party.[62]

The Court is <u>not</u> bound by a lease provision that sets forth the amount of attorney's fees to be awarded to the prevailing Landlord,[63] and the fee agreement between counsel and his or her client is <u>not</u> determinative.[64] Moreover, a prevailing Landlord may <u>not</u> recover attorney's fees directly against a Subtenant, unless contractually agreed otherwise,[65] and a Landlord may <u>not</u> recover the fees incurred defending an unrelated Supreme Court action.[66]

---

60   *See* Weidman v. Tomaselli, 365 N.Y.S.2d 681, 691 (Rockland Cnty. Ct.), *aff'd*, 386 N.Y.S.2d 276 (App. Term, 9th & 10th Jud. Dists. 1975).

61   *See generally Madden*, 13 N.Y.S.3d at 850 (holding where the money judgment was approximately one-third less than the amount claimed, "it cannot be said that [Petitioner] was the prevailing party"); 4702 Chiel Kurtz Realty, LLC v. Molano, 947 N.Y.S.2d 757 (App. Term, 2d, 11th & 13th Jud. Dists. 2012) (holding neither party prevailed where the money judgment was reduced by approximately one-third due to the Landlord's breach of the warranty of habitability).

62   *600 Realty Heights, LLC*, 26 N.Y.S.3d at 216.

63   *See* Queens Fresh Meadows, LLC v. Newberry, 2 N.Y.S.3d 310 (App. Term, 2d, 11th & 13th Jud. Dists. 2014).

64   338 W. 46th St. Realty, LLC v. Leonardi, 930 N.Y.S.2d 177 (App. Term, 1st Dep't 2011).

65   *See* Oakdale Manor Owners, Inc. v. Raimondi, 29 N.Y.S.3d 848 (App. Term, 9th & 10th Jud. Dists. 2015).

66   40-50 Brighton First Rd. Apts. Corp. v. Henderson, 27 N.Y.S.3d 310 (App. Term, 2d, 11th & 13th Jud. Dists. 2015).

b. LATE FEES

An exorbitant late fee may <u>not</u> be enforced.[67] For residential properties, it has been held that a five percent (5%) per month late fee is "unreasonable and confiscatory in nature and therefore unenforceable".[68] Similarly, a $5.00 per day late fee, amounting to seventeen percent (17%) of the monthly rent, was found "unreasonable, excessive and unconscionable".[69]

More recently, the Appellate Term for the Ninth and Tenth Judicial Districts held that a ten percent (10%) late fee, which was clearly disproportionate to the Landlord's monetary losses, was an unenforceable penalty.[70] Further, a lease provision that provided for a rent "discount", which essentially amounted to a late fee and penalty, was rejected by the Court.[71]

To be awarded, the late fee must stem from actual damages sustained as a result of the late payment of rent.[72] For example, if the Landlord is late in making a mortgage payment due to the Tenant's failure to pay the rent in a timely manner, and, as a consequence, the lender imposes a penalty on the Landlord, then the Landlord may recoup a reasonable late fee identified within the rental agreement as "additional" rent.

---

67 *See* Sandra's Jewel Box, Inc. v. 401 Hotel, L.P., 273 A.D.2d 1, at 3, 708 N.Y.S.2d 113 (App. Div., 1st Dep't 2000) (late charge of 365% per annum not recoverable); Mateikis v. Rebmann, Index No. 687-10, 2010 WL 3483918, 2010 N.Y. Misc. LEXIS 4226 (Canandaigua City Ct. July 15, 2010) (60% late fee unenforceable). *See also* Brenner v. General Plumbing Corp., 13 N.Y.S.3d 849 (N.Y. Civ. Ct. 2015) ("This court seeks to be crystal clear that the late fee provision, standing alone, is not unconscionable").

68 943 Lexington Ave., Inc. v. Niarchos, 373 N.Y.S.2d 787 (App. Term, 1st Dep't 1975). *See also* 67-26 Dartmouth St. Corp. v. Silberman, N.Y.L.J., April 2, 1996, at 30, col. 1 (App. Term, 2d & 11th Jud. Dists. 1996) (holding late fee of 5% per month is unenforceable).

69 Rock v. Klepper, 885 N.Y.S.2d 713 (Plattsburgh City Ct. 2009).

70 Wilsdorf v. Fairfield Northport Harbor, LLC, 950 N.Y.S.2d 494 (App. Term, 9th & 10th Jud. Dists. 2012); Diversified Equities, LLC v. Russell, 31 N.Y.S.3d 920 (App. Term, 2d, 11th & 13th Jud. Dists. 2016) (holding a 13% late fee was "excessive and grossly disproportionate to any damages" sustained due to the late payment of rent).

71 Park Haven, LLC v. Robinson, 3 N.Y.S.3d 286 (App. Term, 2d, 11th & 13th Jud. Dists. 2014).

72 *See* Brenner, 13 N.Y.S.3d at 849; Jacob v. Sealey, 28 N.Y.S.3d 648 (App. Term, 1st Dep't 2015) (on appeal, the money judgment was amended to include a $50 late fee); Nu Horizons Manor v. Adderly, 951 N.Y.S.2d 87 (Suffolk Cnty. Dist. Ct. 2012); Spring Valley Gardens Assocs. v. Earle, 447 N.Y.S.2d 629 (N.Y. Civ. Ct. 1982).

With regard to commercial leases, late fee provisions of two percent (2%), four percent (4%) and five percent (5%) have been upheld.[73] However, the Court may consider whether the award is unreasonable or against public policy.[74]

c. RECIPROCAL ATTORNEY'S FEES

Another significant principle of Landlord and Tenant Law is governed by Real Property Law ("RPL") § 234 which involves the situation where a residential lease provides for the award of a prevailing Landlord's attorney's fees, but does not include similar relief for a prevailing Tenant. According to RPL § 234, the lease is deemed to contain a reciprocal provision for the Tenant's attorney's fees (and expenses) should the Tenant prevail in the summary proceeding or the Landlord fails to perform its obligations under the lease.[75]

The purpose of the statute is to dissuade unscrupulous Landlords from engaging in improper conduct while offering an incentive to expeditiously resolve Landlord and Tenant disputes.[76] As a general matter, Courts are disinclined to add a provision "the parties have neglected to specifically include" within a clear and unambiguous negotiated agreement.[77] However, RPL § 234 is clear and prevailing Tenants have recov-

---

73   See 23 E. 39th St. Mgmt. Corp. v. 23 E. 39th St. Developer, 134 A.D.3d 629, 23 N.Y.S.3d 33 (App. Div., 1st Dep't 2015) (2% late fee); K.I.D.E. Assocs., Ltd. v. Garage Estates Co., 280 A.D.2d 251, 720 N.Y.S.2d 114 (App. Div., 1st Dep't 2001) (5% late fee); Goidel & Siegel, LLP v. 122 E. 42nd St., LLC, Index No. 101979-11, 2012 N.Y. Misc. LEXIS 5949 (N.Y. Cnty. Sup. Ct. Dec. 27, 2012) (4% late fee), rev'd on other grounds, 2016 WL 6106888, 2016 N.Y. App. Div. LEXIS 6799 (App. Div., 1st Dep't Oct. 20, 2016); Old Country Rd. Realty, LP v. Zisholtz & Zisholtz, LLP, Index No. 2181-16, 2016 WL 5396005, 2016 N.Y. Misc. LEXIS 3392 (Nassau Cnty Dist. Ct. Sept. 26, 2016) (5% late fee).

74   See K.I.D.E. Assocs., Ltd., 280 A.D.2d at 251, 720 N.Y.S.2d at 114; Goidel & Siegel, LLP, 2012 N.Y. Misc. LEXIS at 5949.

75   N.Y. REAL PROPERTY LAW § 234 (McKinney 2006); see, e.g., Inwood Ventura, LLC v. Ferraira, 7 N.Y.S.3d 242 (App. Term, 1st Dep't 2014).

76   See 251 CPW Hous. LLC v. Pastreich, 124 A.D.3d 401, at 404, 1 N.Y.S.3d 32, 36 (App. Div., 1st Dep't 2015); Marsh v. 300 W. 106th St. Corp., 95 A.D.3d 560, 943 N.Y.S.2d 525 (App. Div., 1st Dep't 2012).

77   Vermont Teddy Bear Co., Inc. v. 538 Madison Realty Co., 1 N.Y.3d 470, at 475, 775 N.Y.S.2d 765 (2004) (internal citations omitted). See W.W.W. Assocs., Inc. v. Giancontieri, 77 N.Y.2d 157, at 162, 565 N.Y.S.2d 440 (1990).

ered attorney's fees in accordance with its terms. The Tenant may be entitled to interest on the fees awarded.[78]

A common issue for the Court to resolve is whether the Landlord's one-sided attorney's fee provision is sufficiently broad to fall within the ambit of RPL § 234. It appears that where the lease explicitly provides for the recovery of attorney's fees "in any action or summary proceeding," a successful Tenant may prevail on its counterclaim for attorney's fees.[79]

For example, the Appellate Division, Second Department awarded the Tenant attorney's fees where the lease provided the Landlord was entitled to recover attorney's fees to recover possession and re-rent the premises.[80] The Appellate Division emphasized that an award of attorney's fees is to be determined on a case-by-case basis following "[a] review of the complete lease provision at issue, within the context of the lease...."[81]

Similar to a prevailing Landlord's request, the Court may deny a prevailing Tenant's counterclaim for attorney's fees where the award is "[m]anifestly unfair or where the successful party engaged in bad faith".[82] In *251 CPW Hous. LLC v. Pastreich*, the Appellate Division, First Department affirmed the Tenant's award of attorney's fees, but denied that portion of the fees related to an Article 78 proceeding and a

---

78 Queens Fresh Meadows, LLC v. Newberry, 2 N.Y.S.3d 310 (App. Term, 2d, 11ᵗʰ & 13ᵗʰ Jud. Dists. 2014) (*citing* Nestor v. Britt, 270 A.D.2d 192, 707 N.Y.S.2d 11 (App. Div., 1ˢᵗ Dep't 2000)).

79 Bunny Realty v. Miller, 180 A.D.2d 460, at 461, 579 N.Y.S.2d 952 (App. Div., 1ˢᵗ Dep't 1992); Stephen, LLC v. Zucchiatti, 890 N.Y.S.2d 371 (N.Y. Civ. Ct. 2009).

80 Casamento v. Juaregui, 88 A.D.3d 345, at 354-55, 929 N.Y.S.2d 286, 292-93 (App. Div., 2d Dep't 2011), *rev'g*, 907 N.Y.S.2d 99 (App. Term, 2d, 11ᵗʰ & 13ᵗʰ Jud. Dists. 2010); *see* Graham Ct. Owners Corp. v. Taylor, 24 N.Y.3d 742, 5 N.Y.S.3d 348 (2015); *Marsh*, 95 A.D.3d at 560, 943 N.Y.S.2d at 525; *but see* Hamilton v. Menalon Realty, LLC, 829 N.Y.S.2d 400, 402-03 (App. Term, 2d & 11ᵗʰ Jud. Dists. 2006) (lease provision unenforceable); Fragiacomo v. Pugliese, 816 N.Y.S.2d 826, 827-28 (App. Term, 9ᵗʰ & 10ᵗʰ Jud. Dists. 2006). *See also* 303 E. 37ᵗʰ Sponsors Corp. v. Goldstein, 918 N.Y.S.2d 400 (App. Term, 1ˢᵗ Dep't 2010) (denying reciprocal right to attorney's fees where the lease was in contravention of the New York City Rent Stabilization Code).

81 *Casamento*, 88 A.D.3d at 361-62, 929 N.Y.S.2d at 298.

82 *251 CPW Hous. LLC*, 124 A.D.3d at 401, 1 N.Y.S.3d at 32.

New York State Division of Housing and Community Renewal hearing because RPL § 234 "does not extend to these types of proceedings".[83] Moreover, the fees incurred for unsuccessful motion practice in the Appellate Court may be deducted from the award.[84]

The dismissal of a summary proceeding "without prejudice" may result in the denial of Tenant's attorney's fees because there has been no final adjudication from which it may be determined that the Tenant was the prevailing party.[85] Although the Tenant may commence a plenary action for attorney's fees or other relief, the reader should be mindful that the principle of res judicata necessitates a dismissal where the claim was previously adjudicated in the summary proceeding.[86]

Interestingly, in *Maplewood Mgmt., Inc. v. Best*, a prevailing Tenant who was represented by a governmentally funded agency, and, thus, had no obligation to pay for the legal services rendered, was awarded attorney's fees pursuant to the statute.[87] The Appellate Division, Second Department held that "[i]t would significantly thwart the accomplishment of the Legislature's intent…if the courts were to hold that the statute requires those landlords who have brought meritless eviction proceedings to pay for their tenant's attorneys' fees only when the tenant himself is of sufficient financial ability to afford his own attorney".[88]

4. ACCELERATED RENT AND SURVIVAL CLAUSES

The Housing Part has subject matter jurisdiction over rent arrears,

---

83 *Id.*, 124 A.D.3d at 406, 1 N.Y.S.3d at 38.

84 Megan Holding LLC v. Conason, 18 N.Y.S.3d 579 (App. Term, 1st Dep't 2015).

85 J.P. & Assocs. Props. Corp. v. Krautter, 128 A.D.3d 963, 9 N.Y.S.3d 626 (App. Div., 2d Dep't 2015); *see also* Horatio Arms, Inc. v. Celbert, 972 N.Y.S.2d 813 (App. Term, 1st Dep't 2013) (Tenant's claim for attorney's fees premature where the summary proceeding was dismissed due to improper service).

86 Hodge v. 26 Ct. Assocs., LLC, 28 N.Y.S.3d 648 (App. Term, 2d, 11th & 13th Jud. Dists. 2015).

87 Maplewood Mgmt., Inc. v. Best, 143 A.D.2d 978, 533 N.Y.S.2d 612 (App. Div., 2d Dep't 1988).

88 *Id.*, 143 A.D.2d at 979, 533 N.Y.S.2d at 613. *See also* Blum v. Stenson, 465 U.S. 886, 104 S.Ct. 1541 (1984) (attorney's fees awarded for representation by the Legal Aid Society pursuant to the Civil Rights Attorney's Fees Awards Act of 1976).

but not future rent or future use and occupancy. Thus, a Landlord in a summary proceeding may <u>not</u> be awarded rent or "additional" rent items not yet due even where the lease includes an acceleration clause.

In this regard, the Court considers the "accelerated" rent provision (i.e., a lease provision that states all remaining months' rent and "additional" rent items become immediately due upon termination) to be damages that are <u>not</u> recoverable in a summary proceeding. Unless waived, the Landlord may commence a plenary action in an appropriate court to enforce the acceleration clause.[89] However, if an acceleration clause is omitted from the lease, then the Landlord may still recover these items in a plenary action provided the lease contains a survival clause, but would have to wait each month as they became due.[90]

The omission of a "survival" clause has significant ramifications on the post-lease termination rights of the parties. As a general principle, the termination of the lease results in the cessation of <u>all</u> future rights and obligations under the agreement. An exception exists where the lease states that post-termination, the Tenant continues to remain liable for all "damages" and financial obligations under the rental agreement.[91] Otherwise, any claims that had not yet accrued at the time of termination, including accelerated rent, would be forfeited and unavailable in a subsequent plenary action.[92]

---

89   *See* 172 Van Duzer Realty Corp. v. Globe Alumni Stud. Assist. Assoc., Inc., 102 A.D.3d 543, 959 N.Y.S.2d 39 (App. Div., 1st Dep't 2013) (doctrine of res judicata does <u>not</u> preclude subsequent plenary action because enforcement of acceleration clause is not available in a summary proceeding), *mod. on other grounds*, 24 N.Y.3d 528 (2014); 30 Broadway, LLC v. Grand Centr. Dental, LLP, 96 A.D.3d 934, 947 N.Y.S.2d 545 (App. Div., 2d Dep't 2012); Ross Realty v. V & A Fabricators, Inc., 42 A.D.3d 246, at 250-51, 836 N.Y.S.2d 242 (App. Div., 2d Dep't 2007); Trumbull Equities, LLC v. City.com Media, LLC, 13 N.Y.S.3d 849 (Queens Cnty. Sup. Ct. 2015).

90   Pikoulas v. Hardina, 36 N.Y.S.3d 340 (App. Term, 9th & 10th Jud. Dists. 2016).

91   H.L. Realty, LLC v. Edwards, 131 A.D.3d 573, 15 N.Y.S.3d 413 (App. Div., 2d Dep't 2015) (guarantor liable in plenary action where the lease contained a survival clause and the guaranty was not rescinded in the stipulation of settlement between Landlord and Tenant).

92   Kings Park 8809, LLC v. Stanton-Spain, 26 N.Y.S.3d 725 (App. Term, 2d, 11th & 13th Jud. Dists. 2015); Patchogue Assocs. v. Sears, Roebuck and Co., 951 N.Y.S.2d 314 (App. Term, 9th & 10th Jud. Dists. 2012).

5. DAMAGES ARE NOT RECOVERABLE

The Housing Part may <u>not</u> award a prevailing Landlord "money damages" for property damage caused by the Tenant.[93] Instead, the Landlord reserves the right to commence a plenary action (civil lawsuit) in the civil part of the Court provided the amount sought is within the maximum dollar jurisdictional limit of the Court (i.e., $25,000 exclusive of costs and interest in the New York City Civil Courts; $15,000 exclusive of costs and interest in the District Courts; or $3,000 exclusive of costs and interest in the Justice Courts).[94] Otherwise, the Landlord may commence an action for damages in either the County Court (up to $25,000) or Supreme Court.[95] It is worth repeating, however, that a claim may be precluded where the claim was raised, or reasonably could have been asserted, in the summary proceeding.[96]

E. INTEREST, COSTS AND DISBURSEMENTS

A summary proceeding based upon a breach of a lease agreement "sounds in contract", and, as a result, a prevailing Landlord may be entitled to prejudgment interest.[97] However, where the Landlord failed to deposit the Tenant's rent checks, the right to prejudgment interest (and attorney's fees) is waived.[98]

---

93 RPAPL § 741(5); *Ross Realty*, 42 A.D.3d at 246, 836 N.Y.S.2d at 242; Bedford Gardens Co. v. Silberstein, 269 A.D.2d 445, 702 N.Y.S.2d 884 (App. Div., 2d Dep't 2000); *Kings Park 8809, LLC*, 26 N.Y.S.3d at 725. *See also* Rostant v. Swersky, 79 A.D.3d 456, 912 N.Y.S.2d 200 (App. Div., 1st Dep't 2010) (Housing Part may <u>not</u> award damages to Petitioner-Tenant seeking to be restored to possession). However, as discussed *infra*, Chapter 7, the Housing Part may award damages on a Tenant's counterclaims.

94 *See* Burke v. Aspland, 56 A.D.3d 1001, 867 N.Y.S.2d 759 (App. Div., 3d Dep't 2008).

95 *See* Chelsea 18 Partners, LP v. Mak, 90 A.D.3d 38, 933 N.Y.S.2d 204 (App. Div. 1st Dep't 2011).

96 Maki v. Bassett Healthcare, 141 A.D.3d 979, 35 N.Y.S.3d 587 (App. Div., 3d Dep't 2016); Tovar v. Tesoros Prop. Mgmt., 119 A.D.3d 1127, 990 N.Y.S.2d 307 (App. Div., 3d Dep't 2014).

97 N.Y. CIVIL PRACTICE LAW AND RULES ("CPLR") § 5001(a) (McKinney 2007). *See, e.g.,* Solow v. Wellner, 86 N.Y.2d 582, at 589-90, 635 N.Y.S.2d 132, 135 (1995); APF 286 MAD, LLC v. Chittur & Assocs., P.C., 28 N.Y.S.3d 647 (App. Term, 1st Dep't 2016) (in a holdover proceeding, interest awarded for the time the commercial Tenant remained in possession).

98 B.N. Realty Assocs. v. Lichtenstein, 96 A.D.3d 434, 949 N.Y.S.2d 1 (App. Div., 1st Dep't 2012) (attorney's fees denied).

A prevailing Landlord is further entitled to recover statutory costs and disbursements.[99] The reader should refer to the rules of the particular Court in which the case is pending for information regarding the specific costs and disbursements that may be recovered. Statutory costs include, but are not limited to, a fee for each "necessary" Respondent served, and, if the award is based upon a default, an additional fee may be awarded to secure an affidavit from the process server stating that the Tenant is <u>not</u> presently in the military.[100] The affidavit stating the Tenant is not in the military is required only where the Tenant does <u>not</u> appear in Court. Unlike the affidavit of service for the Notice of Petition and Petition, a non-military affidavit may be filed at any time prior to submitting an application for the issuance of the final judgment and warrant of eviction.[101]

A prevailing Landlord appearing *pro se* is entitled to recover the filing fee for commencing the summary proceeding.[102] However, the filing fee may <u>not</u> be awarded where the Landlord was represented by counsel.

---

99   *See, e.g.,* N.Y. CITY CIV. CT. ACT §§ 1906-a, 1908 (McKinney 2009); N.Y. UNIFORM CITY CT. ACT §§ 1906-a, 1908 (McKinney 2009); N.Y. UNIFORM DIST. CT. ACT §§ 1906-a, 1908 (McKinney 2009); N.Y. UNIFORM JUST. CT. ACT §§ 1903(d),(m), 1908 (McKinney 2009). *But see* CPLR § 1102(d); Boyle v. Bishop, N.Y.L.J., Apr. 25, 1978, at 11, col. 1 (App. Term, 9th & 10th Jud. Dists. 1978) (holding a "poor person" pursuant to CPLR § 1102(d) is <u>not</u> liable for costs).

100   At the time of publication, the amount awarded for the affidavit is $5.00 except in the Justice Courts where the amount is $1.50. *See* CITY CIV. CT. ACT § 1906-a; UNIFORM CITY CT. ACT § 1906-a; UNIFORM DIST. CT. ACT § 1906-a; UNIFORM JUST. CT. ACT § 1903(d),(m).

101   *See* Avgush v. De La Cruz, 924 N.Y.S.2d 307 (App. Term, 9th & 10th Jud. Dists. 2011).

102   *See* Letter to Hon. Matthew T. Crosson, Formal Op. No. 90-F6, 1990 N.Y. Op. Atty. Gen. 25 (August 8, 1990).

CHAPTER 2

TYPES OF SUMMARY PROCEEDINGS

The Housing Parts throughout the State handle a high volume of cases. In 2015, consistent with the most recent five-year trend, 346,714 new Landlord and Tenant proceedings were commenced in the New York City Civil Courts, the City Courts Outside of New York City and the District Courts. During that same year, 323,457 summary proceedings were disposed of by dismissal, discontinuance, default judgment, settlement or hearing.[103]

It is unfortunate that an exceedingly large number of litigants, both Landlords and Tenants, appear in the Housing Parts without counsel. There have been plenty of "winnable" cases on both sides that ultimately were "lost" for no reason other than the *pro se* litigant's lack of familiarity with the applicable legal standards and/or Court procedures. While many litigants are under the mistaken impression that they do not need representation, others, are in the more perilous position of not being able to afford counsel. Regardless of the reason, a litigant appearing in the highly specialized Landlord and Tenant Housing Parts without legal representation is at a distinct disadvantage. Parenthetically, there is no inherent advantage to being unrepresented because all parties are held to the same laws and procedures.

---

103 *See* New York State Unified Court System Caseload Activity Reporting System, Annual Trial Court Trends, Filings in the Trial Courts (2008 - 2015) and Dispositions in the Trial Courts (2008 - 2015), July 2016. These statistics do <u>not</u> include summary proceedings commenced in the Village Justice Courts.

A. NON-PAYMENT AND HOLDOVER PROCEEDINGS

Commencing the wrong type of summary proceeding is a common mistake by Landlords. If a Landlord brings a non-payment proceeding when a holdover proceeding was proper, or vice versa, the proceeding will be dismissed and the Landlord will have to restart the process.

As discussed previously, the primary relief in a summary proceeding is possession and a warrant of eviction, with or without a money judgment. The rules pertaining to non-payment and holdover proceedings apply to both residential and commercial properties, with limited exceptions, as discussed throughout this Bench Guide. Perhaps the most obvious difference between non-payment and holdover proceedings is that the parties in a non-payment proceeding have a valid Landlord and Tenant relationship, typically demonstrated by the existence of a rental agreement, and the Landlord claims the Tenant failed to pay some or all of the rent due pursuant to that agreement.

In a holdover proceeding, the Landlord and Tenant relationship was either terminated or expired at the time the summary proceeding was commenced, or such a relationship never existed. In accordance with RPAPL §§ 711 and 713, the following situations generally lend themselves to holdover proceedings: (1) where the parties had a rental agreement that expired on its own terms and the Tenant remains in possession without paying any additional rent or use and occupancy; (2) where the parties had a rental agreement that was terminated due to a breach of a material condition; (3) where the parties had a month-to-month tenancy that was terminated by the Landlord; (4) where the owner and the occupant entered into a license agreement or tenancy-at-will that the Landlord revoked or terminated, or that expired; (5) where the occupant is a squatter having unlawfully taken possession of the property; (6) where the occupant is a Tenant of a life tenant following the termination of a life estate;[104] and (7) proceedings to regain possession of post-foreclosed properties.

---

104   Novakovic v. Novakovic, 890 N.Y.S.2d 758 (App. Term, 2d, 11th & 13th Jud. Dists. 2009). A life estate is an agreement that provides the occupant exclusive "[p]ossession, control and enjoyment of the property for the duration of his or her life". *Id.* at 759. The Housing Part may <u>not</u> establish the existence of a life estate, but it must entertain the claim as a defense when asserted. Paladino v. Sotille, 835 N.Y.S.2d 799, 802 (App. Term, 9th & 10th Jud. Dists. 2007). For a discussion on life estates, *see infra*, Chapter 8 subdiv. N.

B. THE DIFFERENCE BETWEEN THE "AWARD" AND "ENTRY" OF JUDGMENT

The distinction between the "award" of the judgment, and the Court's "entry" or "issuance" of the judgment, is critical. The "award" occurs when the Court, either following a trial, which is called a hearing in a summary proceeding, or pursuant to a Stipulation of Settlement negotiated by the parties, directs that the Landlord is entitled to regain possession of the premises. The award of the judgment, while necessary, is just one (1) step in a progression of steps required to terminate the tenancy.

In a non-payment proceeding, the tenancy is <u>not</u> terminated until the Court "issues" (i.e., signs) the judgment and warrant of eviction.[105] Following the award, the onus is on the prevailing Landlord to submit the appropriate paperwork to the Clerk of the Court. Although many prevailing parties choose to file the paperwork immediately or within days of the award, the Landlord may do so within a reasonable period of time.[106] The process is not difficult, and, in fact, if the Landlord is not represented by an attorney, in many Courts, the Landlord may simply complete the forms provided by the Clerk and pay the appropriate fee.

Where the Landlord is represented by counsel, the attorney is required to submit a proposed judgment and warrant for the Court's consideration. In some Courts, the Clerk returns the judgment and warrant prepared by counsel after signed by the Judge, with any necessary modifications. In other courts, such as the District Courts, the Clerk prepares the actual judgment.

1. PAYMENT OF ARREARS PRIOR TO ENTRY OF JUDGMENT (NON-PAYMENT PROCEEDINGS)

Where the Landlord prevails in a non-payment proceeding, the Tenant may avoid the eviction and remain in possession by paying

---

105   RPAPL § 749(3); Fisk Bldg. Assocs., LLC v. Shimazaki II, Inc., 76 A.D.3d 468, at 469, 907 N.Y.S.2d 2 (App. Div., 1st Dep't 2010).

106   Typically, a two (2) or three (3) month delay in seeking the judgment may preclude issuance unless an adequate explanation for the delay is provided.

the amount awarded <u>prior</u> to the issuance of the judgment. In fact, the Landlord has no choice but to accept the payment, which stays issuance of the judgment and warrant, thereby effectively ending further action in the summary proceeding.[107] This commonly occurs where the parties acknowledge rent is owed, but the amount is disputed, or where a Tenant seeks to refrain from tendering the rent until the last possible moment.

If the Landlord refuses to accept the payment, the Tenant may deposit the monies with the Clerk of the Court which similarly stays issuance of the judgment and warrant.[108] Although the deposited funds are maintained in an interest bearing account, the amount tendered to the Landlord will be reduced by the applicable Court and/or statutory fees. If the offer to pay the amount awarded is made <u>after</u> the judgment has been issued, then the Landlord may accept the payment and continue to evict the Tenant provided the warrant was not already executed upon and there was no intent to reinstate the tenancy or other good cause is shown.[109]

---

107 *See* New York City Hous. Auth. v. Torres, 61 A.D.2d 681, at 682 n.1, 403 N.Y.S.2d 527, 529 (App. Div., 1st Dep't 1978) (regarding premises within New York City, "[a] timely tender bars entry of final judgment and therefore logically it must bar issuance of a warrant which is based on that final judgment"); Melick v. Ken's Serv. Stat., Inc., Index No. 1281-12, 2014 WL 4251023, 2014 N.Y. Misc. LEXIS 3874 (App. Term, 9th & 10th Jud. Dists. Aug. 21, 2014) (premises situated outside New York City); Peekskill Hous. Auth. v. Quaintance, 864 N.Y.S.2d 668, 669 (App. Term, 9th & 10th Jud. Dists. 2008); *see also* Keita v. Ottman, 946 N.Y.S.2d 67 (App. Term, 2d, 11th & 13th Jud. Dists. 2011) (where the "[f]inal judgment in [the] nonpayment proceeding was satisfied prior to the issuance of the warrant" and the deadline set forth in the parties' settlement, Landlord's motion to restore the case to the calendar for the purpose of scheduling an inquest against the John Doe and Jane Doe was properly denied); Chester Mamaroneck Gardens, L.L.C. v. Riggsbee, 733 N.Y.S.2d 324 (App. Term, 9th & 10th Jud. Dists. 2001) (arrears offered after entering Stipulation of Settlement, but before issuance of judgment). *Cf.* Chelsea Ridge NY, LLC v. Clarke, 983 N.Y.S.2d 201 (App. Term, 9th & 10th Jud. Dists. 2013) (offering to pay less than the full rent owed is <u>not</u> a lawful tender); *see also* Kew Gardens Realty Co. v. Bank, 958 N.Y.S.2d 61 (App. Term, 2d, 11th & 13th Jud. Dists. 2010) (Tenant failed to provide sworn proof the rent arrears were offered prior to the issuance of the final judgment).

108 RPAPL § 751(1) (outside New York City); *see* Sfaelos v. Farrugia, Index No. 912-00, 2002 WL 31415276, 2002 N.Y. Misc. LEXIS 1361 (App. Term, 9th & 10th Jud. Dists. July 5, 2002).

109 *Torres*, 61 A.D.2d at 684, 403 N.Y.S.2d at 527 (payment of rent "*after* issuance of the warrant does not result in automatic vacatur of the warrant") (emphasis in original); J.A.R.

In a holdover proceeding, the Tenant is <u>not</u> afforded a similar opportunity to remain in possession. This is because a holdover proceeding is typically commenced for reasons other than unpaid rent, and the prevailing Landlord, other than for good cause shown, need not be concerned that the proceeding will be dismissed or that the occupant will be permitted to remain in possession merely because the occupant offers the money awarded prior to the issuance of the judgment. For residential properties within New York City, the reader should consider the statutory stays pursuant to RPAPL § 753 which are discussed *infra*, in Chapter 11.

2. ATTORNEY'S FEES ARE NOT RECOVERABLE WHERE ARREARS ARE PAID PRIOR TO THE AWARD OF JUDGMENT

A Landlord in a non-payment proceeding is <u>not</u> entitled to an award of attorney's fees where the Tenant pays the rent arrears, including permissible late fees, <u>prior</u> to the award. Although exceedingly frustrating to many Landlords and counsel, this rule applies where the Tenant offers to pay the full amount of the arrears during the hearing. The Landlord must not only accept the payment, but she is further precluded from recovering attorney's fees in the summary proceeding even where the lease provides for such fees as "additional" rent.[110] The rationale is that in a non-payment proceeding, the payment of rent prior to the "award" means that the Landlord did <u>not</u> prevail with respect to the central relief sought; i.e., a possessory judgment.[111]

Mgmt. Corp. v. Foster, 442 N.Y.S.2d 723, 724 (App. Term, 2d & 11th Jud. Dists. 1980) ("The acceptance of rent [following issuance of the warrant of eviction] does not automatically revive the tenancy and the landlord's intent when he accepts the rent is controlling with respect to this issue"). An application to vacate the warrant pursuant to RPAPL § 749(3), which permits the Court to vacate a warrant of eviction for "good cause" prior to its execution, is addressed to the sound discretion of the Court. *Torres*, 61 A.D.2d at 684, 403 N.Y.S.2d at 527.

110 *See* Babylon Vill. Equities v. Mitchell, 816 N.Y.S.2d 279 (App. Term, 9th & 10th Jud. Dists. 2006); Russell Place Assocs., L.P. v. Hernandez, 958 N.Y.S.2d 648 (Nassau Cnty. Dist. Ct. 2011).

111 *Babylon Vill. Equities*, 816 N.Y.S.2d at 279; ATM Four, LLC v. Demezier, 881 N.Y.S.2d 361 (Nassau Cnty. Dist. Ct. 2009). *Cf.* 1974-76 Lafontaine Ave. Terr. Corp. v. Rogers, 920 N.Y.S.2d 243 (App. Term, 1st Dep't 2010) (holding that Petitioner "substantially prevailed

3. EARMARKED FUNDS

The parties should pay particular attention to the period for which rent is paid. As a general matter, rent payments are applied towards the oldest arrears. However, when the Tenant writes in the memo portion of the check that the payment is to be applied to a particular month, the earmarked funds may only be applied to the designated month or months.[112]

For example, if the rent has <u>not</u> been paid for April, May and June, and then in the middle of June, the Tenant tenders a check equal to one (1) month's rent and designates those funds are to be applied towards the June rent, then the Landlord, if the check is accepted, must apply the payment to the June rent. The significance is that the acceptance of the check precludes the Landlord from recovering a possessory judgment for a prior month's unpaid rent (i.e., April and May).[113] This is because a Landlord is prohibited from obtaining a judgment of possession and warrant of eviction based on the non-payment of rent where a subsequent month's rent has been paid. The Landlord would, however, be permitted to seek a money judgment for the prior months' unpaid rent in a plenary action.

---

on the central issues" where "all rent arrears [were recovered] pursuant to the 'so ordered' stipulation of settlement" <u>following</u> issuance of a possessory judgment and, as a result, Petitioner was entitled to recover attorney's fees).

112   Greenbrier Garden Apts. v. Eustache, 31 N.Y.S.3d 921 (App. Term, 9th & 10th Jud. Dists. 2016); see 270 E. Props., LLC v. Kent, 18 N.Y.S.3d 260 (App. Term, 2d, 11th & 13th Jud. Dists. 2015) (non-payment proceeding dismissed where Landlord applied "clearly intended" rent payments to legal and late fees, which are <u>not</u> considered rent pursuant to Rent Stabilization Code [9 N.Y.R.R.C.] § 2525.1, even where the lease provides otherwise).

113   See Kew Realty Co. v. Charles, N.Y.L.J., June 3, 1998, at 27, col. 2 (App. Term, 2d & 11th Jud. Dists. 1998).

C. CONDITIONAL LIMITATION VS. CONDITION SUBSEQUENT (HOLDOVER PROCEEDINGS)

The difference between a "conditional limitation" and a "condition subsequent" is another nuance of Landlord and Tenant summary proceedings. A holdover proceeding based upon a conditional limitation is permitted.[114] An example of a conditional limitation is a lease provision that provides for the termination of the lease when a certain event occurs.[115] The most frequently encountered example of a conditional limitation is where the lease expires by its own terms on a date certain.[116] Another example is a lease provision that provides in the event of a breach by the Tenant, such as the failure to maintain adequate insurance for the property, the lease automatically terminates upon service of a Notice of Lease Termination. The critical factor is that there is no discretion for the Landlord to terminate the rental agreement, but rather the agreement is automatically terminated upon the occurrence of a triggering event.[117]

This raises the question whether the non-payment of rent may provide a basis for commencing a holdover proceeding. The Appellate Term answered in the affirmative where the residential lease provided that the lease automatically terminates when the rent is not timely paid following service of a default notice.[118] The Court reasoned that because

---

114 *See generally* Nordica Soho LLC v. Emilia, Inc., 992 N.Y.S.2d 600 (App. Term, 1st Dep't 2014).

115 Oakwood Terr. Hous. Corp. v. Monk, 36 N.Y.S.3d 48 (App. Term, 9th & 10th Jud. Dists. 2016).

116 *See generally* Perrotta v. Western Reg'l Off-Track Betting Corp., 98 A.D.2d 1, at 5, 469 N.Y.S.2d 504 (App. Div., 4th Dep't 1983). *See* Robert F. Dolan, Rasch's Landlord and Tenant Including Summary Proceedings § 23:29, at 190-91 (4th ed. 2010).

117 *See* Dolan, *supra* note 116, §§ 23:25 to 23:27, at 184-87; St. Catherine of Sienna Roman Catholic Church v. 118 Convent Assocs., LLC, 988 N.Y.S.2d 405 (App. Term, 2d, 11th & 13th Jud. Dists. 2014) (lease triggering event that gives the Landlord an "option" of terminating the tenancy "creates a condition, and not a conditional limitation . . ., and a holdover summary proceeding cannot be based thereon").

118 *St. Catherine of Sienna Roman Catholic Church*, 988 N.Y.S.2d at 405; Stadt v. Durkin, Index No. 3173-10, 2012 WL 1123068, 2012 N.Y. Misc. LEXIS 1525 (App. Term, 9th & 10th Jud. Dists. April 2, 2012).

the Landlord and Tenant relationship was terminated prior to the commencement of the summary proceeding, a holdover proceeding was proper and the action was "not void as against public policy".[119] The Appellate Term for the First Department reached a similar conclusion with regard to commercial premises.[120]

On the other hand, a holdover proceeding based upon a "condition subsequent" is <u>not</u> permitted. A condition subsequent is a lease provision that gives the Landlord the option of terminating the tenancy if a certain event occurs (e.g., if the Tenant breaches the lease, then the lease is terminated at the discretion of the Landlord). Under these circumstances, a summary proceeding is improper, and the Landlord may instead commence an action for ejectment in the Supreme Court.[121] Parenthetically, the Housing Parts within New York City may conduct ejectment proceedings where the value of the premises is less than or equal to $25,000 at the time the proceeding was commenced.[122]

---

119   *Stadt*, 2012 WL at 1123068, 2012 N.Y. Misc. LEXIS at 1525. However, the Appellate Term held the following year that where the warranty of habitability defense is established in a holdover proceeding, the summary proceeding must be dismissed. *See* Windy Acres Farm, Inc. v. Penepent, 971 N.Y.S.2d 652 (App. Term, 9ᵗʰ & 10ᵗʰ Jud. Dists. 2013).

120   C & A 483 Broadway, LLC v. KLMNI, Inc., 26 N.Y.S.3d 723 (App. Term, 1ˢᵗ Dep't 2015); Great Location N.Y., Inc. v. Seventh Ave. Fine Foods. Inc., 13 N.Y.S.3d 850 (App. Term, 1ˢᵗ Dep't 2015).

121   *See Perrotta*, 98 A.D.2d at 1, 469 N.Y.S.2d at 504; See Why Gerard, LLC v. Gramro Entm't Corp., 907 N.Y.S.2d 103 (Albany City Ct. 2010), *aff'd*, 94 A.D.3d 1205, 941 N.Y.S.2d 350 (App. Div., 3d Dep't 2012); VNO 100 W. 33ʳᵈ St., LLC v. Square One of Manhattan, Inc., 874 N.Y.S.2d 683, 686 (N.Y. Civ. Ct. 2008); South St. Seaport Ltd. P'ship v. Jade Sea Rest., Inc., 573 N.Y.S.2d 568, 569 (N.Y. Civ. Ct. 1991).

122   N.Y. CITY CIV. CT. ACT § 203(j) (McKinney 2009).

CHAPTER 3

PREDICATE NOTICE

In most cases, the Landlord must provide the Tenant with notice of the breach, default or termination of the tenancy, often referred to as predicate notice, prior to commencing a summary proceeding. The failure to serve a proper predicate notice may result in dismissal of the action, and, as a result, another notice would have to be served before filing a new proceeding.[123]

The parties should review both the statutory service provisions and the rental agreement for any specific service requirements. A lease provision specifying the manner and upon whom the notice must be served will generally be enforced.[124] Certain *de minimis* defects in a predicate notice may be waived. For example, an improper description of the subject premises generally does not constitute a jurisdictional defect absent prejudice to the Tenant or a claim that process was misdirected.[125] Below are some of the common predicate notices associated with summary proceedings.

---

123   *See* NRP, LLC II v. El Gallo Meat Mkt., Inc., Index No. 570007-03, 2003 WL 2246974, 2003 N.Y. Misc. LEXIS 1325 (App. Term, 1ˢᵗ Dep't Oct. 17, 2003). *Cf.* 890 Park LLC v. Rosenfeld, 946 N.Y.S.2d 66 (App. Term, 1ˢᵗ Dep't 2011) (non-renewal notice from prior proceeding sufficient because the earlier proceeding "had not been terminated at the time of commencement" and there was no discernible prejudice).

124   *See* 575 Warren St. HDFC v. Barreto, 983 N.Y.S.2d 203 (App. Term, 2d, 11ᵗʰ & 13ᵗʰ Jud. Dists. 2013); 1626 Second Ave., LLC v. Notte Rest. Corp., 880 N.Y.S.2d 225 (N.Y. Civ. Ct. 2008) ("Service of notices must be done in accordance with the lease provisions in order for service to be proper"); White Plains Galleria Ltd. P'ship v. Woodlawn Partners, 791 N.Y.S.2d 874 (White Plains City Ct. 2004).

125   *See* Kit Ming Corp. v. Tsang, Index No. 234-01, 2001 WL 1535465, 2001 N.Y. Misc. LEXIS 564 (App. Term, 1ˢᵗ Dep't June 1, 2001).

A. NON-PAYMENT PROCEEDINGS (ORAL OR THREE-DAY WRITTEN DEMAND)

A Landlord must make a "demand" for the payment of unpaid rent prior to commencing a non-payment proceeding.[126] The demand may be oral or in writing unless the rental agreement provides otherwise. The rental agreement may provide for additional notice as well.

1. ORAL RENT DEMAND

An oral rent demand is governed by RPAPL § 711(2). It is perhaps the simplest of the predicate notice methods because the demand may simply be made by speaking to the Tenant after the rent has become due.[127] There is no obligation for any prior or follow-up writings from the Landlord.

The demand must be decisive and specify the period of time for which unpaid rent is demanded.[128] "Asking" the Tenant about the shortage of rent or "what is the problem?" have been held to be insufficient rent demands.[129] The demand need not, however, include a date certain by which the arrears must be paid.[130]

The Landlord may commence a non-payment proceeding at any time following a proper oral rent demand. The risk to proceeding in this manner is that the Landlord has the burden of proving a proper rent demand was made, and, absent documentary proof of the demand, an oral demand is obviously more susceptible to challenge. The Landlord need not make an additional rent demand for the rent that becomes due following commencement of the non-payment proceeding.[131]

---

126 Oakwood Terr. Hous. Corp. v. Monk, 36 N.Y.S.3d 48 (App. Term, 9th & 10th Jud. Dists. 2016).

127 See 104 Realty LLC v. Brown, 981 N.Y.S.2d 637 (N.Y. Civ. Ct. 2013) (the Landlord may personally make an oral rent demand).

128 See generally Abart Holdings, LLC v. Hall, 791 N.Y.S.2d 867 (App. Term, 1st Dep't 2004).

129 Claire v. Zellner, N.Y.L.J., June 28, 1990, at 29 (App. Term, 9th & 10th Jud. Dists. 1990) (reversing award in favor of Landlord due to inadequate rent demand).

130 Alexander Muss & Sons v. Rozany, 655 N.Y.S.2d 238, 239 (App. Term, 2d & 11th Jud. Dists. 1996).

131 Main Realty Corp. v. Wang Law Office, PLLC, 19 N.Y.S.3d 654 (App. Term, 2d, 11th &

2. WRITTEN RENT DEMAND

The Landlord may instead choose to provide a "Three-Day Written Demand".[132] Unlike an oral demand, the Landlord must wait at least three (3) days <u>after</u> the written demand is served before commencing a non-payment proceeding.[133] The written demand must state that the Tenant is required to pay the unpaid rent, or, alternatively, return possession of the premises.[134] The demand must further specify the period for which rent is owed and the approximate sum of the arrears.[135]

In the absence of a statutory obligation or lease provision stating that the Landlord must make the rent demand, the Landlord's attorney or agent may provide a written demand.[136] Where the rental agreement states that the Landlord must personally terminate the tenancy, the attorney may still make the demand provided the Tenant has knowledge, or reason to know, that the attorney or agent is authorized to act on behalf of the Landlord.[137]

A written rent demand involving residential property must further comport with the Fair Debt Collection Practices Act ("FDCPA") because the non-payment of rent is considered a consumer debt.[138] Although violations may result in a claim against the offending issuer, non-compliance with the FDCPA may <u>not</u> result in dismissal of

---

13th Jud. Dists. 2015).

132   RPAPL §§ 711(2), 735.

133   *See id.* § 711(2).

134   *Id.*

135   H.S. Realty Assocs., Inc. v. Ilagan, 13 N.Y.S.3d 850 (App. Term, 1st Dep't 2015); See Why Gerard, LLC v. Gramro Entm't Corp., 907 N.Y.S.2d 103 (Albany City Ct. 2010), *aff'd,* 94 A.D.3d 1205, 941 N.Y.S.2d 350 (App. Div., 3d Dep't 2012).

136   *See* Kwong v. Eng, 183 A.D.2d 558, at 560, 583 N.Y.S.2d 457 (App. Div., 1st Dep't 1992).

137   Ashley Realty Corp. v. Knight, 73 A.D.3d 500, at 501, 901 N.Y.S.2d 204, 205 (App. Div., 1st Dep't 2010). *Cf.* Siegel v. Kentucky Fried Chicken of Long Island, Inc., 108 A.D.2d 218, at 220, 448 N.Y.S.2d 744, 746 (App. Div., 2d Dep't 1985) ("[a] notice of termination signed by an agent or attorney who is not named in the lease as authorized to act for the landlord in such matters, and which is not authenticated or accompanied by proof of the latter's authority to bind the landlord in giving such notice, is legally insufficient to terminate the tenancy"), *aff'd,* 67 N.Y.2d 792, 501 N.Y.S.2d 317 (1986).

138   *See* 15 U.S.C. § 1692 *et seq.* (2006); Romea v. Heiberger & Assocs., 163 F.3d 111, 115 (2d Cir. 1998).

the summary proceeding.[139] The statute may not be applicable to commercial leases because the FDCPA defines a "consumer" as "any *natural person* obligated or allegedly obligated to pay a debt".[140]

Counsel should be mindful that the FDCPA, which was enacted for the purpose of curtailing unsavory debt collection practices, imposes strict liability on debt collectors for the "false representation of the character, amount, or legal status of any debt".[141] This includes misstatements in a rent demand. In *Lee v. Krucker & Bruh, LLP*, the United States District Court for the Southern District of New York granted partial summary judgment on liability against the Landlord's attorney because the rent demand overstated the amount of past due rent by several hundred dollars.[142] Apparently, counsel relied upon information provided by the building's billing office which inadvertently failed to credit a partial payment. As a result, Landlord's attorney was liable under the FDCPA for damages, plus attorney's fees.

The implementation of suitable procedures to avoid errors in the rent demand may constitute a viable defense to the otherwise strict liability statute.[143] However, in *Lee*, there was no indication that a credible maintenance procedure had been implemented, and, as a result, Landlord's attorney settled the matter for approximately $130,000 ($22,000 in damages and $108,000 in Tenant's attorney's fees).[144]

Unless otherwise specified within the lease, a written rent demand must be served in the same manner as the Notice of Petition and Petition.[145] This means that the written demand may <u>not</u> simply be mailed to the Tenant, whether by overnight delivery or certified mail.

---

139   *See* Dearie v. Hunter, 705 N.Y.S.2d 519, 520 (App. Term, 1st Dep't 2000).

140   15 U.S.C. § 1692a(3) (emphasis added). *See generally* Castillo v. Balsamo Rosenblatt & Cohen. P.C., 930 N.Y.S.2d 789 (N.Y. Civ. Ct. 2011).

141   15 U.S.C. § 1692e(2)(A).

142   958 F. Supp.2d 524 (S.D.N.Y. 2013).

143   *Id.*

144   *See* Josh Barbanel, "Eviction-Case Settlement Worries Landlord Lawyers", THE WALL ST. JOURNAL, at http://www.wsj.com/articles/SB10001424127887323608504579022850361952282, Aug. 20, 2013.

145   *See* RPAPL §§ 711(2), 735.

Rather, the demand must be personally delivered or left with a person of suitable age and discretion or in a conspicuous place following reasonable efforts to ascertain personal delivery. Follow-up mailings by certified and regular mail are further required where the latter two (2) methods are utilized.

3. RENT DEMAND MUST BE TIMELY

If the demand, whether oral or written, is made <u>prior</u> to the rent being late, then the demand is defective, and upon a motion by the Tenant, the proceeding will be dismissed. An issue that stymies many Landlords is that if the rent is due on the 1st of the month, then a demand may not be made until at least the 2nd. This is because unless the lease specifies otherwise, the rent is not considered late until 12:00 a.m. on the 2nd. Accordingly, a rent demand made on the 1st is premature. If a written demand is made, since at least three (3) days notice must be given, the earliest the Landlord would be permitted to file a summary proceeding is the 5th day of the month.

An exception to the Three-Day Written Demand involves manufactured home parks and mobile homes. Where a manufactured home park owner seeks to evict a Tenant for the non-payment of rent, the owner must provide the Tenant, who may be the owner of the mobile home, a Thirty-Day Written Demand and the notice must be formally served in the manner set forth in RPAPL §735.[146]

Although the demand for rent is an element of the Landlord's case, it is not a jurisdictional issue. Consequently, the defense of an improper rent demand, or the lack of service thereof, is waived unless raised.[147]

---

146 RPL § 233(b)(2).

147 *See* Citi Land Servs., LLC v. McDowell, 926 N.Y.S.2d 343 (App. Term, 2d, 11th & 13th Jud. Dists. 2011); Forest Hills S. Owners, Inc. v. Ishida, 943 N.Y.S.2d 791 (App. Term, 2d, 11th & 13th Jud. Dists. 2011) (defense that the rent demand was improperly served is waived when <u>not</u> asserted within the Answer).

B. HOLDOVER PROCEEDINGS

1. MONTH-TO-MONTH TENANCY (ONE MONTH OR THIRTY-DAY NOTICE)

In a holdover proceeding, the Landlord must demonstrate that the Tenant was in possession of the premises beyond the expiration or termination of the tenancy at the time the proceeding was commenced.[148] Where the tenancy is month-to-month, the Landlord must provide the Tenant with at least one (1) month notice <u>prior</u> to filing suit.[149]

The parties may enter into a month-to-month agreement at their discretion. A month-to-month tenancy need not be in writing, and may result by operation of law, such as when a rental agreement of longer than one (1) month expires and the Tenant remains in possession and continues to pay without entering into a new rental agreement.[150] Parenthetically, the Statute of Frauds does <u>not</u> apply to an oral month-to-month tenancy because the tenancy is capable of being performed within one (1) year; i.e., the tenancy automatically renews upon the payment of rent each month.[151]

A Tenant seeking to terminate a month-to-month tenancy must similarly provide the Landlord with one (1) month notice.[152] The Tenant's failure to provide notice prior to vacating the premises may result in the Tenant being liable for one (1) additional month of rent.[153]

---

148   *See* RPAPL § 711(1).

149   RPL §§ 232-a (within New York City), 232-b (outside New York City). *See* 1400 Broadway Assocs. v. Lee & Co. of NY, Inc., 614 N.Y.S.2d 704 (N.Y. Civ. Ct. 1994).

150   RPL § 232-c; Priegue v. Paulus, 988 N.Y.S.2d 525 (App. Term, 9th & 10th Jud. Dists. 2014); Washington v. Palanzo, 746 N.Y.S.2d 875, 876 (App. Term, 9th & 10th Jud. Dists. 2002).

151   *See* 28 Mott St. Co., Inc. v. Summit Import Corp., 34 A.D.2d 144, at 145-46, 310 N.Y.S.2d 93 (App. Div., 1st Dep't 1970) (RPL § 232-c prohibits the Landlord from declaring a new lease term of more than one (1) month absent an agreement to the contrary), *aff'd*, 28 N.Y.2d 508, 319 N.Y.S.2d 65 (1971). *Cf.* N.Y. GENERAL OBLIGATIONS LAW § 5-703(2) (McKinney 2001) (a lease longer than one (1) year is void unless in writing); 72nd St. Assocs., LLC v. Persson, 13 N.Y.S.3d 853 (App. Term, 1st Dep't 2015) (oral lease extension of two (2) years barred by the statute of frauds).

152   Skinner v. Noy, 856 N.Y.S.2d 503 (App. Term, 9th & 10th Jud. Dists. 2008).

153   Hickey v. Trahan, 31 N.Y.S.3d 921 (App. Term, 9th & 10th Jud. Dists. 2016) (holding "a month-to-month tenant who vacates during the month is liable for the entire month's

The notice terminating a month-to-month tenancy outside New York City may either be oral[154] or in writing. If the notice is in writing, it may be mailed via overnight delivery, certified mail or regular mail.[155] In New York City, the termination of a month-to-month tenancy requires a Thirty-Day Written Notice, and the notice must be served in the same manner as the Notice of Petition and Petition.[156] The distinction between New York City and other jurisdictions of the State is subtle and worth repeating. The termination of a month-to-month tenancy outside New York City requires "one month" notice (as opposed to thirty (30) days within New York City).[157] In addition, outside New York City, the notice to terminate need not be in writing (although it is typically done in writing), and RPL § 232-b does not specify the manner in which the predicate notice must be served. The statute further does <u>not</u> require a statement of the consequences for failing to vacate the premises by the termination date.[158]

Regardless of the type of notice, the termination notice must be "timely, definite [and] unequivocal".[159] The notice must terminate the

rent"); Deban v. Hoevener, 950 N.Y.S.2d 491 (App. Term, 9th & 10th Jud. Dists. 2012) (month-to-month Tenants that vacated on the 8th day of the term are obligated to pay an additional month of rent); Smith v. Woodson, 929 N.Y.S.2d 203 (App. Term, 2d, 11th & 13th Jud. Dists. 2011); Downes v. Obadiah, N.Y.L.J., Feb. 8, 2000, at 29 (App. Term, 9th & 10th Jud. Dists. 2000). *See* RPL §§ 232-a (within New York City), 232-b (outside New York City). For a discussion on the Rule Against Apportionment, *see supra*, Chapter 1 subdiv. D(2).

154   *See* Morse v. Brozzo, 94 A.D.3d 1184, 942 N.Y.S.2d 246 (App. Div., 3d Dep't 2012).

155   Spangenberg v. Chaloupka, 229 A.D.2d 482, at 483, 645 N.Y.S.2d 514 (App. Div., 2d Dep't 1996) ("service by mail is complete upon mailing regardless of delivery"). Where the Petitioner sets forth a procedure for mailing in the regular course of its business, there is a "presumption of mailing" and receipt of the document. *See* We're Assocs. Co. v. Rodin Sportswear Ltd., 288 A.D.2d 465, 734 N.Y.S.2d 104 (App. Div., 2d Dep't 2001); Expressway Vill., Inc. v. Denman, 893 N.Y.S.2d 736, 737 (Niagra Cnty. Ct. 2009) (a Court notice sent via regular mail is presumed to have been received by the recipient when the notice was not returned as "undeliverable").

156   RPL § 232-a.

157   *Id.* § 232-b.

158   Reifield Thompson & Riverside, Inc. v. Ho, N.Y.L.J., Aug. 14, 1995, at 28 (App. Term, 1st Dep't 1995).

159   *See* United Veterans Beacon House, Inc. v. St. James, 781 N.Y.S.2d 628 (App. Term, 9th & 10th Jud. Dists. 2003). *Cf.* Barrett Japaning Inc. v. Bialobroda, 998 N.Y.S.2d 305 (App. Term, 1st Dep't 2014) (re-service of a 4 ½ year-old termination notice from a prior

tenancy on the final day of the rental term because a termination date that extends into the next month is defective.[160] For example, if the rental term ends on the final day of the month (e.g., July 31st), then the proper termination date is the last day of the following month (e.g., August 31st) because at least one (1) month notice must be provided and the tenancy may only be terminated on the last day of the term. In this hypothetical, a noticed termination date of September 1st, or any day other than the last day of the month, would be defective and properly result in dismissal of the summary proceeding following a timely motion to dismiss.

Similar to a rent demand, a termination notice signed by counsel that fails to specify counsel's authority to issue the predicate notice may be defective where counsel's authority to act on behalf of Petitioner was not previously known to the Tenant.[161] It is further well-established that the Landlord may not amend a notice to terminate the tenancy following commencement of the summary proceeding.[162] However, if a defect in the predicate notice "could not have materially misled or confused the tenant or hindered the preparation of [the] defense", then the defect may be overlooked.[163]

2. LEASE EXPIRED BY ITS OWN TERMS (NO NOTICE)

A predicate notice is not required to terminate a rental agreement that expires on a date certain (e.g., a lease that expires by its own terms on December 31, 20__).[164] As a result, where the Tenant holds over

---

proceeding is defective).

160 See Best v. Buday, 841 N.Y.S.2d 818 (App. Term, 9th & 10th Jud. Dists. 2007); Avalonbay Communities, Inc. v. Betts, 791 N.Y.S.2d 867 (App. Term, 9th & 10th Jud Dists. 2004); ATM Four, LLC v. Miller, 961 N.Y.S.2d 356 (Nassau Cnty. Dist. Ct. 2012).

161 See Smith v. Country Serv., Inc., 831 N.Y.S.2d 350 (App. Term, 9th & 10th Jud. Dists. 2006); HSBC Bank, USA, N.A. v. Jeffers, 958 N.Y.S.2d 646 (Nassau Cnty. Dist. Ct. 2011). Cf. GRP/AG REO 2004-1, LLC v. Friedman, 792 N.Y.S.2d 819, 821 (Ramapo Just. Ct. 2005) ("[P]etitioner's attorney was clothed with authority to issue the [termination] notice by virtue of his prior activity known by the respondents and/or their attorneys").

162 See Chinatown Apts., Inc. v. Lam, 51 N.Y.2d 786, at 787, 433 N.Y.S.2d 86 (1980).

163 Oxford Towers Co., LLC v. Leites, 41 A.D.3d 144, at 145, 837 N.Y.S.2d 131 (App. Div., 1st Dep't 2007) (emphasis added).

164 RPL § 232-b; 620 Dahill, LLC v. Berger, 27 N.Y.S.3d 315 (App. Div., 2d Dep't 2016);

<u>without</u> paying for the additional time, the Landlord need not provide a predicate notice before commencing a holdover proceeding.[165]

However, the Landlord may <u>not</u> hold the Tenant to a new rental term or renew the expired lease without consent. In other words, the Landlord may not unilaterally elect to re-new the expired lease based on the holdover. An exception may apply where the expired lease contained an automatic lease renewal provision.[166]

In addition to a judgment of possession, a warrant of eviction, rent arrears and "added" rent, the Landlord may seek use and occupancy for the time the Tenant remains in possession following the termination of the lease.[167] This raises the question whether a non-payment proceeding is permitted where the Tenant holds over following the expiration of the lease and pays rent for an additional month (or months), but thereafter stops making payment without notice.

There is a split in the Appellate Terms regarding this issue. As previously discussed, where the Tenant holds over and pays rent or use and occupancy for a period subsequent to the expiration of the rental agreement, the tenancy typically becomes a month-to-month tenancy.[168] According to the Appellate Term in the First Department, if the Tenant thereafter fails to pay rent, the Landlord's recourse is to commence a holdover proceeding, as opposed to a non-payment proceeding, after giving thirty (30) days notice. The reasoning is that the Landlord and Tenant do <u>not</u> have a rental agreement for the payment of rent in any month other than the current month in a month-to-month tenancy. Therefore, it would be inconsistent to permit a non-payment proceeding absent an agreement to pay rent.[169]

BGB Realty, LLC v. Annunziata, 820 N.Y.S.2d 841 (App. Term, 9th & 10th Jud. Dists. 2006).

165   RPL § 232-c.

166   *See* Affirmative Defenses *infra*, Chapter 8 subdiv. K.

167   *See* Jaroslow v. Lehigh Valley R.R. Co., 23 N.Y.2d 991, at 993, 298 N.Y.S.2d 999 (1969); Krantz & Phillips, LLP v. Sedaghati, Index No. 570718-02, 2003 WL 222778, 2003 N.Y. Misc. LEXIS 58 (App. Term, 1st Dep't Jan. 23, 2003).

168   RPL § 232-c; Bahamonde v. Grabel, 939 N.Y.S.2d 226 (App. Term, 9th & 10th Jud. Dists. 2011).

169   *See Krantz & Phillips, LLP*, 2003 WL at 222778, 2003 N.Y. Misc. LEXIS at 58;

On the other hand, the Appellate Term for the Ninth and Tenth Judicial Districts has held that the Landlord may commence either a non-payment or a holdover proceeding because RPL § 232-c is inapplicable to month-to-month tenancies. The rent demand and commencement of the non-payment proceeding is considered a permissible election to "[t]reat the holdover tenants as tenants for a new term" on "[t]he same terms as were in the expired lease".[170]

Others have argued that because the Tenant is liable for an additional month's rent due to its failure to give the Landlord one (1) month notice, the parties implicitly agreed to another term thereby making a non-payment proceeding proper. This argument, however, does not appear to be supported by case law. Regardless, the Landlord may always elect to commence a holdover proceeding after giving the Tenant one month (30 days in New York City) notice.

3. LICENSEES AND SQUATTERS (TEN-DAY NOTICE TO QUIT) VS. TENANTS-AT-WILL (THIRTY-DAY NOTICE)

Where the occupant is either a "licensee" or a "squatter", a Landlord and Tenant relationship does not exist.[171] However, the RPAPL permits a summary proceeding provided the occupant is served with a Ten-Day Notice to Quit in the manner set forth in RPAPL § 735 prior to the commencement of the proceeding.[172]

The pertinent statutes offer little assistance in identifying when a licensor and licensee relationship exists. For instance, a "licensee" is defined in the RPAPL as someone who was "entitled to possession of the

---

Eshaghian v. Adames, 957 N.Y.S.2d 635 (N.Y. Civ. Ct. 2010); 1400 Broadway Assocs. v. Lee & Co. of NY, Inc., 614 N.Y.S.2d 704 (N.Y. Civ. Ct. 1994); *see* Dashnaw v. Shiflett, 862 N.Y.S.2d 807 (Plattsburgh City Ct. 2005).

170   Tricarichi v. Moran, 959 N.Y.S.2d 372 (App. Term, 9th & 10th Jud. Dists. 2012). *See* Priegue v. Paulus, 988 N.Y.S.2d 525 (App. Term, 9th & 10th Jud. Dists. 2014).

171   Federal Nat'l Mtg. Assoc. v. Simmons, 12 N.Y.S.3d 487 (App. Term, 1st Dep't 2015) (licensee holdover proceeding dismissed where Respondent entered into possession as a Tenant pursuant to a proprietary lease).

172   RPAPL §§ 713(3),(7). RPAPL § 713 lists the grounds for commencing a summary proceeding following service of a Ten-Day Notice to Quit when a Landlord and Tenant relationship does not exist. *Id.* § 713.

property at the time of the license" and the license has expired, been revoked or the occupant is no longer entitled to possession.[173]

The relevant case law has since provided some instruction by holding that a licensee is a person who lawfully gained entry to the subject premises with the express or implicit permission of the owner, or pursuant to a "[p]ersonal, revocable, non[-]assignable privilege from the owner, without possessing any interest in the property, and who becomes a trespasser thereon upon revocation of the permission of the privilege".[174] Conversely, a "squatter" is an individual who gained possession <u>without</u> permission or consent and remains in possession without permission, or, if at some point after unlawful entry permission to occupy was granted, it has since been revoked.[175]

On the other hand, a "tenant-at-will" is an individual who took lawful possession of the premises for an undetermined duration. A tenant-at-will must be given a written Thirty-Day Notice, not necessarily one (1) month, prior to the commencement of a summary proceeding.[176] Unlike a notice terminating a month-to-month tenancy, the thirty (30) days need not end on any particular date. Real Property Law § 228 permits the Landlord to provide more than thirty (30) days notice; i.e., no fewer than thirty (30) days notice is required. The termination notice must be formally served unless otherwise agreed.[177]

A critical distinction between a tenant-at-will and a licensee is whether the occupant has "exclusive possession" of the premises.[178] The distinction is the difference between the Landlord having to serve a Thirty-Day Notice (tenant-at-will) or a Ten-Day Notice (licensee) prior to commencing suit. Generally, where the occupant has complete

173   *Id.* § 713(7).

174   Rosenstiel v. Rosenstiel, 20 A.D.2d 71, at 76, 245 N.Y.S.2d 395 (App. Div., 1st Dep't 1963) (citations omitted).

175   Robert F. Dolan, Rasch's Landlord and Tenant Including Summary Proceedings §§ 35:14 to 35:16, at 537-40 (4th ed. 2010).

176   RPL § 228.

177   *Id.*

178   Rodriguez v. Greco, 927 N.Y.S.2d 819 (App. Term, 9th & 10th Jud. Dists. 2011).

and unfettered access to all or a portion of the property (e.g., the bedroom and full and complete access to the kitchen, laundry room and bathroom at all times without restriction), the occupant is more likely to be considered a tenant-at-will notwithstanding the absence of an agreement to pay rent.[179] Otherwise, the occupant may be considered a licensee.

Although the Notice to Quit must clearly denominate the parties' relationship and relief sought, the RPAPL omits any specific requirements regarding the content of the Ten-Day Notice. A Ten-Day Notice to Quit entitled "Ten-Day Notice to Vacate" that failed to include the date by which the occupant was required to vacate was deemed adequate notice.[180] However, the inclusion of incorrect and/or incomplete information, such as omitting the facts upon which the proceeding is based or failing to properly define the type of occupancy, may render the Notice to Quit defective. Thus, if the occupant is a licensee but the Notice to Quit identifies the occupant as a squatter, then the Notice, and the proceeding upon which it was based, may be defective and the proceeding dismissed.[181]

---

179   *Id.*; Nextel of New York, Inc. v. Time Mgmt. Corp., 297 A.D.2d 282, at 283, 746 N.Y.S.2d 169 (App. Div., 2d Dep't 2002); DiStasio v. Macaluso, 16 N.Y.S.3d 791 (App. Term, 9th & 10th Jud. Dists. 2015); Sherhan v. Numyal Food, Inc., 862 N.Y.S.2d 709, 712 (App. Term, 2d & 11th Jud. Dists 2008) ("[w]hether...exclusive possession or control of any specific area is granted is of great importance in determining whether a license or a lease is constituted....") (citation omitted); City of New York v. Utsey, 714 N.Y.S.2d 410, 412 (App. Term, 2d & 11th Jud. Dists. 2000).

180   *See* Washington Mutual Bank, F.A. v. Hanspal, 856 N.Y.S.2d 27 (App. Term, 9th & 10th Jud. Dists. 2007).

181   *See* City of New York v. Bullock, 606 N.Y.S.2d 552, 554 (N.Y. Civ. Ct. 1993) (predicate notice defective where it identified the occupant as either a licensee or squatter), *aff'd*, 630 N.Y.S.2d 652 (App. Term, 2d, 11th & 13th Jud. Dists. 1995). *Cf.* Retained Realty Inc. v. Zwicker, 7 N.Y.S.3d 245 (App. Term, 1st Dep't 2014) (licensee holdover proceeding dismissed where the occupant entered possession as a Tenant pursuant to a rental agreement); *but see* United Veterans Beacon House, Inc. v. St. James, 781 N.Y.S.2d 628 (App. Term, 9th & 10th Jud. Dists. 2003) (improperly identifying the Tenant as a licensee did not warrant dismissal absent a showing of prejudice).

4. POST-FORECLOSURES (TEN-DAY, NINETY-DAY OR LONGER NOTICE)

There have been many occasions where Tenants have been evicted following foreclosures due to no fault of their own. Often these cases involve "short sales", mortgage defaults and other attempts at reconciliation between the lender and the former owner. Until mid-2009, when the owner lost title in a foreclosure action, the occupants were entitled to the same predicate notice as squatters; i.e., a Ten-Day Notice to Quit.[182] Both the Federal and State governments have since enacted legislation enlarging many of the notice requirements for occupants of foreclosed dwellings.

The Federal Title VII Protecting Tenants at Foreclosure Act ("PTFA"), which took effect on May 20, 2009, substantially expanded the notice provisions for "bona fide Tenants" occupying foreclosed residential premises and properties involving federally-related mortgage loans.[183] A "bona fide Tenant" is defined as an individual rightfully in possession of the premises having entered into an agreement with the then owner, or other person with a superior interest in the property, prior to the Notice of Foreclosure.

The PTFA requires that the new owner provides a bona fide Tenant a minimum of Ninety-Days written notice <u>prior</u> to the commencement of a holdover proceeding. A bona fide Tenant with a written lease is entitled to remain in possession of the foreclosed property for either the Ninety-Day notice period or the remainder of the lease, whichever is greater, except where the new owner intends to occupy the property as a primary residence, in which case, a Ninety-Day Notice will suffice.[184] As a practical matter, a bona fide Tenant will typically present a copy of the lease to justify the extended notice period.

A bona fide Tenant does <u>not</u> include the mortgagor (former owner) or the child, spouse, or parent of the mortgagor under the contract. In addition, the tenancy must have been the result of an "arm's length

---

182   RPAPL § 713(5).

183   Protecting Tenants at Foreclosure Act of 2009, Pub. Law No. 111-22, §§ 701-04, 123 Stat. 1660 (2009).

184   *Id.* § 702(a)(2).

transaction", and the rent may <u>not</u> be substantially less than the fair market value. If the rent is for a significantly reduced amount, then the rent must have been reduced or subsidized by a Federal, State or local subsidy.[185] An occupant who is <u>not</u> a bona fide Tenant is entitled to a Ten-Day Notice.

The re-service of the Notice to Quit <u>following</u> commencement of the summary proceeding is improper because the notice is a prerequisite to the commencement of the action, and the Petition must accurately allege that the occupant was in possession at the time the proceeding was commenced.[186] The reader should be mindful that the Supreme Court's findings in the underlying foreclosure proceeding may <u>not</u> be challenged in the Housing Part.[187]

A lessee in possession of the premises who was not joined in the mortgage foreclosure action may remain in possession for the remainder of the lease.[188] This is because a Tenant is a necessary party to the foreclosure action, and the failure to name the Tenant "[l]eaves that party's rights unaffected by the judgment and sale, and the foreclosure sale may be considered void as to the omitted party".[189] However,

---

185   *Id.*

186   TD Bank, N.A. v. Yeshiva Chofetz Chaim, Inc., 17 N.Y.S.3d 386 (App. Term, 9th & 10th Jud. Dists. 2015).

187   Nassau Homes Corp. v. Shuster, 941 N.Y.S.2d 539 (App. Term, 9th & 10th Jud. Dists. 2011); M & T Mortgage Corp. v. Larkins, 910 N.Y.S.2d 763 (App. Term, 2d, 11th & 13th Jud. Dists. 2010); Federal Nat'l Mtg. Assoc. v. Williams, 943 N.Y.S.2d 791 (Nassau Cnty. Dist. Ct. 2012).

188   1426 46th St., LLC v. Klein, 60 A.D.3d 740, at 742, 876 N.Y.S.2d 425 (App. Div., 2d Dep't 2009). A lease longer than three (3) years not recorded with the County Clerk is void as against a bona fide purchaser for value whose interest is first recorded. *See* RPL § 291; Hi-Rise Laundry Equip. Corp. v. Matrix Props., Inc., 96 A.D.2d 930, 466 N.Y.S.2d 375 (App. Div., 2d Dep't 1983).

189   Development Strategies Co., LLC v. Astoria Equities, Inc., 924 N.Y.S.2d 308 (App. Term, 9th & 10th Jud. Dists. 2011) (internal citations omitted). A party acquiring an interest in real property by conveyance recorded <u>following</u> the filing of the notice of pendency of the mortgage foreclosure action is not a necessary party to the foreclosure action and "[i]s bound by all proceedings taken in the action…to the same extent as a party". *See* CPLR § 6501; Green Point Savings Bank v. St. Hilaire, 267 A.D.2d 203, 699 N.Y.S.2d 458 (App. Div., 2d Dep't 1999).

a month-to-month Tenant is <u>not</u> a necessary party to the foreclosure,[190] and, as a result, neither be named nor provided notice of the mortgage foreclosure action.[191]

Where the foreclosed premises contains multiple families living independently in separate units, the owner must commence a separate summary proceeding for each independent living area.[192] The PTFA does <u>not</u> create a private right of action for relief, but rather is intended to protect the rights of those impacted by the foreclosure.[193] New York has since enacted a statute comparable to the PTFA regarding judgments of foreclosure issued after January 13, 2010.[194]

The successor owner has the burden of demonstrating (1) compliance with the relevant statutory notice provisions and (2) that the occupant is <u>not</u> a bona fide Tenant.[195] In *Bank of Am. v. Owens*, the post-foreclosure action was dismissed because the lender notified the occupants that they would be evicted unless they provided a response to its questionnaire within five (5) days, rather than serving a proper termination notice.[196]

RPAPL § 713(5) provides that a certified copy of the deed must be "exhibited" (i.e., presented for inspection) to the occupants prior to the

---

190 Eastern Savings Bank, FSB v. Whyte, Index No. 6111-CV-13, 2016 U.S. Dist. LEXIS 45880 (E.D.N.Y. April 4, 2016).

191 *Id.* (*citing* In re Roberto Oligbo, 328 B.R. 619, 638 (Bankr. Ct. E.D.N.Y. 2005)); *see* 585 A.P. Lenox Assocs. v. 585 Lenox Ave. Assocs., 194 A.D.2d 380, 598 N.Y.S.2d 264, 265 (App. Div., 1st Dep't 1993).

192 *See* First Cent. Savings Bank v. Yglesia, Index No. 2618-10, 2012 WL 5053024, 2012 N.Y. Misc. LEXIS 4911 (App. Term, 9th & 10th Jud. Dists. Oct. 11, 2012).

193 Nativi v. Deutsche Bank Nat'l Trust Co., Index No. 6096-09, 2010 WL 2179885, at *3-4, 2010 U.S. Dist. LEXIS 51697, at *9-10 (N.D. Cal. May 24, 2010).

194 RPAPL § 1305. Under New York's law, the notice period for bona fide Tenants is the greater of 90 days or the duration of the rental agreement provided the Tenant is <u>not</u> the owner of the premises and the rent is not substantially less than the fair market rental value, except where the premises is subject to a federal or state system of subsidy or statutory scheme. *See id.*

195 Bank of Am., N.A. v. Owens, 903 N.Y.S.2d 667, 671 (Rochester City Ct. 2010). *See also* First Nat'l Bank of Chicago v. Silver, 73 A.D.3d 162, at 169-70, 899 N.Y.S.2d 256, 262 (App. Div., 2d Dep't 2010) (holding the foreclosing party has the burden of demonstrating compliance with the Home Equity Theft Prevention Act).

196 *Bank of Am.*, 903 N.Y.S.2d at 667.

commencement of a summary proceeding. It has been held that attaching a certified copy of the referee's deed to the Notice to Quit, which was served by "nail and mail" delivery following four (4) unsuccessful attempts at personal delivery, failed to satisfy "[t]he requirement of exhibition of the deed pursuant to RPAPL 713(5)".[197]

Due to the high volume of foreclosures within the State, there have been questions regarding the standing of foreign banks (out of state) to commence summary proceedings. Pursuant to § 200 of the Banking Law, foreign banks that loan money within New York may "commence actions to enforce obligations under those mortgages", and, as a result, they have standing to commence a summary proceeding.[198]

5. TENANCY BY SUFFERANCE (THIRTY-DAY NOTICE)

A tenancy by sufferance is a hybrid situation where the occupant previously had lawful possession but refuses to vacate the premises following termination of the primary Tenant's possessory interest. A tenancy by sufferance may result when a Subtenant, who was not named in the underlying summary proceeding, fails to leave after the Tenant vacated the premises due to the termination or expiration of the Tenant's rental agreement.

Describing the relationship as a "tenancy" is a misnomer because the relationship is not that of Landlord and Tenant, but rather a claim by the occupant for adverse possession. The owner must provide a tenant by sufferance a Thirty-Day Notice, not necessarily one (1) month, prior to commencing a holdover proceeding, and the notice must be

---

197 Home Loan Servs., Inc. v. Moskowitz, 920 N.Y.S.2d 569 (App. Term, 2d, 11ᵗʰ & 13ᵗʰ Jud. Dists. 2011); see IFS Props. LLC v. Willins, 970 N.Y.S.2d 865 (Nassau Cnty. Dist. Ct. 2013); Deutsche Bank Nat'l Trust Co. v. Dirende, 21 N.Y.S.3d 842 (Pound Ridge Just. Ct. 2015). But see Hudson City Savings Bank v. Lorenz, 959 N.Y.S.2d 844 (Suffolk Cnty. Dist. Ct. 2013) (although not the accepted standard, the Court reasoned that requiring personal exhibition of the deed "[w]ould create a higher standard of service for the presentment of the deed than is needed for the Notice of Petition in an eviction").

198 See First Wisconsin Trust Co. v. Hakimian, 237 A.D.2d 249, at 250, 654 N.Y.S.2d 808 (App. Div., 2d Dep't 1997); Deutsche Bank Nat'l Trust Co. v. Fleurimond, Index No. 509893-15, 2016 N.Y. Misc. LEXIS 1259 (Kings Cnty. Sup. Ct. Feb. 29, 2016).

formally served in accordance with the CPLR and RPAPL.[199] Similar to a tenancy-at-will, the thirty (30) days need not end on any particular date, only that no fewer than thirty (30) days must be provided following service of the notice.

Many of the tenancies discussed in this Bench Guide are fluid, and, as a result, the type of tenancy and the requisite predicate notice are subject to change. For example, a squatter may convert into a tenancy-at-will by express agreement or the acceptance of rent by the owner which would require a Thirty-Day Notice (tenant-at-will), as opposed to a Ten-Day Notice to Quit (squatter).[200] However, other tenancies are restricted by definition. For instance, a squatter (trespasser) cannot convert into a tenancy by sufferance, and vice versa, because a tenancy by sufferance requires initial lawful possession by the occupant.

6. UNLAWFUL ACTIVITY

A rental agreement is void when the premises are used for "any illegal trade, manufacture or other business".[201] Where the premises and its occupants participate in a federally assisted low income housing program governed by the United States Housing and Urban Development, a local public agency may seek to evict the Tenants pursuant to either (1) the federal strict liability standards set forth in 42 U.S.C. §1437d or (2) RPAPL §§ 711(5) and 715.[202]

Under the federal statute, the decision to commence an eviction

---

199 *See* RPL § 228; ROBERT F. DOLAN, RASCH'S LANDLORD AND TENANT INCLUDING SUMMARY PROCEEDINGS § 30:39, at 446-47 (4th ed. 2010). *See also* Lippe v. Professional Surgical Supply Co., Inc., 503 N.Y.S.2d 254 (N.Y. Civ. Ct. 1986).

200 City of New York v. Utsey, 714 N.Y.S.2d 410, 412 (App. Term, 2d & 11th Jud. Dists. 2000).

201 RPL § 231. The owner or any Tenant within 200 feet of the unlawfully utilized premises has standing to seek an injunction enjoining the unlawful business. *Id.* § 231(6).

202 New York City Hous. Auth. v. Williams, 957 N.Y.S.2d 637 (N.Y. Civ. Ct. 2010). Section 1437d(l)(6) of Title 42 of the United States Code provides that "any criminal activity that threatens the health, safety, or right to peaceful enjoyment of the premises by other tenants or any drug-related criminal activity on or off such premises, engaged in by a public housing tenant, any member of the tenant's household, or any guest or other person under the tenant's control, shall be cause for termination of [the tenancy]".

proceeding is left to the discretion of the public housing agency.[203] Where the public agency elects to proceed in this manner, the local housing agency's administrative procedures and protocols must be followed.[204] An advantage for the Petitioner is that she does not have to establish that the Tenant had actual "knowledge", or even a "reason to know", of the unlawful activity.[205] Congress authorized no-fault evictions under these circumstances because "[r]egardless of knowledge, a tenant who 'cannot control drug crime, or other criminal activities by a household member which threaten health or safety of other residents, is a threat to other residents'".[206]

On the other hand, an eviction proceeding pursuant to the State provisions of RPAPL §§ 711(5)[207] and 715 requires a showing that the Tenant "knew or should have known" of the unlawful activity.[208] The evidence must further credibly establish that the premises was used "customarily

---

203 Department of Hous. and Urban Dev. v. Rucker, 535 U.S. 125, 122 S.Ct. 1230 (2002).

204 *See, e.g.*, Matthews v. Hernandez, Index No. 401300-08, 2009 WL 1207166 , 2009 N.Y. Misc. LEXIS 4726 (N.Y. Cnty. Sup. Ct. April 28, 2009), *reargument granted*, 2009 WL 2355631, 2009 N.Y. Misc. LEXIS 6015 (N.Y. Cnty. Sup. Ct. July 10, 2009).

205 *Rucker*, 535 U.S. at 125, 122 S.Ct. at 1230.

206 *Id.*

207 A special proceeding may be maintained where "[t]he premises, or any part thereof, are used or occupied as a bawdy-house, or house or place of assignation for lewd persons, or for the purposes of prostitution, or for any illegal trade or manufacture, or other illegal business". *See* RPAPL § 711(5).

208 Beautiful Vill. Assocs. Redevelop. Co. v. Gomez, 966 N.Y.S.2d 788 (App. Term, 1st Dep't 2012); *see* Douglas v. New York City Hous. Auth., 126 A.D.3d 647, 4 N.Y.S.3d 495 (App. Div., 1st Dep't 2015) (eviction upheld following arrest and conviction of Tenant's son for drug activity in the premises); Waterside Plaza Ground Lessee, LLC v. Hirsch, 18 N.Y.S.3d 582 (N.Y. Civ. Ct. 2015) (holding Tenant knew or should have known the premises was utilized for the sale of heroin by a recovering occupant with a known drug addiction who "kept the door to his room locked at all times"); *but see* WHGA Renaissance Apts., L.P. v. Jackson, 37 N.Y.S.3d 809 (App. Term, 1st Dep't 2016) (whether the Tenant had the capacity to know or should have known that her son was engaging in unlawful drug activities in the apartment is a question of fact). *Cf.* 518 W. 184th St. LLC v. Guzman, 7 N.Y.S.3d 818 (App. Term, 1st Dep't 2015) (elderly Tenant, who suffered from epilepsy, depression and memory loss, did not have the requisite knowledge or reason to know that her adult son was using the premises to sell drugs); Second Farms Neighborhood HDFC v. Lessington, 932 N.Y.S.2d 763 (App. Term, 1st Dep't 2011) (Petitioner failed to prove that "the subject premises were used to facilitate trade in drugs and that the tenant knew or should have known of the activities and acquiesced in the illegal drug activity in the apartment").

or habitually" for the illegal purpose, rather than the unlawful activity being a sporadic or isolated incident.[209]

No predicate notice is required, and the Landlord need not terminate the tenancy prior to commencing a summary proceeding pursuant to RPAPL § 711(5).[210] Recognizing the possibility that the Landlord may not be inclined to actively pursue the eviction, whether due to willing participation, implicit consent or fear of retribution, RPAPL § 715(1) authorizes additional parties to commence a summary proceeding.

For example, both the District Attorney's Office (law enforcement agencies) and other tenants have standing to commence an eviction proceeding to remove occupants engaged in unlawful activity at the premises.[211] Where an authorized party other than the Landlord seeks to commence a summary proceeding, the interested party must first provide the Landlord a Five-Day written notice stating that a summary proceeding to remove the Tenant will be commenced unless, within the notice period, the Landlord makes application for removal, or, if having already done so, "good faith" measures are taken to obtain a judgment and warrant of eviction.[212]

In *New York City Hous. Auth. v. Fashaw*, the Housing Authority commenced a summary proceeding pursuant to RPL §§ 231, 711(5) and 715 at the direction of the New York County District Attorney alleging unlawful drug activity at the residential premises. The proceeding was dismissed after the Court concluded there was inadequate evidence of "customary and habitual" illegal drug trade at the premises and/or that the Respondent had constructive knowledge of the illegal activity.[213]

---

209 Riverside Park Comm., LLC v. Ventura, Index No. 53434-12, 2012 WL 4876041, 2012 N.Y. Misc. LEXIS 4857 (N.Y. Civ. Ct. Oct. 12, 2012); New York City Hous. Auth. v. Grillasca, 852 N.Y.S.2d 610 (N.Y. Civ. Ct. 2007). *Cf.* 436-438 Assocs. v. Alvardo, 981 N.Y.S.2d 635 (N.Y. Civ. Ct. 2013) ("the mere fact that an arrest occurred at the subject apartment does not establish any guilt or that the subject apartment was used for illegal trade, manufacture, or other illegal business").

210 Spira v. Spiratone, Inc., 561 N.Y.S.2d 881 (N.Y. Civ. Ct. 1990); 410 Lenox Ave. Apts., Inc. v. Community II Supermarket, Inc., 516 N.Y.S.2d 432 (N.Y. Civ. Ct 1987).

211 RPAPL § 715(1).

212 *Id.*

213 *See* New York Hous. Auth. v. Fashaw, Index No. 19793-15, 2016 WL 6209468, 2016 N.Y.

When RPAPL § 715 is invoked, the Petitioner's case takes "precedence over any similar proceeding thereafter brought" by the Landlord.[214] However, where the Landlord prosecutes a summary proceeding in good-faith, and over the objection of the non-Landlord interested party reaches a settlement with the Tenant, the Landlord's decision prevails and the non-Landlord interested party may neither compel the Landlord to pursue an appeal nor pursue an appeal on its own.[215]

7. VICTIMS OF DOMESTIC VIOLENCE (TEN-DAY NOTICE)

The RPL recognizes the plight of victims of domestic violence in residential leaseholds. Specifically, RPL § 227-c sets forth the protocol for terminating the tenancy where an order of protection has been issued in favor of the victim.

Any time while an order of protection is in effect, the Tenant may terminate the tenancy after giving the Landlord and all co-Tenants a written Ten-Day Notice.[216] The Criminal Court must entertain the application even where the underlying domestic violence dispute has been resolved provided the order of protection remains in effect.[217]

The Tenant must demonstrate that notwithstanding the order of protection, (1) a substantial risk of physical and/or emotional harm to the Tenant and/or his or her children will continue to persist if they remain in the premises and (2) the Tenant's request for early termination was refused by the Landlord.[218] If the application is granted, the Court must terminate the tenancy between thirty (30) and 150 days following

Misc. LEXIS 3874 (N.Y. Civ. Ct. Sept. 29, 2016).

214   RPAPL § 715(1).

215   *See* 37-01 31st Ave. Realty Corp. v. Mohammed, 960 N.Y.S.2d 679 (App. Term, 2d, 11th & 13th Jud. Dists. 2010) (law enforcement agency's Five-Day Notice of intent to seek removal does not take priority over Landlord's good-faith efforts to resolve the controversy).

216   RPL § 227-c(2)(a).

217   *Id.*

218   *Id.* § 227-c(2)(b).

the due date of the next rent payment.[219]

The Court must further condition the termination on the payment of all rent due as of the termination date.[220] A lease provision waiving the rights afforded under RPL § 227-c is void as against public policy.[221]

8. NOTICE TO TERMINATE DUE TO BREACH OF LEASE (OTHER THAN NON-PAYMENT)

A Notice to Terminate based upon a breach other than the non-payment of rent must state the consequences of failing to vacate the premises by the termination date. The parties should review their lease provisions regarding predicate notice and the manner in which the notice must be served. Regardless of any heightened obligations, the Landlord may <u>not</u> file a summary proceeding until after the termination date set forth in the notice.

The Notice to Terminate must (1) unequivocally and unambiguously state the Landlord's basis for recovering possession; (2) advise the Tenant of the termination date; (3) it must be signed by the Landlord (or attorney or agent known by the Tenant); and (4) notify the Tenant that a summary proceeding will be commenced if the Tenant does not vacate the premises by the termination date. The Notice to Terminate must further identify the breached lease provisions.[222] No notice is required where the lease expired by its own terms.

9. NOTICE TO CURE

A Notice to Cure provides the Tenant with notice of an alleged breach(es) of the lease that must be corrected during a "cure period" or a summary proceeding will be commenced.[223] The Notice to Cure must

---

219   *Id.* § 227-c(2)(d).

220   *Id.* § 227-c(2)[c].

221   *Id.* § 227-c(4).

222   *See generally* 69 E.M. LLC v. Mejia, 29 N.Y.S.3d 849 (App. Term, 1st Dep't 2015).

223   Lucky Dollar, Inc. v. Mount Cavalry Pentecostal Church, Index No. 651840-14, 2016 WL 613816, 2016 N.Y. Misc. LEXIS 474 (N.Y. Cnty. Sup. Ct. Feb. 8, 2016) (Notice to Cure for failing to maintain liability insurance defective due to a lack of specificity).

be served in the manner set forth within the rental agreement.[224] If service requirements are not specified, then the service provisions of the RPAPL and CPLR would presumably suffice, but, at minimum, proof of service should be memorialized.

The Notice to Cure is defective, and otherwise not amendable, where it fails to instruct the Tenant of the condition(s) that must be cured and the lease provision(s) claimed to have been breached.[225] The cure period may be extended based upon the parties' conduct. For example, in an illegal-sublet holdover proceeding, the "cure period" was extended to the commencement of the summary proceeding where the parties engaged in "extensive settlement negotiations" and the Landlord accepted a sublet application and cashier's checks.[226] For residential properties within New York City, there is a mandatory post-award "cure period" of ten (10) days during which the Tenant may cure the breach and avoid eviction.[227]

10. SECTION 8 HOUSING

There are several Section 8 federally subsidized rental programs, including the Housing Choice Voucher Program pursuant to 42 U.S.C. § 1437(f) and 24 C.F.R. § 982 *et seq.* Under this program, the Landlord

---

224   *See* Benben v. DiMartini, 791 N.Y.S.2d 868 (App. Term, 9th & 10th Jud. Dists. 2004) (service of a notice of default is governed by the terms of the lease, and not CPLR § 2103(a) which is applicable "only from the summons through post-judgment notices").

225   *See* 1346 Park Pl. HDFC v. Wright, 34 N.Y.S.3d 561 (App. Term, 2d, 11th & 13th Jud. Dists. 2016). *See also* Chinatown Apts., Inc. v. Lam, 51 N.Y.2d 786, at 787, 433 N.Y.S.2d 86 (1980) (action dismissed where unlawful free-standing structure mistakenly described as a "partition"); Westhampton Cabins & Cabanas Owners Corp. v. Westhampton Bath & Tennis Club Owners Corp., 62 A.D.3d 987, at 988, 882 N.Y.S.2d 124 (App. Div., 2d Dep't 2009). Where the Landlord accepts rent with knowledge of the breach, the breach may be waived. In the event the lease contains a 'no waiver' provision, the parties' intent is crucial in determining whether the notice is enforceable. *See* Jefpaul Garage Corp. v. Presbyterian Hosp. in the City of New York, 61 N.Y.2d 442, 474 N.Y.S.2d 458 (1984); Atkins Waste Materials, Inc. v. May, 34 N.Y.2d 422, 358 N.Y.S.2d 129 (1974).

226   Mansfield Owners, Inc. v. Bridgeman, 31 N.Y.S.3d 922 (App. Term, 2d, 11th & 13th Jud. Dists. 2016).

227   1346 E. Pkwy. HDFC v. Robinson, 936 N.Y.S.2d 59 (App. Term, 2d, 11th & 13th Jud. Dists. 2011).

and Section 8 Tenant enter into a lease agreement for at least one (1) year.[228] In addition, a Housing Assistance Payment ("HAP") contract is executed between the Landlord and the Public Housing Agency ("PHA") that (1) authorizes the PHA to send subsidized rent payments to the Landlord and (2) binds the parties to the Section 8 regulations.

For rent stabilized premises, the Landlord's acceptance of a Section 8 rent subsidy becomes a "term and condition" of the lease agreement which must continue in the renewal lease.[229] Federal rent subsidy payments must be applied to the month in which the payments were received, and may <u>not</u> be utilized for prior arrears.[230]

A Section 8 Tenant is responsible for only the Tenant's portion of the rent, which according to the Brooke Amendment of the United States Housing Act, is limited to the greater of thirty (30) percent of the family's monthly adjusted income, ten (10) percent of the family's income or other amount determined by the public agency.[231] When the lease expires, a Section 8 tenancy (for leases entered into after 1995) may be terminated in the same manner as other tenancies.[232] The Landlord, Tenant and PHA have standing to terminate a HAP contract. The contract is also terminated when the PHA "terminates assistance for the family".[233] If the parties elect to continue the leasehold, they will typi-

---

228   See 24 C.F.R. § 982.309(a). An initial lease for a duration of less than one (1) year may be approved by the Public Housing Agency if the shorter term improves the Tenant's housing opportunities and is the "prevailing local market practice". Id. § 982.309(a)(2).

229   Rosario v. Diagonal Realty, LLC, 8 N.Y.3d 755, 840 N.Y.S.2d 748 (2007) (holding that once accepted, the Landlord may not change the terms and conditions by "opting out" of the Section 8 rent subsidy payments in a renewal lease).

230   Ioppolo v. Haerle, N.Y.L.J., Oct. 30, 2001, at 20, col. 6 (App. Term, 9th & 10th Jud. Dists. 2001).

231   See 42 U.S.C. § 1437a; Riverview II Preserv., L.P. v. Brice-Frazier, 13 N.Y.S.3d 852 (App. Term, 9th & 10th Jud. Dists. 2015) (dismissing summary proceeding where the rent and electricity charges exceeded 30% of the Tenant's monthly adjusted income).

232   See Numme v. Lemon, 741 N.Y.S.2d 384 (App. Term, 9th & 10th Jud. Dists. 2002). Leases with Section 8 Tenants entered into prior to 1996 are automatically renewed absent "good cause" for an eviction. Id. The automatic renewal provision was changed pursuant to 42 U.S.C. § 1437f(d)(1)(B)(ii). Id.

233   24 C.F.R. § 982.309(b)(2). The decision to terminate a Section 8 Tenant's rent subsidy may be challenged in an Article 78 Proceeding in Supreme Court, and not a summary proceeding. See 60 St. Nicholas Ave. HDFC v. Edwards, 13 N.Y.S.3d 853 (App. Term, 1st

cally enter into a month-to-month tenancy.

In *Underhill Ave. Realty v. Ramos*, the Appellate Term for the Second, Eleventh and Thirteenth Judicial Districts held that a non-payment proceeding may <u>not</u> be maintained against a Section 8 Tenant where it is undisputed that the Tenant remained in possession after the Landlord's predecessor "refused to issue a renewal lease" and no additional monies were paid after the lease expired.[234] The fact that the Section 8 subsidy was approved was insufficient to re-establish a Landlord and Tenant relationship, and, as a result, the non-payment proceeding was dismissed.[235]

The termination notice must be served on the public housing authority at the same time as the Tenant.[236] The rationale for simultaneous service is to allow the agency ample opportunity to withhold payments, to monitor the Landlord's conduct and the conditions of the premises, and to determine whether intervention on behalf of the Section 8 Tenant is required. The Notice must allege sufficient grounds to terminate the tenancy as set forth in 24 C.F.R. § 982.310, but upon expiration of a lease of a definite term or in a month-to-month Section 8 tenancy, the termination notice need not allege the cause for the termination.

The Petition must allege the relevant regulatory status of the tenancy (e.g., Section 8) and compliance with the Section 8 regulations.[237] The

---

Dep't 2015).

234   Underhill Ave. Realty, LLC v. Ramos, 29 N.Y.S.3d 850 (App. Term, 2d, 11th & 13th Jud. Dists. 2015) (noting that the Landlord may commence a plenary action for use and occupancy).

235   *Id.*

236   *See, e.g.*, Douglas v. Latimer, 901 N.Y.S.2d 905 (Nassau Cnty. Dist. Ct. 2009); Lamlon Dev. Corp. v. Owens, 533 N.Y.S.2d 186, 191 (Nassau Cnty. Dist. Ct. 1988) (holding the failure to simultaneously serve notice on the public housing authority is a jurisdictional defect). In addition to the Section 8 Tenant, 24 C.F.R. § 247.4(b) permits service of the termination notice on an individual of suitable discretion at least 18 years of age or on a minor under the age of 18 "[e]mancipated to act on his or her own behalf, including the ability to execute a contract or lease". *But see* Cromwell Towers Redev. Co., L.P. v. Blackwell, 966 N.Y.S.2d 345 (App. Term, 9th & 10th Jud. Dists. 2012) (dismissing summary proceeding where the termination notice was served on the Section 8 Tenant's 16-year-old son).

237   Brookwood Coram I, LLC v. Oliva, 15 N.Y.S.3d 710 (App. Term, 9th & 10th Jud. Dists. 2015).

omission of these allegations is a defense to the action but does <u>not</u> render the Petition jurisdictionally defective.[238]

A Section 8 Tenant may <u>not</u> be evicted due to the failure to pay late charges and/or attorney's fees.[239] As stated previously, a Section 8 Tenant is only liable for his or her share of the rent. This is the case even where the disputed items are listed in the agreement as "added" rent.[240] However, where it is agreed between the parties, the Tenant may be responsible for use and occupancy (the full amount) in the event the Tenant holds over following termination of the Section 8 Agreement.[241]

In many locations throughout the State, a Landlord may refuse to rent residential property to a prospective Tenant based upon the Tenant's source of income, such as the fact the Tenant receives public financial assistance. However, in Nassau and Suffolk counties, for example, this practice is unlawful provided the Tenant's income is obtained from a lawful source.[242]

---

238 Rippy v. Kyer, 885 N.Y.S.2d 713 (App. Term, 9th & 10th Jud. Dists. 2009); Wyandanch Comm. Dev. Corp. v. Nesbitt, Index No. 439-02, 2003 WL 21402061, 2003 N.Y. Misc. LEXIS 778 (App. Term, 9th & 10th Jud. Dists. May 20, 2003); 17th Holding LLC v. Rivera, 758 N.Y.S.2d 758 (App. Term, 2d & 11th Jud. Dists. 2002); Town of Oyster Bay Hous. Auth. v. Kohler, 950 N.Y.S.2d 611 (Nassau Cnty. Dist. Ct. 2012); 35 Ossining LLC v. Thornton, 981 N.Y.S.2d 503 (Ossining Just. Ct. 2014).

239 Poughkeepsie Hous. Auth. v. Lee, N.Y.L.J., Dec. 18, 1998, at 36 (App. Term, 9th & 10th Jud. Dists. 1998). *See also* Fairview Hous., LLC v. Wilson, 967 N.Y.S.2d 866 (App. Term, 9th & 10th Jud. Dists. 2012) (attorney's fees not recoverable against Section 8 Tenant in a summary proceeding even where the fees are listed in the lease as "additional" rent).

240 Port Chester Hous. Auth. v. Turner, 734 N.Y.S.2d 805 (App. Term, 9th & 10th Jud. Dists. 2001); Douglas v. Nole, 867 N.Y.S.2d 16 (Nassau Cnty. Dist. Ct. 2008).

241 Zappala v. Caputo, 851 N.Y.S.2d 62 (App. Term, 9th & 10th Jud. Dists. 2007); McCurdy v. Williams, 953 N.Y.S.2d 550 (App. Term, 2d, 11th & 13th Jud. Dists. 2012); Community Props. v. McCloud, Index No. 177-01, 2003 WL 21730080, 2003 N.Y. Misc. LEXIS 905 (App. Term, 9th & 10th Jud. Dists. June 3, 2003).

242 *See, e.g.*, NASSAU COUNTY LOCAL LAW No. 9-2006 (Nassau County's Human Rights Law); SUFFOLK COUNTY LOCAL LAW No. 25-2014, § 528-9 (Suffolk County's Human Rights Law). Exceptions to the Suffolk County law include, but are not limited to, individuals under the age of 18, age 55-and-over communities, and owner occupied single- and two-family dwellings. SUFFOLK COUNTY LOCAL LAW No. 25-2014, at § 528-9[c].

11. CHRONIC RENT DELINQUENCY (NO NOTICE)

A Landlord does <u>not</u> have to serve a predicate notice prior to commencing a holdover proceeding due to the Tenant's "chronic non-payment" of rent.[243] Chronic non-payment of rent is different from the occasional non-payment of rent, and, as a result, the Landlord has the option of commencing a non-payment proceeding (predicate notice required) or a holdover proceeding (no predicate notice) even where the rental agreement states that a non-payment proceeding is required.[244] The reasoning is that where the Tenant chronically fails to pay rent on time, a holdover proceeding is appropriate because there has been a violation of a substantial obligation of the leasehold.[245]

The Landlord will typically demonstrate that "[i]t was compelled to bring numerous nonpayment proceedings within a relatively short period of time and that the tenant's non-payment was willful, unjustified, without explanation, or accompanied by an intent to harass the landlord…."[246] Although the frequency and merits of the non-payments are evaluated on a case-by-case basis, summary judgment was awarded in favor of the Landlord where it brought five (5) non-payment proceedings over three and one-half (3½) years, and, in each of those proceedings, the Tenant failed to assert a viable defense.[247] Similarly, the Landlord successfully pursued chronic non-payment of rent claims where it commenced six (6) non-payment proceedings in four and one-half (4½) years[248] and, in another situation, four (4) non-payment

---

243 Definitions Personal Fitness, Inc. v. 133 E. 58th St. LLC, 107 A.D.3d 617, 967 N.Y.S.2d 647 (App. Div., 1st Dep't 2013); 3363 Sedgewick, L.L.C. v. Medina, 723 N.Y.S.2d 592 (App. Term, 1st Dep't 2000).

244 *Definitions Personal Fitness, Inc.*, 107 A.D.3d at 617, 967 N.Y.S.2d at 647.

245 *See* Adam's Tower Lim. P'ship v. Richter, 717 N.Y.S.2d 825 (App. Term, 1st Dep't 2000).

246 25th Realty Assocs. v. Griggs, 150 A.D.2d 155, 540 N.Y.S.2d 434 (App. Div., 1st Dep't 1989).

247 Tenth St. Holdings, LLC v. McKowen, 31 N.Y.S.3d 924 (App. Term, 1st Dep't 2016).

248 Zevrone Realty Corp. v. Gumaneh, 37 N.Y.S.3d 209 (App. Term, 1st Dep't 2016); *Definitions Personal Fitness, Inc.*, 107 A.D.3d at 617, 967 N.Y.S.2d at 647 (Tenant's motion for a Yellowstone injunction denied where Landlord brought ten (10) non-payment proceedings in seven (7) years).

proceedings in three (3) years.[249]

It has been held that the execution of a renewal lease for a rent-stabilized apartment, as required by § 2523.5(a) of the New York City Rent Stabilization Code ("RSC"), does <u>not</u> necessitate dismissal of the Landlord's holdover proceeding for chronic rent delinquency.[250] The Appellate Term reasoned that the holdover proceeding could continue because the "act of renewing the lease was not one of free will but of adhering to the requirements of law".[251]

12. NUISANCE (RENT STABILIZED PREMISES) (SEVEN-DAY NOTICE)

The Landlord of a rent stabilized property in New York City may commence a holdover proceeding to evict a Tenant whose misconduct arises to a nuisance, or where the Tenant allows others to partake in such misconduct within the premises. The New York Codes, Rules and Regulations at [9 N.Y.C.R.R.] § 2524.3(b) provides that a "nuisance" occurs where the Tenant (1) with malicious intent or by gross negligence "substantially" damages the premises or (2) "engages in a persistent and continuing course of conduct evidencing an unwarrantable, unreasonable or unlawful use of the property to the annoyance, inconvenience, discomfort or damage of others, the primary purpose of which is intended to harass the owner or other tenants or occupants of the same or adjacent building".[252] In other words, the Petitioner must demonstrate that the Tenant's conduct "interfered with the use or enjoyment" of the premises over a period of time.[253]

Although there is no bright-line rule as to the number and frequency of incidents required to give rise to a nuisance claim, it has been held that a "handful of [obnoxious noise] complaints over the course of

---

249 GIT LEB, LLC v. Golphin, Index No. 1006-14, 2016 WL 2584968, 2016 N.Y. Misc. LEXIS 1636 (App. Term, 2d, 11th & 13th Jud. Dists. April 27, 2016).

250 *See* FM United LLC v. Dulle-Wollin, 5 N.Y.S.3d 327 (App. Term, 1st Dep't 2014).

251 *Id.*

252 *See* RSC [9 N.Y.C.R.R.] § 2524.3(b); *see* 1806 Caton, LLC v. Ngyuen, 29 N.Y.S.3d 848 (App. Term, 2d, 11th & 13th Jud. Dists. 2015).

253 Sharp v. Norwood, 89 N.Y.2d 1068, 659 N.Y.S.2d 834 (1997).

more than one year" do <u>not</u> constitute an ongoing pattern that threatens the comfort and safety of the other occupants.[254] However, making repeated threats and participating in "physically violent conduct" towards the property manager, which resulted in the Tenant's conviction for harassment in the second degree, was an actionable nuisance.[255]

The spouse of an evicted Tenant does <u>not</u> automatically assume the lease of a rent-regulated apartment. Instead, the rights of the spouse, similar to any other family member, are governed by [9 N.Y.C.R.R.] § 2204.6(d) which provides that a family member assumes succession rights where he or she co-occupied the premises as a primary residence for at least the two (2) years (one (1) year if the Tenant is a senior citizen or disabled) immediately prior to the Tenant's death or removal.[256]

The Tenant is entitled to at least seven (7) days notice prior to the commencement of a summary proceeding.[257] The notice is not an opportunity to cure. However, the notice must be sufficiently detailed to provide the Tenant a reasonable opportunity to prepare a defense.[258] Overly broad conclusory allegations that the Tenant acted in "some undefined 'anti-social, disruptive, destructive and/or illegal behavior'" are inadequate.[259]

---

254   150 W. 21ˢᵗ LLC v. "John Doe", 31 N.Y.S.3d 922 (App. Term, 1ˢᵗ Dep't 2016); 125 Rockaway Pkwy. LLC v. Robinson, N.Y.L.J., April 28, 2014, at 1202655058331, at *1 (N.Y. Civ. Ct. 2014) (holding two (2) water overflow episodes were "consistent with unintentional and accidental incidents", not arising to a nuisance). *Cf.* 443 E. 78 Realty LLC v. Tupas, 14 N.Y.S.3d 610 (App. Term, 1ˢᵗ Dep't 2015) (the collection of refuse and debris "from the floor to ceiling" constitutes a nuisance).

255   Peters v. Owens, 18 N.Y.S.3d 581 (App. Term, 1ˢᵗ Dep't 2015) (ongoing "belligerent and aggressive" behavior towards Tenants and building staff constitutes a nuisance); Mautner-Glick Corp. v. Tunne, 966 N.Y.S.2d 347 (App. Term, 2d, 11ᵗʰ & 13ᵗʰ Jud. Dists. 2012) (Tenant's abusive conduct towards the superintendent's spouse and building staff substantiated nuisance claim).

256   *See* M. M. I. Realty Co., L.L.C. v. Gargano, 998 N.Y.S.2d 556 (App. Term, 2d, 11ᵗʰ & 13ᵗʰ Jud. Dists. 2014). *See* RSC [9 N.Y.C.R.R.] § 2204.6(d)(1),(3).

257   *See* RSC [9 N.Y.C.R.R.] § 2524.2[c](2).

258   69 E.M. LLC v. Mejia, 29 N.Y.S.3d 849 (App. Term, 1ˢᵗ Dep't 2015); West 97ᵗʰ St. Realty Corp. v. Aptaker, Index No. 78484-15, 2016 WL 344157, 2016 N.Y. Misc. LEXIS 230 (N.Y. Civ. Ct. Jan. 25, 2016).

259   *69 E.M. LLC*, 29 N.Y.S.3d at 849.

13. REFUSAL TO RENEW (RENT STABILIZED PREMISES)

Unique to rent stabilized apartments and hotel tenancies in New York City, the Landlord must offer a renewal lease provided the Tenant continues to pay rent.[260] However, there are limited exceptions to this rule, some of which are discussed below.

a. OWNER OCCUPANCY (90 TO 150-DAY NOTICE)

An owner who seeks to recover possession for the purpose of occupying the premises as his primary residence or the primary residence of an "immediate family member"[261] is <u>not</u> required to offer the Tenant a renewal lease.[262] To regain possession, the Landlord must provide the Tenant written notice to vacate the premises between ninety (90) and 150 days prior to the expiration of the lease. Where the occupant is a hotel permanent tenant, the notice provision must be given between ninety (90) and 150 days before the commencement of the summary proceeding.[263] If the Tenant or the spouse of the Tenant is a senior citizen[264] or disabled,[265] then the owner must offer the Tenant an equal or superior alternative housing accommodation in close proximity at the same or lower rent.[266]

In *Sendowski v. Pilzer*, the Appellate Term for the First Department affirmed the final judgment of possession where the owner elected not to re-new the lease so that his daughter could use the premises as her

---

260 RSC [9 N.Y.C.R.R.] § 2524.1.

261 The term "immediate family" under the Rent Stabilization Code includes a spouse, son, daughter, stepson, stepdaughter, father, mother, stepfather, stepmother, brother, sister, grandfather, grandmother, grandson, granddaughter, father-in-law, mother-in-law, son-in-law and daughter-in-law. *See id.* § 2520.6(n).

262 *Id.* § 2524.4(a).

263 *Id.* § 2524.2[c](3).

264 A person 62 years of age or older. *See id.* § 2520.6(p).

265 The term "disabled person" is defined as "a person who has an impairment which results from anatomical, physiological or psychological conditions, other than addiction to alcohol, gambling, or any controlled substance, ..., and which are expected to be permanent and which prevent such person from engaging in any substantial gainful employment". *See id.* § 2520.6(q).

266 *Id.* § 2524.4(a)(2).

primary residence.[267] The factors cited as evidence of good faith included the proximity of the premises to both the employment and the residences of the Landlord's adult children.[268]

b. PRIMARY RESIDENCE ((a) 90 TO 150-DAY NOTICE and (b) THIRTY-DAY NOTICE)

The Landlord may refuse to renew the lease where the Tenant does not occupy the premises as his or her primary residence.[269] In determining primary residence, the Court typically examines whether the Tenant (1) utilized a different address on his or her tax returns, motor vehicle registration, driver's license or any other document filed with a government agency; (2) used the premises as his or her voting address; and (3) lived in the apartment "for an aggregate of less than 183 days in the most recent calendar year", not including periods of temporary relocation due to active military duty, matriculation as a full-time student, Court Order, employment, hospitalization or other reasonable ground determined by the Division of Homes and Community Renewal.[270]

In *RSP 86 Prop. LLC v. Sylvester*, the Appellate Term dismissed the Petition after concluding the 89-year old Tenant "maintained a substantial physical nexus" to the rent stabilized apartment notwithstanding the fact he spent the weekends and summer months in the Hamptons, Long Island and the winter in Florida.[271] The Court noted that the Tenant continued to list the New York residence on his tax returns, driver's license, voter registration and bank and credit card accounts,

---

267 Sendowski v. Pilzer, 16 N.Y.S.3d 794 (App. Term, 1st Dep't 2015).

268 *Id.*

269 RSC [9 N.Y.C.R.R.] § 2524.4[c]; *see* Kalikow Family P'ship, LP v. Seidemann, 18 N.Y.S.3d 579 (App. Term, 2d, 11th & 13th Jud. Dists. 2015) (affirming judgment in favor of Landlord where the Tenant and his family primarily resided in Connecticut).

270 RSC [9 N.Y.C.R.R.] §§ 2520.6(u), 2523.5(b)(2). *See* Hyatt Ave. Assocs., LLC v. Rahman, 17 N.Y.S.3d 579 (App. Term, 2d, 11th & 13th Jud. Dists. 2015) (summary judgment denied where there was an issue of fact regarding the Tenant's primary residence).

271 RSP 86 Prop. LLC v. Sylvester, 15 N.Y.S.3d 714 (App. Term, 1st Dep't 2015).

mail was delivered to the premises, and he received medical care in New York City.[272]

A Tenant may not take a position that is inconsistent with "the declarations made under the penalty of perjury on income tax returns".[273] For example, where the Tenant deducted the entire rent on her tax returns as a "business expense", she could not then assert the apartment was her primary residence.[274] However, where only a portion of the rent is deducted as a business expense, the Court must make a determination regarding primary residence status.[275]

Prior to commencing a holdover proceeding, the Landlord must provide the Tenant (1) written notice between ninety (90) and 150 days before the expiration of the lease stating the Landlord's intention not to renew the lease, and (2) an additional thirty (30) day written notice stating the Landlord will commence a summary proceeding on the grounds that the Tenant does not use the premises as his or her primary residence.[276] The two (2) notices may be served simultaneously in a combined predicate notice, which is commonly referred to as a "Golub Notice".[277] The notices are only required to be served upon a party to the lease, and no other occupant has standing to challenge their sufficiency.[278]

---

272   *Id.; see also* Budhu v. Castro, Index No. 570004-16, 2016 WL 5395990, 2016 N.Y. Misc. LEXIS 3388 (App. Term, 1st Dep't Sept. 27, 2016) (Landlord failed to demonstrate that the 82-year old Tenant, who frequently visited his former girlfriend at a nearby apartment, did not maintain the rent controlled apartment as his primary residence).

273   Goldman v. Davis, 17 N.Y.S.3d 624 (App. Term, 1st Dep't 2015) (citations omitted).

274   Ansonia Assocs. L.P. v. Unwin, 130 A.D.3d 453, 13 N.Y.S.3d 67 (App. Div., 1st Dep't 2015); *Goldman*, 17 N.Y.S.3d at 624.

275   *See* BDS Assocs, LLC v. Lin, 31 N.Y.S.3d 920 (N.Y. Civ. Ct. 2016).

276   RSC [9 N.Y.C.R.R.] §§ 2524.2(a),[c](2), 2524.4[c].

277   *See* Georgetown Unsold Shares, LLC v. Ledet, 130 A.D.3d 99, 12 N.Y.S.3d 160 (App. Div., 2d Dep't 2015); 149th Partners LP v. Watts, Index No. 570732-15, 2015 WL 6633098, 2015 N.Y. Misc. LEXIS 3877 (App. Term, 1st Dep't Oct. 30, 2015).

278   *149th Partners LP*, 2015 WL at 6633098, 2015 N.Y. Misc. LEXIS at 3877 (non-party to the lease "[m]ay not be heard to argue that the combined (Golub) notice of lease non-renewal and termination utilized by landlord was not a proper predicate for this holdover proceeding seeking possession based upon the record tenant's alleged nonprimary residence"); 1700 First Ave. LLC v. Parsons-Novak, 998 N.Y.S.2d 757 (App. Term, 1st Dep't

The predicate notice must provide sufficient facts to establish that the premises are <u>not</u> being used by the Tenant as his or her primary residence. It is well-established that the conclusory claims that "[b]uilding personnel have not seen the tenant and the tenant has not spent 183 days in the past year residing in the apartment" are insufficient.[279]

Parenthetically, the Landlord's acceptance of rent, without more, during the period between the expiration of the lease and the commencement of the holdover proceeding does <u>not</u> vitiate the predicate notice.[280] Rather, a determination must be made whether there was an intent by the Landlord to waive the right to pursue a non-primary residence proceeding.[281]

C. YELLOWSTONE INJUNCTIONS

For commercial leases, where the Tenant is served with a Notice to Cure, the Tenant may seek to toll the "cure period" by obtaining a Yellowstone injunction.[282] The application for a Yellowstone injunction is typically made in conjunction with a declaratory judgment action in Supreme Court. The Supreme Court's decision on the injunction is <u>not</u> an "adjudication on the merits of the validity of landlord's termination of the lease and does not constitute law of the case".[283]

A Yellowstone injunction is intended to maintain the *status quo* during the pendency of the dispute.[284] Similar to other Landlord and

---

2014).

279   325 Third Ave. LLC v. Vargas, 30 N.Y.S.3d 536 (N.Y. Civ. Ct. 2016) (citations omitted); 2363 ACP Pineapple, LLC v. Iris House, Inc., 992 N.Y.S.2d 161 (App. Term, 1ˢᵗ Dep't 2014).

280   *Georgetown Unsold Shares, LLC*, 130 A.D.3d at 99, 12 N.Y.S.3d at 160; Goldman v. Becraft, 800 N.Y.S.2d 346 (App. Term, 1ˢᵗ Dep't 2001).

281   *Georgetown Unsold Shares, LLC*, 130 A.D.3d at 99, 12 N.Y.S.3d at 160.

282   See First Nat'l Stores v. Yellowstone Shopping Ctr., Inc., 21 N.Y.2d 630, at 637-38, 290 N.Y.S.2d 721 (1968); Hopp v. Raimondi, 51 A.D.3d 726, at 728, 858 N.Y.S.2d 300 (App. Div., 2d Dep't 2008).

283   River Park Residences, LP v. Richman Plaza Garage Corp., 17 N.Y.S.3d 385 (App. Term, 1ˢᵗ Dep't 2015).

284   Graubard, Mollen, Horowitz, Pomeranz & Shapiro v. 600 Third Ave. Assocs., 93 N.Y.2d 508, at 514, 693 N.Y.S.2d 91 (1999).

Tenant proceedings, the Tenant must provide the Landlord with notice of the application in accordance with the lease terms.

To obtain a Yellowstone injunction, a commercial Tenant must demonstrate that it (1) holds a commercial lease; (2) received a Notice of Default, Notice to Cure or other indicator that the rental agreement may be terminated; (3) made its request for the injunction prior to the termination of the rental agreement; and (4) is capable of curing the breach by any means short of vacating the premises.[285] Courts will typically grant the application with "[f]ar less than the showing normally required for the grant of preliminary injunctive relief".[286]

The District Court, similar to other local Housing Parts, may not issue injunctive relief, thus the need to make the application in Supreme Court. The request for a Yellowstone injunction must be made before the rental agreement terminates, whether upon its own expiration or the due date set forth in the Landlord's notice. An untimely request may be fatal to the Tenant's claim because the Courts are generally "[p]owerless to revive [a terminated or] expired lease".[287]

The Court is further without authority to "rewrite" the lease by extending the deadline for the repairs.[288] A Tenant may also pursue injunctive relief in a Court of competent jurisdiction pursuant to CPLR § 6301 by demonstrating (1) a likelihood of success on the merits; (2) irreparable harm; and (3) a balance of the inequities favoring

---

285 Trump on the Ocean, LLC v. Ash, 81 A.D.3d 713, at 716, 916 N.Y.S.2d 177, 181 (App. Div., 2d Dep't 2011); Purdue Pharma, LP v. Ardsley Partners, LP, 5 A.D.3d 654, at 655, 774 N.Y.S.2d 540 (App. Div., 2d Dep't 2004).

286 *Trump on the Ocean, LLC*, 81 A.D.3d at 716, 916 N.Y.S.2d at 181 (*citing* Post v. 120 E. End Ave. Corp., 62 N.Y.2d 19, at 24-25, 475 N.Y.S.2d 821, 823 (1984)).

287 *Post*, 62 N.Y.2d at 24-25, 475 N.Y.S.2d at 823; 276-43 Gourmet Grocery, Inc. v. 250 W. 43 Owner LLC, Index No. 157468-15, 2016 N.Y. App. Div. LEXIS 6407 (App. Div., 1st Dep't Oct. 4, 2016); Barsyl Supermarkets, Inc. v. Avenue P Assocs., LLC, 86 A.D.3d 545, at 546-47, 928 N.Y.S.2d 45, 47 (App. Div., 2d Dep't 2011). *But see* Village Ctr. for Care v. Sligo Realty and Serv. Corp., 95 A.D.3d 219, 943 N.Y.S.2d 11 (App. Div., 1st Dep't 2012) (application for Yellowstone injunction was timely, even when made after the initial cure date and service of the notice of termination, where the lease contemplated Tenant's inability to cure the default within the cure period).

288 *Trump on the Ocean, LLC*, 81 A.D.3d at 716, 916 N.Y.S.2d at 181.

injunctive relief.[289]

Although the overwhelming majority of Yellowstone injunctions involve commercial properties, the relief has been granted, on limited occasions, where the occupants were residential Tenants.[290] In addition, a Yellowstone injunction may be granted "where [the] nonpayment of rent is the only issue" and the lease provides that the tenancy is terminated if the rent is not timely paid following service of a Notice to Cure.[291]

The movant must typically post an undertaking in an amount rationally related to the Landlord's damages in the event it is determined that the injunction was unwarranted.[292] In New York City, RPAPL §§ 751(1) and 753(4) have combined largely to eliminate the need for injunctive relief in residential holdover proceedings because the Court must grant a Ten-Day stay to allow the Tenant an opportunity to cure the breach (RPAPL § 753(4)). Alternatively, the Tenant may avoid an eviction in a non-payment proceeding by depositing the rent arrears with the Court at any time prior to the issuance of the judgment and warrant (RPAPL § 751(1)).

---

289 See, e.g., Jones v. Park Front Apts., LLC, 73 A.D.3d 612, 901 N.Y.S.2d 46 (App. Div., 1st Dep't 2010).

290 See Hopp, 51 A.D.3d at 728, 858 N.Y.S.2d at 300 (residential property outside New York City); Caldwell v. American Package Co., Inc., 57 A.D.3d 15, 866 N.Y.S.2d 275 (App. Div., 2d Dep't 2008) (residential Tenants with a lease commercial in form); Gabai v. 130 Diamond St. LLC, 932 N.Y.S.2d 760 (Kings Cnty. Sup. Ct. 2011) (although a Yellowstone injunction may be extended to residential Tenants where the Landlord served a rent demand for the non-payment of rent, the Tenant must demonstrate "[s]ome equity or defense that could not be raised in the summary proceeding").

291 3636 Greystone Owners, Inc. v. Greystone Bldg., 4 A.D.3d 122, 771 N.Y.S.2d 341 (App. Div., 1st Dep't 2004).

292 See Medical Bldgs. Assocs., Inc. v. Abner Props. Co., 959 N.Y.S.2d 476 (App. Div., 1st Dep't 2013).

CHAPTER 4

PROPER AND NECESSARY PARTIES

The Landlord must name each "proper" and "necessary" party in a summary proceeding, which includes all <u>known</u> Tenants. A distinction is made between <u>known</u> Tenants and other occupants because a Tenant may sublet the premises or permit other occupants to take possession unbeknownst to the Landlord.

A. TENANTS

The requirement that the Landlord names each and every Tenant is a jurisdictional requirement. Although Tenants are jointly and severally liable for a money judgment in favor of the Landlord (i.e., the Landlord may enforce the judgment against any or all of the Tenants until the judgment is satisfied),[293] the Landlord may <u>not</u> pick and choose against which Tenants to commence a summary proceeding.

This is the case even where the Landlord leases the premises to multiple Tenants but only some of the occupants pay rent. Due to the fact that Tenants are both "proper" and "necessary" parties in a summary proceeding, each Tenant must be afforded an opportunity to be heard.[294]

---

[293] *See* Priegue v. Paulus, 988 N.Y.S.2d 525 (App. Term, 9ᵗʰ & 10ᵗʰ Jud. Dists. 2014); Armour v. McDermott, 906 N.Y.S.2d 770 (App. Term, 9ᵗʰ & 10ᵗʰ Jud. Dists. 2009) (Tenants named on the lease are presumed to be joint obligors due to their status as tenants in common). A joint obligor that pays more than its proportionate share is entitled to contribution from another joint obligor. *See* NY Artistic, LLC v. Archetype, LLC, Index No. 650871-13, 2014 WL 3381984, 2014 N.Y. Misc. LEXIS 3070 (N.Y. Cnty. Sup. Ct. July 7, 2014).

[294] *See generally* 45ᵗʰ & Broadway Assocs. v. Skyline Enters., 544 N.Y.S.2d 975 (N.Y. Civ. Ct. 1989).

It is to the Landlord's benefit to name all of the Tenants because only those persons named in the proceeding may appear on the warrant and, as a result, be evicted should an eviction become necessary. The spouse of a Tenant need not be named unless he or she has an "independent possessory right" to the premises.[295] The same holds true for adult children,[296] and minor children should not be named in the summary proceeding because they will be removed along with their parent or guardian.[297]

An interesting situation involves the assignment of a lease. It is well-established that a summary proceeding may <u>not</u> be maintained against a Tenant who, with the knowledge of the Landlord, assigns (as opposed to sublets) the lease and all obligations thereunder to a third party. Where the assignment occurs <u>prior</u> to the commencement of the summary proceeding, the Landlord may only proceed against the assignee.[298] The Landlord may, however, be permitted to seek monetary damages against the assignor in a plenary action.

1. ROOMMATE RULE (IMMEDIATE FAMILY PLUS ONE)

A residential leasehold entered into by one (1) Tenant permits the Tenant's immediate family members plus one (1) additional guest, and the guest's dependent children, to take possession along with the Tenant provided the Tenant and/or the Tenant's spouse occupies the premises as their primary residence.[299] This rule is commonly referred

---

295 Kuprewicz v. Muktadir, Index No. 1648-01, 2002 WL 31940887, 2002 N.Y. Misc. LEXIS 1672 (App. Term, 2d & 11th Jud. Dists. September 19, 2002).

296 *See* Loira v. Anagnastopolous, 204 A.D.2d 608, 612 N.Y.S.2d 189 (App. Div., 2d Dep't 1994); JLNT Realty, LLC v. Liautaud, 26 N.Y.S.3d 213 (App. Term, 2d, 11th & 13th Jud. Dists. 2015); New York City Hous. Auth. v. Kilafofski, N.Y.L.J., June 6, 1996, at 36 (App. Term, 2d & 11th Jud. Dists. 1996); Crossroads Assocs., LLC v. Amenya, 16 N.Y.S.3d 791 (Peekskill City Ct. 2015).

297 Daley v. Billinghurst, 799 N.Y.S.2d 159 (App. Term, 2d & 11th Jud. Dists. 2004).

298 Dun-Donnelly Pub'g Corp. v. Kenvic Assocs., 225 A.D.2d 373, at 374, 639 N.Y.S.2d 42 (App. Div., 1st Dep't 1996); I & T Petroleum, Inc. v. Lascalia, 880 N.Y.S.2d 873 (Nassau Cnty. Sup. Ct. 2009).

299 RPL § 235-f(3). *See* Roxborough Apts. Corp. v. Becker, 296 A.D.2d 358, 745 N.Y.S.2d 173 (App. Div., 1st Dep't 2002) (noting that the Tenant had three (3) roommates in violation

to as The Roommate Rule, and is applicable to all residential premises regardless of whether the premises is subject to the Multiple Dwelling Law.[300] Although a lease provision waiving these rights is unenforceable, the Landlord reserves the right to "restrict occupancy" to comply with federal, state and local ordinances.[301]

A residential lease agreement entered into by two (2) or more Tenants permits the "immediate family of tenants, occupants and dependent children of occupants [to take possession as well]; provided that the total number of tenants and occupants, excluding occupants' dependent children, does not exceed the number of tenants specified in the current lease or rental agreement".[302] At least one (1) of the Tenants and/or their spouses must occupy the premises as their primary residence.[303]

2. SENIOR CITIZENS

Real Property Law § 227-a permits the early termination of a residential lease where the Tenant or the Tenant's spouse reaches or will reach the age of sixty-two (62) during its term. A lease provision waiving the rights afforded under this section is "void as contrary to public policy".[304]

The lease termination date must be at least thirty (30) days <u>after</u> the due date of the next rent payment.[305] The Tenant may invoke this right in two (2) ways. First, the Tenant may provide certified documentation from a physician stating that due to medical reasons, the Tenant is unable to independently reside in the premises and requires assistance to

---

of RPL § 235-f).

300   *See* Barrett Japaning, Inc. v. Bialobroda, 68 A.D.3d 474, 892 N.Y.S.2d 35 (App. Div., 1st Dep't 2009).

301   RPL §§ 235-f(7),(8).

302   *Id.* § 235-f(4).

303   *Id.*

304   *Id.* § 227-a(4).

305   *Id.* § 227-a(2); *see* Plotkin v. Fairfield at Setauket, LLC, 819 N.Y.S.2d 212 (App. Term, 9th & 10th Jud. Dists. 2006) (two-week notice inadequate pursuant to RPL § 227-a(2)).

perform daily activities, and, as a result, will be moving into the residence of a family member.[306] The termination notice must further include a notarized statement from a family member (1) verifying the familial relationship and (2) confirming that the Tenant and/or Tenant's spouse will be moving into his or her residence "for a period of not less than six months".[307]

Alternatively, the qualifying Tenant may terminate the lease by providing proof that he or she will be moving into an adult care facility pursuant to section 2(21) of the Social Services Law,[308] a residential health care facility pursuant to Public Health Law § 2801,[309] or other qualifying subsidized housing unit.[310] The termination notice must be accompanied by an executed copy of the lease or contract between the Tenant and facility demonstrating admission or pending admission.[311]

B. SUBTENANTS

A Subtenant is a "proper" but <u>not</u> a "necessary" party in a summary proceeding.[312] This means that the Landlord may, in its discretion, commence a summary proceeding against a Subtenant provided all of the Tenants are also named in the Petition.

---

306   RPL § 227-a(1).

307   *Id.* § 227-a(2).

308   Effective July 1, 2017, an "adult care facility" is defined as "a family type home for adults, a shelter for adults, a residence for adults, an enriched housing program or an adult home, which provides temporary or long-term residential care and services to adults who, though not requiring continual medical or nursing care as provided by facilities licensed pursuant to article twenty-eight of the public health law or articles nineteen, twenty-three and thirty-one of the mental hygiene law, are by reason of physical or other limitations associated with age, physical or mental disabilities or other factors, unable or substantially unable to live independently". *See* SOCIAL SERVS. LAW § 2(21).

309   The term "residential health care facility" is defined as "a nursing home or a facility providing health-related service". PUBLIC HEALTH LAW § 2801(3).

310   RPL § 227-a(1).

311   *Id.* § 227-a(2). *See* Windsor Realty LLC v. Sadacca, 801 N.Y.S.2d 244 (N.Y. Civ. Ct. 2005) (failure to provide documentation demonstrating admission or pending admission necessitates denial of claim).

312   *See* 117-119 Leasing Corp. v. Reliable Wool Stock, LLC, 139 A.D.3d 420, 30 N.Y.S.3d 622

The Landlord may <u>not</u> under any circumstance commence a summary proceeding against a Subtenant without also naming the Tenants because the Landlord is <u>not</u> in privity with a Subtenant.[313] It is for this reason that where the Landlord prevails against the Tenants, the subtenancy is automatically terminated.[314] However, only those Subtenants named in the summary proceeding may be evicted.[315]

Where the summary proceeding is dismissed against the Tenants, the proceeding will also be dismissed against the Subtenant.[316] On the other hand, if the proceeding is dismissed against the Subtenant, then the Landlord may continue to proceed against the Tenant.[317]

A judgment of possession and a warrant of eviction, without a money judgment, is typically the relief sought against Subtenants. Notably, a Tenant may commence a summary proceeding directly against a Subtenant.[318] Tenants and Subtenants may further assert claims against one another regarding damages, but this usually occurs in a plenary action outside the context of a summary proceeding. It has been held that where a commercial Subtenant agrees within the sublease to be bound by "all of the provisions and restrictions in the master lease" between the Landlord and Tenant, the Subtenant may be liable

---

(App. Div., 1st Dep't 2016); 1234 Broadway LLC v. Ying, 31 N.Y.S.3d 922 (App. Term, 1st Dep't 2016).

313   Triborough Bridge & Tunnel Auth. v. Wimpfheimer, 633 N.Y.S.2d 695, 696-97 (App. Term, 1st Dep't 1995); see 7001 E. 71st St., LLC v. Millenium Health Servs., 138 A.D.3d 573, 28 N.Y.S.3d 604 (App. Div., 1st Dep't 2016); 170 W. 85th St. Tenants Assoc. v. Cruz, 173 A.D.2d 338, 569 N.Y.S.2d 705 (App. Div., 1st Dep't 1991).

314   117-119 Leasing Corp., 139 A.D.3d at 420, 30 N.Y.S.3d at 622; 170 W. 85th St. Tenants Assoc., 173 A.D.2d at 338, 569 N.Y.S.2d at 705.

315   Farchester Gardens, Inc. v. Elwell, 525 N.Y.S.2d 111 (Yonkers City Ct. 1987).

316   See Tefft v. Apex Pawnbroking & Jewelry Co., Inc., 75 A.D.2d 891, 428 N.Y.S.2d 52 (App. Div., 2d Dep't 1980).

317   1234 Broadway LLC, 31 N.Y.S.3d at 922 (summary proceeding continued against Tenant following dismissal against "John Doe").

318   See, e.g., Sow v. Thanvi, 31 N.Y.S.3d 924 (App. Term, 2d, 11th & 13th Jud. Dists. 2016) (commercial non-payment proceeding dismissed absent agreement between the Tenant and Subtenant for the payment of rent); Subway Rests., Inc. v. Mannetti, Index No. 957-02, 2003 WL 22038450, 2003 N.Y. Misc. LEXIS 1115 (App. Term, 9th & 10th Jud. Dists. July 11, 2003).

for damages to "the entire leasehold premises" even where its holdover included only a portion of the property.[319]

A peculiar situation arises where the Landlord prevails against the Tenants but the Subtenant, who was not named in the summary proceeding, refuses to leave. Notwithstanding the possible establishment of a tenancy by sufferance, the Subtenant may continue to occupy the premises even after the Tenants have been evicted. If in fact a tenancy by sufferance was established, the Petitioner may bring another summary proceeding to regain possession after giving the Subtenant a Thirty-Day Notice. Otherwise, the Landlord may be left with no recourse other than an ejectment proceeding in a court of competent jurisdiction.

Unique to New York City Rent Stabilized properties, a Tenant may sublet the apartment provided he or she (1) simultaneously maintains the premises as his or her primary residence and (2) the rent charged to the Subtenant does not exceed the regulated rent, plus a ten (10) percent surcharge where the premises are provided fully furnished.[320] The premises may not be subleased for more than two (2) out of the four (4) years preceding the expiration of the sublease.[321]

C. JOHN AND JANE "DOES"—UNNAMED RESPONDENTS

The Landlord will typically identify unknown individuals in both the predicate notice and the Notice of Petition and Petition as "John Doe" and "Jane Doe". Service of the appropriate documents, and the requisite number of copies of each, must be made on each "Doe" in the same manner as a named individual. Parenthetically, a friend of the "Doe" lacks standing to appear on his or her behalf.[322]

---

319 PHH Mtg. Corp. v. Ferro, Kuba, Mangano, Skylar, Gacovino & Lake, P.C., 113 A.D.3d 831, 979 N.Y.S.2d 536 (App. Div., 2d Dep't 2014).

320 RSC [9 N.Y.C.R.R.] § 2525.6(a),(b). A violation may result in an award of treble damages. *Id.*

321 *Id.* § 2525.6[c].

322 *See* Medhat O'Kelly, As Administrator of the Estate of Magdy O'Kelly v. "John Doe", 36 N.Y.S.3d 408 (App. Term, 2d, 11th & 13th Jud. Dists. 2016).

The Landlord <u>must</u> move to amend the caption to substitute the proper name of an occupant identified as a "Doe" when the individual's name is learned. The failure to do so may result in dismissal where it can be demonstrated that the person's name was disclosed <u>prior</u> to the commencement of the summary proceeding.[323] However, as previously mentioned, the proceeding may continue against the Tenant even where the case is dismissed against the "Doe" because the "Doe" is a "proper" but <u>not</u> a "necessary" party.[324]

D. GUARANTORS

A summary proceeding may <u>not</u> be maintained against the guarantor of a rental agreement unless the guarantor has an independent possessory interest in the premises.[325] The Landlord may, however, commence a plenary action to enforce the guaranty in a court of competent jurisdiction.[326] This is the case even where the lease is terminated early, provided the lease contains a survival clause continuing the Tenant's obligations under the lease (and the guarantor's obligations) post-termination.[327] Otherwise, the right to enforce not-yet accrued lease provisions against the guarantor (and Tenant) may be forfeited upon the termination or expiration of the rental agreement.[328] Depending on the

---

323   CPLR § 1024. *See 1234 Broadway LLC*, 31 N.Y.S.3d at 922; Cymo Trading Corp. v. Manhattan Inn Hostel, LLC, 943 N.Y.S.2d 791 (App. Term, 1st Dep't 2012).

324   *See Triborough Bridge & Tunnel Auth.*, 633 N.Y.S.2d at 696-97.

325   *See* MTC Commons, LLC v. Millbrook Training Ctr. & Spa, Ltd., 31 N.Y.S.3d 922 (App. Term, 9th & 10th Jud. Dists. 2016); Phoenix Indus., Inc. v. Ultimate Sports, LLC, 859 N.Y.S.2d 906 (App. Term, 9th & 10th Jud. Dists. 2008); 26-44 Lincoln Ave., LLC v. Iranian Jewish Ctr. of Roslyn, Inc., 901 N.Y.S.2d 911 (Nassau Cnty. Dist. Ct. 2009).

326   *See* Hawthorne Gardens, LLC v. Salman Home, Inc., 94 A.D.3d 425, 941 N.Y.S.2d 489 (App. Div., 1st Dep't 2012) (guarantor held liable for accelerated rent through end of lease term when the guaranty was "[o]nly for the first two years of the lease").

327   *See* H.L. Realty, LLC v. Edwards, 131 A.D.3d 573, 15 N.Y.S.3d 413 (App. Div., 2d Dep't 2015) (summary judgment granted in favor of Landlord against guarantor where the lease contained a survival clause and the parties' stipulation terminating the rental agreement did not terminate the obligations of either the Tenant or the guarantor); Brusco v. Soclof, 899 N.Y.S.2d 57 (App. Term, 1st Dep't 2009).

328   *See generally* 300 E. 96th St. LLC v. Saka, 28 N.Y.S.3d 651 (App. Term, 1st Dep't 2015)

guaranty provision, it is possible that the "[g]uarantor's liability may exceed the scope of the principal's liability".[329]

There have been occasions where a guarantor has appeared in the Housing Part, either voluntarily or after being improperly named as a Respondent in a summary proceeding. Even if the guarantor consents to the jurisdiction of the Court, such as to avoid being named in a subsequent plenary action, the summary proceeding must be dismissed against the guarantor because the Court may not expand its jurisdictional authority even with the consent of the parties.[330]

E. FAMILY MEMBERS

With limited exceptions, a family member may not evict another family member in a summary proceeding where the occupancy arises out of the "familial relationship", such as an adult child who has lived in the family home since birth.[331] In other words, the absence of an identifiable Landlord and Tenant relationship necessitates dismissal due to the Housing Part's lack of subject matter jurisdiction. Instead, the owner may commence an ejectment proceeding in an appropriate court of competent jurisdiction. Parenthetically, an ejectment proceeding may be commenced by either the owner or the occupant, but, unlike a summary proceeding, monetary damages may be awarded.

A summary proceeding may be permitted to evict a family member whose occupancy is not the result of the "familial relationship".[332] For example, where a parent and adult child enter into a rental agreement for the payment of rent for a specific period of time or where a recent

(summary judgment denied due to issues of fact regarding the guaranty and whether it applied to the renewal lease).

329   See International Plaza Assocs., L.P. v. Lacher, 104 A.D.3d 578, 961 N.Y.S.2d 427 (App. Div., 1st Dep't 2013).

330   26-44 Lincoln Ave., LLC, 901 N.Y.S.2d at 911.

331   See O'Neill v. O'Neill, 36 N.Y.S.3d 48 (N.Y. Civ. Ct. 2016) (summary proceeding to evict adult son who resided in the family home for more than 30 years dismissed).

332   See generally Pugliese v. Pugliese, 37 N.Y.S.3d 208 (App. Term, 2d, 11th & 13th Jud. Dists. 2016) (summary proceeding to evict Petitioner's mother would have been permitted had there been credible proof of a Landlord and Tenant relationship).

college graduate returns home with the understanding that he or she will "assist around the house" and remain only until enough money is saved to find another residence, a summary proceeding on proper notice may be appropriate.

Although summary proceedings are generally an emotional experience, the emotion is heightened when family members are involved. These matters often involve Family Court and/or Criminal Court issues, including Orders of Protection, which may impact the right to possess the property. Of course, the Housing Part will <u>not</u> modify or supersede a prior Court's Order, and this often has to be explained to *pro se* litigants.

Case law has evolved by extending the breadth of "familial relationships" beyond that of a stereotypical traditional family. Below is a brief synopsis of family member eviction cases. The cases are neither exhaustive nor cumulative, but rather a diverse sampling of efforts to evict family members in summary proceedings.

In *Rosenstiel v. Rosenstiel,* the Appellate Division, First Department held that a separated spouse may <u>not</u> be evicted in a summary proceeding. The Court reasoned that the occupation of the marital home by a spouse exists "[b]ecause of special rights incidental to the marriage contract and relationship" that cannot be abridged as long as the marital relationship remains intact.[333] In *Kakwani v. Kakwani,* the licensee holdover proceeding to evict Petitioner's sister-in-law was dismissed where the Respondent's husband (i.e., Petitioner's brother) "moved out of the master bedroom [of his brother's home] and into another room in the house".[334] The Court reasoned that since the Respondent entered the premises due to her marriage to Petitioner's brother, where they lived as a family for four (4) years, the familial relationship precluded an eviction by summary proceeding.

Following the termination or nullification of the marriage, a

---

333   Rosenstiel v. Rosenstiel, 20 A.D.2d 71, at 76-77, 245 N.Y.S.2d 395 (App. Div., 1st Dep't 1963). *But see* Halaby v. Halaby, 44 A.D.2d 495, 355 N.Y.S.2d 671 (App. Div., 4th Dep't 1974) (summary proceeding may be maintained against a spouse where the couple entered into a license agreement in connection with the divorce proceeding).

334   Kakwani v. Kakwani, 967 N.Y.S.2d 827 (Nassau Cnty. Dist. Ct. 2013).

summary proceeding to regain possession may be appropriate but that depends on the particular circumstances and the terms of the divorce. For example, an ex-wife's motion to dismiss the licensee holdover proceeding was granted where she and her former husband shared the family home as a married couple for approximately sixteen (16) years during which time she financially contributed to the household.[335] A different result, however, was reached in *Piotrowski v. Little* where a summary proceeding was permitted against a licensee co-resident same-sex partner pursuant to RPAPL § 713(7).[336] The previous year, the District Court of Nassau County held that a daughter-in-law could be evicted in a holdover proceeding because "[t]he primary basis for finding that a family member was exempt from licensee status" was that "[t]he parties lived together 'in a family unit' with 'some indicia of permanence or continuity'", which the Court held had not been established.[337]

Generally, efforts to evict children and grandchildren have not been successful. For example, in *Sirota v. Sirota*, the Appellate Term held that the familial exception prohibited a parent from evicting his adult children who had lived in the home for nearly thirty (30) years.[338] Moreover, in *Sears v. Okin*, a dispute between domestic partners, it was held that a parent may <u>not</u> evict his minor children absent a Court Order.[339] In *Williams v. Williams*, the summary proceeding to evict adult grandchildren was dismissed because the grandchildren had resided in the residence with their grandparents as a family for more than a decade since age eleven (11).[340]

---

335 *See* Nauth v. Nauth, 981 N.Y.S.2d 266 (N.Y. Civ. Ct. 2013); *see also* Saoidoh v. Saoidoh, 26 N.Y.S.3d 727 (N.Y. Civ. Ct. 2015) (dismissing summary proceeding against former spouse and daughter where the family home, which was acquired during the marriage, was not addressed in the Judgment of Divorce).

336 Piotrowski v. Little, 911 N.Y.S.2d 583 (Middletown City Ct. 2010).

337 Lally v. Fasano, 875 N.Y.S.2d 750, 753 (Nassau Cnty. Dist. Ct. 2009).

338 Sirota v. Sirota, 626 N.Y.S.2d 672, 673 (N.Y. Civ. Ct. 1995), *modified*, 644 N.Y.S.2d 950 (App. Term, 2d & 11th Jud. Dists. 1996).

339 Sears, Jr. v. Okin, 847 N.Y.S.2d 899 (App. Term, 9th & 10th Jud. Dists. 2007). *See also* Isler v. Isler, Index No. 66819-08, 2008 N.Y. Misc. LEXIS 7511, at *3 (N.Y. Cnty. Sup. Ct. Dec. 11, 2008).

340 Williams v. Williams, 822 N.Y.S.2d 415 (N.Y. Civ. Ct. 2006).

In *Robinson v. Holder*, the licensee holdover proceeding commenced by an incarcerated father and his mother to evict the father's paramour and the minor child they had in common was dismissed.[341] The evidence established that the paramour originally moved into the premises due to the then expectant child with co-Petitioner to whom she was once engaged but did not marry. Although a one-half interest in the property, which was in foreclosure, was conveyed to the co-Petitioner, it was unclear whether the father sought the eviction because he did not sign the Notice of Petition or Petition, and did not attend the hearing due to his incarceration. The co-Petitioner testified that she did not consider the relationship to be that of a Landlord and Tenant, and further expressed frustration that she had been denied visits with her grandson.[342] Unable to satisfy their burden, the proceeding was dismissed.

The *Robinson* case further stands for the proposition that a parent may not, as a matter of law, evict his or her minor child without a Court Order. This protection is afforded to all children whether born in or out of wedlock.[343]

F. EXPRESS TRUST

Where the premises are placed in an express trust, the trust generally vests in the trustee.[344] Accordingly, the proper party to sue or be sued is the trustee named in the trust agreement, and the failure to name the trustee as a party on behalf of the trust will result in dismissal.[345]

---

341 Robinson v. Holder, 901 N.Y.S.2d 902 (Suffolk Cnty. Dist. Ct. 2009).

342 *Id.*

343 *See* N.Y. Fam. Ct. Act §§ 413, 513 (McKinney 2008). *See* Jimenez v. Weinberger, 417 U.S. 628, 94 S.Ct. 2496 (1974).

344 Estate, Powers and Trust Law ("EPTL") § 7-2.1(a).

345 CPLR § 1004; *see* Salanitro Family Trust v. Gorina, 29 N.Y.S.3d 849 (App. Term, 2d, 11th & 13th Jud. Dists. 2015); Ronald Henry Land Trust v. Sasmor, 990 N.Y.S.3d 767 (App. Term, 2d, 11th & 13th Jud. Dists. 2014).

NOTICE OF PETITION
AND PETITION

In most of the Housing Parts, the Petitioner commences a summary proceeding to recover possession by filing a Notice of Petition and Petition with the Clerk of the Court. Regardless of whether the proceeding is a non-payment or a holdover proceeding, the Petitioner must pay a filing fee.[346]

A. NOTICE OF PETITION

The purpose of the Notice of Petition is to provide the Tenant or occupant, referred to as the Respondent in a summary proceeding, ample notice of the proceeding and the relief sought. The Notice of Petition must provide (1) the time and location of the hearing; (2) notice that the failure to assert and establish a defense may preclude the Respondent from asserting the defense or related claim in another proceeding; and (3) a description of the premises for venue purposes.[347]

For non-payment proceedings in the New York City Housing Parts, the Notice of Petition must further state that (1) the proceeding is

---

346   At the time of publication, the filing fee to commence a summary proceeding was $45.00. In 2005, the change was made such that civil actions in the City and District Courts are commenced at the time of "filing" (as opposed to "service") which comports with the Supreme and County Court standards. As a general matter, in the Justice Courts the proceeding continues to be commenced upon "service" of the Notice of Petition and Petition.

347   RPAPL § 731(2); see N.Y. UNIFORM CITY CT. ACT § 204 (McKinney 2009); N.Y. CITY CIV. CT. ACT § 303 (McKinney 2009); N.Y. UNIFORM DIST. CT. ACT § 303 (McKinney 2009); N.Y. UNIFORM JUST. CT. ACT § 204 (McKinney 2009).

returnable within five (5) days of service; (2) if the Respondent answers the Petition, a hearing will be scheduled between three (3) and eight (8) days from the answer; and (3) if the Respondent fails to answer or appear, the Court may enter a judgment against the Respondent and stay issuance of the warrant of eviction for a maximum of ten (10) days.[348]

A judge, attorney or the Clerk of the Court (for *pro se* Petitioners) may issue a Notice of Petition.[349] The Clerk of the Court assigns the proceeding an index number at the time of filing. In New York City, an attorney may <u>not</u> issue a Notice of Petition.[350]

B. THE PETITION

The Petition expands upon the Notice of Petition by asserting specific allegations. At minimum, the Petition <u>must</u> include the following information: (1) the Petitioner's interest in the premises;[351] (2) the Respondent's interest in the premises and relationship to the Petitioner;[352] (3) a description of the premises from which removal is sought;[353] (4) sufficient facts upon which the proceeding is based;[354] and

---

348 RPAPL § 732; N.Y. Uniform Rules for Trial Cts. [22 N.Y.C.R.R.] § 208.42(d); Augoshe v. Sitar, Index No. 895-01, 2002 WL 860821, 2002 N.Y. Misc. LEXIS 363 (App. Term, 9th & 10th Jud. Dists. Feb. 21, 2002) (RPAPL § 732 only applies to proceedings pending in the Civil Court of the City of New York).

349 RPAPL § 731(1).

350 N.Y. City Civ. Ct. Act § 401[c].

351 RPAPL § 741(1).

352 *Id.* § 741(2). *See* Brookwood Coram I, LLC v. Oliva, 15 N.Y.S.3d 710 (App. Term, 9th & 10th Jud. Dists. 2015); 287 Realty Corp. v. Livathinos, 967 N.Y.S.2d 87 (App. Term, 2d, 11th & 13th Jud. Dists. 2013); Cintron v. Pandis, 950 N.Y.S.2d 490 (App. Term, 9th & 10th Jud. Dists. 2012); Jeffco Mgmt. Corp. v. Local Dev. Corp. of Crown Heights, 881 N.Y.S.2d 364 (App. Term, 2d, 11th & 13th Jud. Dists. 2009).

353 RPAPL § 741(3). *See* Clarke v. Wallace Oil Co., Inc., 284 A.D.2d 492, 727 N.Y.S.2d 139 (App. Div., 2d Dep't 2001).

354 RPAPL § 741(4); Oakwood Terr. Hous. Corp. v. Monk, 36 N.Y.S.3d 48 (App. Term, 9th & 10th Jud. Dists. 2016); Ropshitz v. Schwartz, 927 N.Y.S.2d 819 (App. Term, 9th & 10th Jud. Dists. 2011); McFadden v. Sassower, 907 N.Y.S.2d 101 (App. Term, 9th & 10th Jud. Dists. 2010).

(5) a statement of the relief sought.[355]

The failure to include "the name of the village [or hamlet] in the address for the property...does not constitute a fatal defect, particularly [where] the address was fully set forth elsewhere in the petition".[356] Where the occupant is a Section 8 Tenant, or in possession pursuant to another government sponsored program, the Petition must describe the Tenant's "[r]egulatory status, because [the] status may determine the scope of the tenant's rights".[357] A summary proceeding may be dismissed where the Petitioner fails to allege the reason for the termination of a Section 8 Tenant's subsidy.[358]

The Petition typically states that the Petitioner is seeking (1) a final judgment of possession, which means lawful possession of the premises; (2) a warrant of eviction; and (3) if a monetary award for unpaid rent is sought, the amount claimed and the period during which the claim accrued.[359] The Petition must further set forth the dollar amount sought for items "other than base rent".[360] In a holdover proceeding, where a monetary award is sought, the Petition will state both the amount of unpaid rent claimed prior to the expiration or termination of the lease, and the fair value for the continued use and occupancy of the premises.

The Petition must be verified by a person authorized pursuant to RPAPL § 721 or by the Petitioner's attorney.[361] Unlike civil practice in other courts, an attorney may verify the Petition where the Petitioner

---

355 RPAPL § 741(5).

356 Birchwood Ct. Owners, Inc. v. Toner, 37 N.Y.S.3d 206 (App. Term, 9th & 10th Jud. Dists. 2016).

357 *Cintron*, 950 N.Y.S.2d at 490.

358 See 2025 Regent, LLC v. Bennet, 930 N.Y.S.2d 177 (App. Term, 2d, 11th & 13th Jud. Dists. 2011).

359 RPAPL § 741(5); Poughkeepsie Hous. Auth. v. Lee, N.Y.L.J., Dec. 18, 1998, at 36 (App. Term, 9th & 10th Jud. Dists. 1998).

360 *Oakwood Terr. Hous. Corp.*, 36 N.Y.S.3d at 48.

361 1346 Park Pl. HDFC v. Wright, 34 N.Y.S.3d 561 (App. Term, 2d, 11th & 13th Jud. Dists. 2016).

and attorney are situated in the same county.[362]

The failure to verify (or to properly verify) the Petition is <u>not</u> a jurisdictional defect. However, pursuant to CPLR § 3022, the Petition may be deemed a nullity where the Tenant immediately raises an objection, which has been defined as "within 24 hours of the receipt of the defective pleading".[363]

An attorney's verification may delay the proceeding in the event of a default. For instance, where the Respondent defaults in a non-payment proceeding, the Court typically awards a default judgment, without an inquest, provided the pleadings are facially sufficient, the Notice of Petition includes the requisite information, and proper service is alleged.[364] However, where the Petition is verified by counsel, it has been held that a default judgment should <u>not</u> be awarded unless the application is accompanied by the sworn affidavit or testimony of an individual with personal knowledge of the claims.[365] If the Petitioner does not have such a person in Court at the time of the default, the Court may deny the default application without prejudice to renew at an inquest or upon the submission of a sworn affidavit from the Landlord or property manager.[366]

1. AMENDING THE PETITION

At or prior to the hearing, where both the Petitioner and Respondent are present, the Petitioner may amend the Petition to include the rent and "additional" rent that accrued since the commencement of the

---

362   RPAPL § 741.

363   *1346 Park Pl. HDFC*, 34 N.Y.S.3d at 561.

364   *See* RPAPL §§ 732(3),(4) (within New York City); Brusco v. Braun, 84 N.Y.2d 674, 621 N.Y.S.2d 291 (1994).

365   77 Commercial Holding, LLC v. Central Plastic, Inc., 4 N.Y.S.3d 464 (App. Term, 2d, 11th & 13th Jud. Dists. 2014); Sella Props. v. DeLeon, 890 N.Y.S.2d 254, 255-56 (App. Term, 2d, 11th & 13th Jud. Dists. 2009); Kentpark Realty Corp. v. Lasertone Corp., 779 N.Y.S.2d 324, 326 (App. Term, 2d & 11th Jud. Dists. 2004).

366   1081 Flatbush Ave., LLC v. Jadoo, 946 N.Y.S.2d 67 (App. Term, 2d, 11th & 13th Jud. Dists. 2011); *see* 285 Schenectady LLC v. Williams, Index No. 51905-16, 2016 WL 3583928, 2016 N.Y. Misc. LEXIS 2409 (N.Y. Civ. Ct. May 11, 2016) (granting default judgment following submission of sworn affidavit from an individual with firsthand knowledge of the claims); 104 Realty LLC v. Brown, 981 N.Y.S.2d 637 n.14 (N.Y. Civ. Ct. 2013).

summary proceeding. As a practical matter, the Petitioner does <u>not</u> have to make another rent demand for the newly accrued rent.[367] The parties should be mindful that the Petition may be amended to conform to the proof at the hearing.[368]

Leave to amend the Petition will be "freely" granted without advanced notice to the Respondent provided there is no prejudice or undue surprise.[369] The amendment may be made orally, but, regardless of form, a request to amend the Petition must be timely.[370]

For example, an amendment request made on the 1st of the month to include the month's rent may be denied as premature because typically the rent is not considered late until the 2nd or other date specified within the rental agreement. In addition, an amendment to include newly accrued rent and "additional" rent items should <u>not</u> be permitted if the Tenant is not present.[371] The rationale is that although the Respondent may have accepted the outcome and chose not to appear, she did not consent to a money judgment for an amount higher than that set forth in the Petition.

An amendment request may similarly be denied where the Tenant appeared on the initial Court date but failed to return for the hearing. This commonly occurs when the proceeding is adjourned on the initial date, and the Landlord either failed to or was unable to amend because the rent had not yet become due. In other words, the Petitioner may proceed based on the default, but may <u>not</u> amend the Petition for the

---

367   *See* 36 Main Realty Corp. v. Wang Law Office, PLLC, 19 N.Y.S.3d 654 (App. Term, 2d, 11th & 13th Jud. Dists. 2015); Building Mgmt. Co., Inc. v. Benmen, 959 N.Y.S.2d 87 (N.Y. Civ. Ct. 2012); JDM Washington St., LLC v. 90 Washington Rest. Assocs., 950 N.Y.S.2d 647 (N.Y. Civ. Ct. 2012).

368   *JDM Washington St., LLC,* 950 N.Y.S.2d at 647 (granting motion to conform pleading to the proof at the hearing, but the case was nevertheless dismissed due to a discrepancy in the dollar amounts).

369   *36 Main Realty Corp.,* 19 N.Y.S.3d at 654.

370   *See, e.g.,* Regensburg v. Rzonca, 836 N.Y.S.2d 489 (Suffolk Cnty. Dist. Ct. 2007); Jefferson House Assocs., LLC v. Boyle, 800 N.Y.S.2d 348 (Ossining Just. Ct. 2005).

371   *See generally* Mustafa v. Plein, 950 N.Y.S.2d 492 (App. Term, 2d, 11th & 13th Jud. Dists. 2012) (in a holdover proceeding, default judgment limited to the amount in the Petition); Port Chester Hous. Auth. v. Turner, 734 N.Y.S.2d 805 (App. Term, 9th & 10th Jud. Dists. 2001) (same result in a non-payment proceeding).

higher dollar amount. The declination of the amendment may result in a shorter stay, if any, on the execution of the warrant of eviction.

Amendments with respect to parties' names and the proper spelling of names are routinely granted. For example, Petitioner was permitted to substitute the proper name of the person to whom the premises was transferred after a certified copy of the transfer deed was provided.[372] However, a request to substitute the name of an individual who was neither served nor listed in the caption is <u>not</u> permitted without the individual's consent.

An amendment may also be granted to correct a mistake in the address or description of the property, either pre- or post-judgment, provided there is no prejudice to the Respondent.[373] For example, in *Najjar v. Cooper*, the Court granted the Landlord's cross-motion to amend the Petition to state that the apartment was situated on the first floor.[374] In *Gnosis, LLC v. Soforte*, the Petitioner's post-judgment motion to amend the judgment and warrant to include the proper village and street suffix was similarly granted.[375]

2. NON-PAYMENT PROCEEDING

The Petition in a non-payment proceeding must allege that a rent demand was made, either oral or written.[376] If the rent demand was made in writing, then the Landlord must state the manner of service or attach the affidavit of service to the Petition.[377] If the affidavit was

---

372 Blue Mountain Homes, LLC v. Betancourt, 16 N.Y.S.3d 791 (App. Term, 9th & 10th Jud. Dists. 2015).

373 Najjar v. Cooper, 950 N.Y.S.2d 724 (App. Term, 2d, 11th & 13th Jud. Dists. 2012); Gnosis, LLC v. Soforte, LLC, 958 N.Y.S.2d 307 (Nassau Cnty. Dist. Ct. 2010).

374 *Najjar*, 950 N.Y.S.2d at 724.

375 *Gnosis, LLC*, 958 N.Y.S.2d at 307 (noting that ample notice had been provided, including additional notices listing the correct address).

376 Oakwood Terr. Hous. Corp. v. Monk, 36 N.Y.S.3d 48 (App. Term, 9th & 10th Jud. Dists. 2016) (dismissing non-payment proceeding where Petitioner failed to prove or plead a rent demand was made); Pepe v. Miller & Miller Consulting Actuaries, Inc., 221 A.D.2d 545, at 546, 634 N.Y.S.2d 490, 491 (App. Div., 2d Dep't 1995).

377 *See* Kentpark Realty Corp. v. Lasertone Corp., 779 N.Y.S.2d 324, 326 (App. Term, 2d & 11th Jud. Dists. 2004); Sears, Jr. v. Okin, 800 N.Y.S.2d 357 (App. Term, 9th & 10th Jud. Dists.

inadvertently omitted, then the Landlord may cure the defect by attaching the affidavit of service to its opposition to the Tenant's motion to dismiss.[378]

If the rent demand was oral, simply alleging within the Petition that an oral demand was made is sufficient. Whether the demand was actually made, and, if so, was it done properly, is a matter for the Court to determine at the hearing (rather than on a motion to dismiss).[379]

3. HOLDOVER PROCEEDING

In a holdover proceeding, the Petition must allege that a predicate notice, to the extent required, was timely provided to the Respondent. Similar to a non-payment proceeding, the Petitioner should attach a copy of the proof of service to the Petition, but the failure to do so is not a jurisdictional defect.

Although pleading requirements are specific, the Appellate Term for the Ninth and Tenth Judicial Districts has held that the inappropriate use of the term "rent" (which implies the parties have a valid Landlord and Tenant relationship), when "use and occupancy" was proper, does not warrant dismissal of a licensee holdover proceeding.[380] The Court reasoned that when viewed as a whole, the Petition could not be "[d]eemed a judicial admission of the existence of a landlord-tenant relationship, as the petition sets forth at length the basis for petitioner's claim that occupant is a licensee [and not a Tenant]".[381]

2004).

378 Reckson Operating P'ship, L.P. v. LJC Corp., 856 N.Y.S.2d 26 (App. Term, 9th & 10th Jud. Dists. 2007).

379 ROBERT F. DOLAN, RASCH'S LANDLORD AND TENANT INCLUDING SUMMARY PROCEEDINGS § 32:15, at 501 (4th ed. 2010).

380 East Ramapo Cent. Sch. Dist. v. Mosdos Chofetz Chaim, Inc., 36 N.Y.S.3d 344 (App. Term, 9th & 10th Jud. Dists. 2016).

381 Id.

SERVICE REQUIREMENTS— "5 AND 12 RULE"

The Notice of Petition and Petition must be served upon each Respondent. It is worth repeating that in a majority of the Housing Parts, a summary proceeding is commenced when the Notice of Petition and Petition are "filed" with the Court.[382] However, in the Justice Courts, the proceeding continues to be commenced upon "service". Regardless of whether the Housing Part is a filing Court or a service Court, effectuating proper service is a strictly enforced statutory obligation.

If the Respondent defaults by failing to appear on the return date, the Petitioner must still demonstrate proper service. Where service is inadequate, the Court is devoid of personal jurisdiction and the proceeding will be dismissed "without prejudice".[383] This means that an-

---

382   See generally 92 Bergenbrooklyn, LLC v. Cisarano, 21 N.Y.S.3d 810 (App. Term, 2d, 11th & 13th Jud. Dists. 2015). The 92 Bergenbrooklyn, LLC Court held that commencement of a holdover proceeding is "keyed" to service. Under this approach, where the Landlord accepts payment after filing but before service of the Notice of Petition and Petition, the termination notice is vitiated and the proceeding is dismissed. Id. The decision is in direct contradiction with the Appellate Term of the First Department and several other jurisdictions which maintain that "commencement" occurs upon filing, and, as a result, any moneys tendered following the filing but before service may be accepted without vitiating the notice. See ABN Assocs., LLC v. Citizens Advice Bureau, Inc., 910 N.Y.S.2d 760 (App. Term, 1st Dep't 2010). It remains undisputed, however, that payment accepted following service is considered use and occupancy which may be accepted at any time without vitiating the termination notice. For a discussion regarding the Landlord's ability to accept payment following service of a termination notice, see infra, Ch. 8 subdiv. C.

383   When the Tenant appears but fails to dispute service in a timely manner, the Tenant consents to personal jurisdiction. See, e.g., Citi Land Servs., LLC v. McDowell, 926 N.Y.S.2d 343 (App. Term, 2d, 11th & 13th Jud. Dists. 2011).

other summary proceeding may be commenced <u>after</u> the Petitioner serves a new predicate notice and pays another filing fee. The new proceeding may be commenced only if the Respondent remains in possession of the premises. Where the Tenant appears, the defense of defective service must be raised or it is waived.

In New York, there are three (3) acceptable ways to serve the Notice of Petition and Petition: (1) personal delivery upon the Respondent; (2) substituted service; or (3) conspicuous place service, commonly referred to as "nail and mail". Since a party to the proceeding may <u>not</u> serve the Notice of Petition and Petition, the Petitioner will typically retain a licensed process server. However, any individual over the age of eighteen (18) and not a party to the proceeding may serve the papers.[384]

Excluding non-payment proceedings in New York City, service must be completed no fewer than five (5) days but no more than twelve (12) days <u>prior</u> to the original hearing date set forth in the Notice of Petition.[385] This is known as the "5 and 12 Rule", and is applicable in a majority of summary proceedings. Regardless of the type of service utilized, service must be completed during this limited window period.

In determining whether service was completed in a timely manner, the Court does <u>not</u> include the "day of reckoning" (i.e., the date service is completed), but the day the proceeding is to be heard is counted.[386] If the final day is a "Saturday, Sunday or public holiday", then the time to complete service is extended to the next business day. Service of "legal process" may <u>not</u> be made on Sunday or other religious observance day.[387]

---

384 CPLR § 2103(a). Within a city of more than one (1) million residents, a non-party, non-attorney who has "effectuated service of process in five or more actions or proceedings in the twelve month period immediately preceding the service in question" may be considered a process server. N.Y. GENERAL BUSINESS LAW § 89-bb (McKinney 2009).

385 RPAPL § 733(1).

386 *See* N.Y. GENERAL CONSTRUCTION LAW § 20 (McKinney 2003).

387 N.Y. GENERAL BUSINESS LAW § 11 (McKinney 2013). Interestingly, the Appellate Division, Second Department permitted service of a termination notice on Sunday where the lease did <u>not</u> specify that the notice was "legal process" or that service was required to be completed in accordance with the statutory requirements. *See* Glenball, Ltd. v. TLY Coney, LLC, 57 A.D.3d 843, 874 N.Y.S.2d 128 (App. Div., 2d Dep't 2008). Although it is not

Computing the window period is a source of considerable confusion for many litigants. However, the beginning and end dates may be charted by days of the week. For example, excluding holidays, if the return date is on a Wednesday, then the latest service may be completed is the previous Friday (i.e., five (5) days before the return date not counting the date of service) and the earliest is the Friday prior (i.e., twelve (12) days before the return date not counting the date of service).[388] Of course, service may be completed on any day in between the beginning and end dates, except Sundays and/or holidays.

A. TYPE OF SERVICE

1. PERSONAL DELIVERY

Personal delivery is the preferred method of service. This is achieved by handing the Notice of Petition and Petition to the Respondent. The papers need <u>not</u> be personally delivered at the premises.[389] Service in

clear whether the same result would be achieved at present, the case stands for the proposition that documents that are not "legal process" may be served on Sunday. *Id.*; *cf.* Di Perna v. Black, 62 N.Y.S.2d 69 (App. Term, 1st Dep't 1946) (service of a termination notice on Sunday regarding a rent stabilized apartment is defective). Since the Notice of Petition and Petition are "legal process", they may <u>not</u> be served on Sunday under any circumstance.

388   The following lists the general service windows, excluding holidays, in Courts adhering to the "5 and 12" Rule. These dates are not determinative, as each Court may have its own procedures for filing the affidavit of service. As a general matter, if the return date is on a Monday, then service may be performed between the two (2) prior Wednesdays. If the return date is on a Tuesday, then service may be performed between the two (2) prior Thursdays. As previously indicated, if the return date is on a Wednesday, then service may be completed between the two (2) previous Fridays. Where the return date is on a Thursday, service may be performed between the two (2) prior Saturdays, but if service is achieved on the Saturday closest to the return date in a manner other than personal delivery, the requisite mailings should be mailed the same day and the affidavit of service filed the next day the Court is open; i.e., Monday. Finally, if the return date is on a Friday, since service may not be performed on Sunday, the service may be performed on the same schedule as a Thursday return date.

389   *See* AMB Fund III New York III & IV, LLC v. WWTL Logistics, Inc., 942 N.Y.S.2d 307 (App. Term, 2d, 11th & 13th Jud. Dists. 2012) (service on the corporation's general manager at the place of business, rather than the subject premises, satisfied personal service requirements pursuant to CPLR § 311(a)(1)); 126 Spruce St., LLC v. Club Centr., LLC, 830 N.Y.S.2d 506 (Nassau Cnty. Dist. Ct. 2007).

this manner is considered "complete" when the papers are handed, or personally delivered, to the Respondent, which again, must be done not less than five (5) but no more than twelve (12) days prior to the hearing date. Although service is considered "complete" when the papers are handed to the Respondent, the term "complete" is not entirely accurate because the process server **must** further file proof of service with the Clerk of the Court in the form of a sworn affidavit of service within three (3) days of service.[390]

Notwithstanding RPAPL § 735(2)(a), which requires the affidavit of service to be filed within three (3) days of personal delivery, it has been held that the failure to comply constitutes a mere ministerial error (as opposed to a jurisdictional defect) that warrants the denial of a motion to dismiss.[391] The Petitioner may move to cure the filing date of the affidavit of service *nunc pro tunc*.[392]

A process server must utilize "reasonable" efforts to serve each Respondent at a time and place when the occupant is expected to be present.[393] In other words, if the process server knows that the Tenant will not be present when service is attempted, that generally is not considered a reasonable attempt.[394] Attempts at service exclusively during normal working hours are inadequate.[395]

---

390 RPAPL § 735(2)(a).

391 Siedlecki v. Doscher, 931 N.Y.S.2d 203 (App. Term, 2d, 11th & 13th Jud. Dists. 2011); Martin, Jr. v. Sandoval, 9 N.Y.S.3d 594 (Peekskill City Ct. 2015) (service proper where the affidavit of service was filed five (5) days following delivery); Mangano v. Ikinko, 958 N.Y.S.2d 308 (Ossining Just. Ct. 2010) (late affidavit of service "deemed to have been timely filed" where the Notice of Petition and Petition were properly served).

392 *Martin, Jr.*, 9 N.Y.S.3d at 594.

393 RPAPL § 735. *See* Doji Bak, LLC v. Alta Plastics, Index No. 751-15, 2016 WL 2946090, 2016 N.Y. Misc. LEXIS 1851 (App. Term, 9th & 10th Jud. Dists. May 12, 2016); 809-811 Kings Hwy., LLC v. Pulse Laser Skin Care, 901 N.Y.S.2d 906 (App. Term, 2d, 11th & 13th Jud. Dists. 2009).

394 *See, e.g.*, Brooklyn Heights Realty Co. v. Gliwa, 92 A.D.2d 602, 459 N.Y.S.2d 793, 794 (App. Div., 2d Dep't 1983) (attempts at service exclusively when a person is reasonably expected to be at work); Gomiela v. Ottimo, Index No. 94061212 (Southampton Just. Ct. Nov. 8, 1994) (unreported decision) (dismissing summary proceeding against occupant of a summer rental "[u]sed primarily on weekends" where all attempts at service were made on weekdays).

395 *Brooklyn Heights Realty Co.*, 92 A.D.2d at 602, 459 N.Y.S.2d at 793.

2. SUBSTITUTED SERVICE

Substituted service is another method of service. Unlike the personal delivery method, substituted service is considered "complete" when the affidavit of service is filed with the Clerk of the Court.[396] Strict compliance with the statute is required.[397]

Substituted service is a byproduct of an unsuccessful effort to personally deliver the papers. For example, if the Respondent is not home when service is attempted, the process server may leave the papers with the individual who answers the door provided that person is of an appropriate age and has the appropriate judgment. Although a precise description of a "person of suitable age and discretion" is not clearly defined, leaving the Notice of Petition and Petition with a spouse, adult child, or other mature adult at the residence or with the office manager at a place of business will generally suffice.[398]

The process server must leave the same number of copies of both the Notice of Petition and Petition with a person of suitable age and discretion as there are named Respondents. In other words, if there are two (2) named Tenants, then the process server must leave two (2) copies of the Notice of Petition and Petition. The process server must further mail two (2) copies of the papers to each Respondent at the subject premises the following business day; one (1) copy via certified mail and one (1) by regular mail.[399] For commercial properties, a copy of the papers must be mailed to the Tenant's known corporate address, whether on or off the subject premises, by regular and certified or registered

---

396   RPAPL § 735(2)(b).

397   *See* Riverside Syndicate, Inc. v. Saltzman, 49 A.D.3d 402, 852 N.Y.S.2d 840 (App. Div., 1st Dep't 2008); Berkeley Assocs. Co. v. Di Nolfi, 122 A.D.2d 703, at 705-06, 505 N.Y.S.2d 630, 632 (App. Div., 1st Dep't 1986); Ron Rose Group, Inc. v. Gavish & G-R Bea Corp., Index No. 524-01, 2002 WL 1162445, 2002 N.Y. Misc. LEXIS 553 (App. Term, 9th & 10th Jud. Dists. March 13, 2002); *but see* ZOT, Inc. v. Watson, 867 N.Y.S.2d 379 (N.Y. Civ. Ct. 2008) (holding the late filing of the affidavit of service does not deny the court of jurisdiction).

398   *Cf.* O'Connell v. Singletary, 926 N.Y.S.2d 345 (App. Term, 9th & 10th Jud. Dists. 2011) (substituted service on a person of suitable age and discretion at the premises after the Respondent surrendered possession was not proper service).

399   RPAPL § 735(1)(b).

mail the following business day.[400]

In order to complete service, the process server must file with the Court a sworn affidavit of service within three (3) days of the mailing. Again, all of this must be completed no more than twelve (12) but no fewer than five (5) days prior to the initial Court date.

3. CONSPICUOUS PLACE SERVICE ("NAIL AND MAIL")

The third and final method of service is conspicuous place service which is commonly referred to as "nail and mail". If on the initial attempt of service no one answers the door, the process server must return at least one (1) additional time during a different time of day to attempt service. If on the second visit there is still no answer and the Petitioner is willing to forego a money judgment if the Tenant fails to appear in Court, then the process server may fasten the papers (one (1) copy per Respondent) to the door or slide them beneath the entrance of the residence. The process server may not "wedge" the papers between the door knob and door frame without the use of tape or another fastening device.[401] Where a money judgment is sought in the event of a default, the process server must make a third attempt at service before resorting to "nail and mail".[402]

Leaving the Notice of Petition and Petition on an outer fence surrounding the premises is sufficient where the fence "blocks" the process server's access to the front door.[403] It has been held that where the building's exterior door impedes the process server's ability to reach the Tenant's particular unit, the "outer bounds of tenant's actual dwelling

---

400 *Id.; see* George Doulaveris & Son, Inc. v. P.J. 37 Food Corp., 961 N.Y.S.2d 722 (App. Term, 2d, 11th & 13th Jud. Dists. 2013) (service defective where follow-up mailings bore the name of an entity other than the corporate Tenant); F & Realty Corp. v. 1014 Flatbush Ave., Inc., 969 N.Y.S.2d 802 (App. Term, 2d, 11th & 13th Jud. Dists. 2013) (dismissing proceeding because the papers were not mailed to Respondent's known corporate address following substituted service).

401 *See* Bruckner by the Bridge, LLC v. Gonzales, 18 N.Y.S.3d 577 (N.Y. Civ. Ct. 2015).

402 *See* Default Judgments *infra*, Chapter 6 subdiv. B.

403 *See* Res Land, Inc. v. SHS Baisley, LLC, 939 N.Y.S.2d 743 (App. Term, 2d, 11th & 13th Jud. Dists. 2011).

place must be deemed to extend to the exterior door of the building".[404]

The use of "nail and mail" service at a commercial property is defective where the Landlord and/or Landlord's representatives were aware that the Tenant previously vacated the premises.[405] The Appellate Term for the Ninth and Tenth Judicial Districts concluded that attempts at service at a location where there is not "at least a reasonable expectation of success in finding a person on the premises to whom delivery may be made" fails to satisfy the reasonable application standards of RPAPL § 735. This was the case even though the rental agreement stated that notices were to be mailed to the premises.[406]

Similar to substituted service, two (2) copies of the Notice of Petition and Petition must be mailed the following business day to each Respondent at the premises; one (1) via certified mail and one (1) by regular mail.[407] The process server must further file a sworn affidavit of service within three (3) days of the mailing.[408] Once again, all of this must be completed between five (5) and twelve (12) days before the initial Court date.

---

404   322 W. 47th St. HDFC v. Loo, 31 N.Y.S.3d 924 (App. Term, 1st Dep't 2016).

405   *Doji Bak, LLC*, 2016 WL at 2946090, 2016 N.Y. Misc. LEXIS at 1851; 91 Fifth Ave. Corp. v. Brookhill Prop. Holdings LLC, 28 N.Y.S.3d 263 (N.Y. Civ. Ct. 2016) (holding that an attempt at service "predestined to failure" is the "equivalent of no attempt at all").

406   *Doji Bak, LLC*, 2016 at WL 2946090, 2016 N.Y. Misc. LEXIS at 1851.

407   Where Tenant's address in France was known, Landlord was required to mail a copy of the Notice of Petition and Petition to that alternative address the day after leaving the papers at the premises. Horatio Arms, Inc. v. Celbert, 972 N.Y.S.2d 813 (App. Term, 1st Dep't 2013).

408   RPAPL § 735(2)(b). *See* Abakporo v. Gardner, 875 N.Y.S.2d 818 (N.Y. Civ. Ct. 2008); Zajaczkowska v. Zeranska, Index No. 72293-07, 2007 N.Y. Misc. LEXIS 7819 (N.Y. Civ. Ct. Oct. 4, 2007).

B. DEFAULT JUDGMENTS

The Respondent's failure to appear on the hearing date may result in a default judgment in favor of the Landlord. This means that the Landlord will be awarded a judgment of possession and a warrant of eviction provided service was proper.[409] The content of the process server's affidavit of service is *prima facie* proof that service was performed in the manner and at the time and location alleged.[410] The attempts at service must satisfy the "reasonable application" standard pursuant to RPAPL § 735.[411] Where the principal place of business of a corporate Respondent "[i]s not located on the property sought to be recovered" and the Landlord has "[w]ritten information of the principal office or principal place of business within the state", the Petition must be mailed to the principal place of business when conspicuous place service is utilized.[412]

Petitioner may further be entitled to a money judgment for unpaid rent, "additional" rent and/or use and occupancy.[413] Unless previously amended, the money judgement is limited to the amount sought in the Petition.[414] To obtain a money judgment where "nail and mail" service

---

409   809-811 Kings Hwy., LLC v. Pulse Laser Skin Care, 901 N.Y.S.2d 906 (App. Term, 2d, 11th & 13th Jud. Dists. 2009) ("nail and mail" service after two (2) unsuccessful attempts during normal business hours on two (2) different days sufficient for a possessory judgment).

410   Iodice v. Academics R Us, Inc., 26 N.Y.S.3d 724 (App. Term, 1st Dep't 2015).

411   ZOT, LLC v. Crown Assocs., 880 N.Y.S.2d 877 (App. Term, 2d, 11th & 13th Jud. Dists. 2009); Martine Assocs., LLC v. Minck, 785 N.Y.S.2d 648, 649 (App. Term, 9th & 10th Jud. Dists. 2004) ("[a]t least two attempts at personal service, one during normal working hours and one attempt when a person working normal hours could reasonably be expected to be home, are required to satisfy the 'reasonable application' standard").

412   RPAPL § 735(1). *See* Tradito v. The 815 Yonkers Ave. Series TDS Leasing, LLC, 913 N.Y.S.2d 867, 869-70 (App. Term, 9th & 10th Jud. Dists. 2010). There is a similar mailing requirement when service is effectuated on a person of suitable age and discretion. *See* F & Realty Corp. v. 1014 Flatbush Ave., Inc., 969 N.Y.S.2d 802 (App. Term, 2d, 11th & 13th Jud. Dists. 2013).

413   *See* RH Apts., LP v. Eliot, 946 N.Y.S.2d 69 (Rochester City Ct. 2012) (granting a default, but denying use and occupancy absent testimony or a sworn affidavit from a person with firsthand knowledge that the occupants continued to occupy the premises following commencement of the summary proceeding).

414   Mustafa v. Plein, 950 N.Y.S.2d 492 (App. Term, 2d, 11th & 13th Jud. Dists. 2012); Port Chester Hous. Auth. v. Turner, 734 N.Y.S.2d 805 (App. Term, 9th & 10th Jud. Dists. 2001).

is utilized, the process server must satisfy the heightened "due diligence" requirements pursuant to CPLR § 308(4). Although left to the discretion of the Court, "due diligence" has routinely been interpreted to require a minimum of three (3) attempts at service over two (2) days at different times of the day, and not on Sunday or public holiday.[415]

The previous standard required personal delivery to obtain a money judgment, which, at minimum, continues to be the law in the Fourth Judicial Department.[416] Where there is a "split" in the Judicial Departments, it is axiomatic that the Courts follow the precedent set by the Appellate Division within their own Department. However, if a particular issue has <u>not</u> been decided within the Department, then the doctrine of *stare decisis* requires that the Court adheres to the precedent set by another Department until either the Court of Appeals or the local Appellate Division rules on the matter.[417]

To obtain a money judgment where service was adequate, the Petitioner must further file with the Court a non-military affidavit attesting that the process server made a reasonable inquiry regarding the Tenant's military status. Since there is no set time to file the non-military affidavit, the failure to file the affidavit by the return date is <u>not</u> a jurisdictional defect. Instead, the Court may adjourn the case to allow

---

415 *See generally* CPLR § 308. *See also* Florestal v. Coleman-Florestal, 124 A.D.3d 578, 2 N.Y.S.3d 153 (App. Div., 2d Dep't 2015) (several attempts at service, including two (2) Saturdays, a weekday evening and a weekday morning, was sufficient to satisfy the due diligence requirement); Wells Fargo Bank, N.A. v. Cherot, 102 A.D.3d 768, 957 N.Y.S.2d 886, 887 (App. Div., 2d Dep't 2013) (three (3) attempts to effect personal service at the appellant's residence at various times on different days, including a Saturday, was sufficient to satisfy the due diligence requirement); JP Morgan Chase Bank, N.A. v. Szajna, 72 A.D.3d 902, 898 N.Y.S.2d 524 (App. Div., 2d Dep't 2010) (three (3) attempts over three (3) days satisfies due diligence); Avgush v. Berrahu, 847 N.Y.S.2d 343, 344-47 (App. Term, 9th & 10th Jud. Dists. 2007) (five (5) attempts over two (2) days sufficient service for a money judgment).

416 *Avgush*, 847 N.Y.S.2d at 345-46. In the Fourth Judicial Department, personal delivery is required to obtain a money judgment where the Tenant defaults. *See* In re McDonald, 225 A.D. 403, 233 N.Y.S. 368 (App. Div., 4th Dep't 1929). Parenthetically, in 2009 the Niagara County Court issued a decision rejecting the *McDonald* holding. *See* Expressway Vill., Inc. v. Denman, 893 N.Y.S.2d 736, 738 (Niagara Cnty. Ct. 2009). The Rochester City Court has since refuted the County Court and challenged the Court's authority to disregard Appellate Division authority. *See* Cornhill LLC v. Sposato, 26 N.Y.S.3d 831 (Rochester City Ct. 2016).

417 Halpern v. Tunne, 966 N.Y.S.2d 346 (App. Term, 2d, 11th & 13th Jud. Dists. 2012).

for the filing of the affidavit, at which time, should the Tenant again fail to appear, a default judgment may be entered.[418]

The purpose of the service requirements is to insure adequate notice of the claims.[419] Another interesting situation arises when the Respondent appears in Court after service was effectuated by "nail and mail" following two (2) unsuccessful attempts. If the Respondent consents to the issuance of a judgment of possession but disputes the award of a money judgment, the Respondent may be in a more favorable position by defaulting so as to avoid the money judgment. On the other hand, if the Tenant appears, then a prevailing Petitioner may be awarded a money judgment.

This is <u>not</u> to suggest that it is in the best interest of the Respondent to default because the Respondent would then waive the opportunity to assert defenses in the proceeding (and possibly a related action) and the right to request a stay on execution of the warrant of eviction prior to the issuance of the judgment. Moreover, the Tenant may remain liable for damages in a subsequent plenary action. Seeking the advice of counsel is always in the individual's best interest.

---

418   Avgush v. De La Cruz, 924 N.Y.S.2d 307 (App. Term, 9th & 10th Jud. Dists. 2011).

419   *See* Grounds to Vacate a Default Judgment and Traverse Hearings *infra*, Chapter 13 subdiv. A(2).

CHAPTER 7

ANSWER, COUNTERCLAIMS AND DISCOVERY

The Respondent may (not required) respond to the Petition at or before the hearing, either orally or in writing, by denying all or a portion of the allegations and asserting affirmative defenses. The Answer, unlike the Petition, need <u>not</u> be verified when in writing.[420] Notwithstanding the Housing Part's limited authority to grant equitable relief, the Respondent may assert any affirmative defense, whether based in law or equity, in a summary proceeding.[421]

The purpose of answering the Petition is threefold: (1) frame the issues before the Court; (2) preserve the right of appeal; and (3) preserve the right to assert related claims in another action. A personal jurisdiction defense, such as the lack of proper service, may be waived if not asserted in the Answer or at the initial Court appearance.[422] The Appellate Term for the First Department has held that where the Tenant fails to assert a lack of personal jurisdiction as a defense in the original Answer, it is precluded from asserting the defense in an Amended Answer.[423] In addition, the doctrine of res judicata prohibits the assertion of a claim in a subsequent plenary action that could have been raised in the summary proceeding.[424]

---

420   *See* Stein v. Jeff's Express, Inc., 955 N.Y.S.2d 713 (App. Term, 2d, 11th & 13th Jud. Dists. 2012).

421   *See* Yacoob v. Persaud, 950 N.Y.S.2d 611 (App. Term, 2d, 11th & 13th Jud. Dists. 2012).

422   Iodice v. Academics R Us, Inc., 26 N.Y.S.3d 724 (App. Term, 1st Dep't 2015).

423   *Id.*

424   *See* IG Second Generation Partners, L.P. v. La Motta, 133 A.D.3d 415, 21 N.Y.S.3d 2

A. ANSWER AND MOTIONS TO DISMISS

Unlike other civil actions, the failure to respond to the Petition does <u>not</u> preclude the Respondent from asserting defenses at the hearing. The parties should be mindful that where the Tenant serves an Answer but fails to appear on the return date, a default judgment may be entered.[425]

There is an exception to the rule that the Tenant need <u>not</u> submit an Answer. This occurs when the Petition is served at least eight (8) but no more than twelve (12) days before the return date, and the Petitioner demands that an Answer is served at least three (3) days prior to the hearing.[426] The reader should be mindful that in New York City, with respect to non-payment proceedings, the Tenant <u>must</u> answer the Petition within five (5) days of service.[427] The Clerk of the Court will thereafter schedule the hearing in three (3) to eight (8) days.[428]

Instead of answering, the Respondent may move to dismiss the proceeding. Typically, a motion to dismiss will be based upon defects in service and/or the Petition. Although the Court may determine from a cursory review whether proper service is alleged or if the Petition states a *prima facie* case, disputes concerning material issues of fact require a hearing.[429] The Landlord's submission of the rental agreement, without an accompanying affidavit, may be sufficient to withstand a motion to dismiss where the rental agreement contradicts the Tenant's claims.[430] Since a defense must be timely asserted, the Court may not consider a

---

(App. Div., 1st Dep't 2015); Tewksbury Mgmt. Group, LLC v. Rogers Invests. NV LP, 110 A.D.3d 546, 973 N.Y.S.2d 591 (App. Div., 1st Dep't 2013).

425   191 St. Assocs. LLC v. Cruz, 29 N.Y.S.3d 848 (App. Term, 1st Dep't 2016).

426   RPAPL § 743. Local Rule 212.42[c] provides that where the Petition is served at least eight (8) but not more than twelve (12) days <u>before</u> the hearing date, the Landlord may require that an Answer is served at least three (3) days prior. N.Y. UNIFORM RULES FOR TRIAL CTS. [22 N.Y.C.R.R.] § 212.42[c]; *see* Development Strategies Co., LLC v. Astoria Equities, Inc., 924 N.Y.S.2d 308 (App. Term, 9th & 10th Jud. Dists. 2011).

427   RPAPL § 732(3).

428   *Id.* § 732(2).

429   706 Realty Corp. v. Mohammed, 941 N.Y.S.2d 541 (App. Term, 1st Dep't 2011).

430   1935 Andrews Ave. Equities v. Diaz, 31 N.Y.S.3d 922 (App. Term, 1st Dep't 2016).

defense asserted for the first time in support of Respondent's motion to renew a prior Order.[431]

In *Kirschenbaum v. Gianelli*, the Appellate Division, Third Department held that the untimely filing of a motion does <u>not</u> extend the time to answer.[432] In that case, a demand was made in the Petition for an Answer to be served within three (3) days of the return date. However, the former owner, who lost the property in foreclosure, moved to dismiss the action <u>after</u> the time to answer expired. The Court noted that a ten (10) day extension to serve and file an Answer following the entry of its Order denying the motion may have been proper pursuant to CPLR § 3211(f) had the motion been made earlier.[433]

CPLR §§ 3012(d), 2004 and 2005 permit extensions to file late pleadings where a reasonable excuse is shown or in the interest of justice, including law office failure. It should be noted that a *pro se* Tenant's request for an adjournment on the initial Court date for the purpose of seeking counsel extends the time to answer.[434]

The denial of Respondent's motion to dismiss and/or for summary judgment is typically <u>not</u> an adjudication on the merits, and, therefore, the same arguments may be reasserted at the hearing.[435] The rule prohibiting a party from making successive summary judgment motions is applicable to summary proceedings, and further will be upheld where an Amended Answer is served provided there are no new issues regarding the Landlord's possessory claim.[436] Similar to motion practice in a plenary action, the Court should <u>not</u> consider evidence introduced for the first time in reply papers following receipt of the non-movant's opposition.[437]

---

431 Tenth St. Holdings, LLC v. McKowen, 31 N.Y.S.3d 924 (App. Term, 1st Dep't 2016).

432 Kirschenbaum v. Gianelli, 63 A.D.2d 1057, 405 N.Y.S.2d 820 (App. Div., 3d Dep't 1978).

433 *Id.*, 63 A.D.2d at 1058, 405 N.Y.S.2d at 821; Djokic v. Perez, 872 N.Y.S.2d 263 (N.Y. Civ. Ct. 2008).

434 In-Towne Shopping Ctrs. Co. v. DeMottie, 851 N.Y.S.2d 70 (App. Term, 9th & 10th Jud. Dists. 2007).

435 *See* Karagiannis v. Nasar, 943 N.Y.S.2d 816 (App. Term, 2d, 11th & 13th Jud. Dists. 2012).

436 Bruckner Realty LLC v. Cruz, 13 N.Y.S.3d 849 (App. Term, 1st Dep't 2015).

437 *See* Patchogue Assocs. v. Sears, Roebuck and Co., 951 N.Y.S.2d 314 (App. Term, 9th & 10th Jud. Dists. 2012) (summary proceeding); Master v. Boiakhtchion, 122 A.D.3d 589, at

The return date of a motion is typically the initial date the parties are due to appear in Court or a date shortly thereafter. If the parties cannot agree on a return date, then the Court will select a reasonable date. The Court may further direct a briefing schedule to avoid delay and/or confusion.

The Landlord may similarly move for summary judgment on its claims. In *Chew v. McKenzie*, the Appellate Term, First Department granted Landlords' cross-motion for summary judgment where there was no question that the Tenant violated the rental agreement by subleasing the rent stabilized apartment for approximately two (2) years without permission.[438]

B. COUNTERCLAIMS

1. PROCEDURAL MATTERS

Although Respondents often seek to orally place counterclaims on the Record, the Court may require that the counterclaims be asserted in writing. Unlike the Petitioner's claims, a Respondent may be awarded damages on its counterclaims in a summary proceeding. Equitable counterclaims are <u>not</u> permitted.[439]

The Court's maximum dollar jurisdictional limit in civil actions, which in many of the local Courts equals $15,000, excluding costs and interest, does <u>not</u> apply to either the Petitioner's claim for rent and "added" rent[440] or the Respondent's counterclaims, with the exception of counterclaims asserted in the Justice Courts which are limited

---

590, 996 N.Y.S.2d 116, 117 (App. Div., 2d Dep't 2014) (personal injury action).

438   Chew v. McKenzie, 941 N.Y.S.2d 536 (App. Term, 1ˢᵗ Dep't 2011) (warrant of eviction permanently stayed where the Tenant cured the defect). *Cf.* 13775 Realty, LLC v. Foglino, 36 N.Y.S.3d 48 (App. Term, 1ˢᵗ Dep't 2016) (hearsay evidence insufficient to establish Landlord's *prima facie* entitlement to summary judgment).

439   ROBERT F. DOLAN, RASCH'S LANDLORD AND TENANT INCLUDING SUMMARY PROCEEDINGS § 43:38, at 137-38 (4ᵗʰ ed. 2010).

440   N.Y. CITY CIV. CT. ACT § 204; N.Y. UNIFORM CITY CT. ACT § 204; N.Y. UNIFORM DIST. CT. ACT § 204; N.Y. UNIFORM JUST. CT. ACT § 204.

to $3,000.[441] A counterclaim sought in that Court in excess of $3,000 is deemed waived.[442] In *2094-2096 Boston Post Rd., LLC*, the Appellate Term directed the Housing Part Judge to permit the Tenant to withdraw any portion of the counterclaim exceeding $3,000, without prejudice, prior to ruling on the underlying motion.[443]

Counterclaims are <u>not</u> restricted to the time period for which unpaid rent is sought. However, the assertion of an unrelated counterclaim may constitute a waiver of a personal jurisdiction defense.[444] Personal jurisdictional defenses previously waived, whether intentional or otherwise, are <u>not</u> revived by the Tenant's withdrawal of the counterclaims.[445]

The Court may dismiss and sever the counterclaims, without prejudice, to filing a plenary action where the claims are insufficiently pled, unrelated to the underlying action and/or otherwise improperly before the Court. For example, a Tenant's counterclaims were severed where the claims "[w]ere not so intertwined with [the] landlord's claim for rent as to require that they be disposed of in one proceeding".[446] Similarly, the Tenant's efforts to assert a counterclaim on the eve of the hearing may be denied as untimely.[447] Where the Tenant's claim is asserted in a separate plenary action, the Landlord may continue to seek possession in the summary proceeding, and the Tenant's damages in

---

441 N.Y. City Civ. Ct. Act § 208; Uniform City Ct. Act § 208; Uniform Dist. Ct. Act § 208; *see also* Uniform Just. Ct. Act § 208.

442 2094-2096 Boston Post Rd., LLC v. Mackies Am. Grill, Inc., Index No. 2023-15, 2016 WL 3083340, 2016 N.Y. Misc. LEXIS 1975 (App. Term, 9th & 10th Jud. Dists. May 25, 2016); Siodlak v. Light, 31 N.Y.S.3d 924 (App. Term, 9th & 10th Jud. Dists. 2016).

443 *2094-2096 Boston Post Rd., LLC*, 2016 WL at 3083340, 2016 N.Y. Misc. LEXIS at 1975.

444 Halberstam v. Kramer, 969 N.Y.S.2d 803 (App. Term, 2d, 11th & 13th Jud. Dists. 2013) (asserting counterclaims for mental and emotional distress waives the right to challenge the "adequacy of the service").

445 *Id.*; ROL Realty Co., LLC v. Gordon, 920 N.Y.S.2d 244 (App. Term, 1st Dep't 2010) (withdrawing an unrelated counterclaim does not "revive" personal jurisdictional objection).

446 V & J Inc. v. 2320 Rte. 112, LLC, 822 N.Y.S.2d 367, 368 (App. Term, 9th & 10th Jud. Dists. 2006) (internal citation omitted).

447 *See* LGS Realty Partners LLC v. Kyle, 26 N.Y.S.3d 725 (App. Term, 1st Dep't 2015).

the plenary action may be offset against the rent arrears or enforced in the form of a money judgment.[448]

A lease provision barring counterclaims will generally be enforced.[449] There is an exception where the counterclaims are "inextricably intertwined" with the Petitioner's claims for unpaid rent and/or use and occupancy, in which case, the counterclaims may be permitted notwithstanding the lease provision to the contrary.[450]

2. TENANT'S SAFETY

It is well-established that "[a] landlord is not the insurer of the safety of its tenants".[451] Under common law, a Landlord is merely required to "[t]ake minimal precautions to protect tenants from foreseeable harm, including foreseeable criminal conduct by a third person".[452]

Absent a lease provision to the contrary, the Landlord has no duty to clean-up or otherwise make the premises secure during a storm.[453] In fact, the Landlord's obligation to take "reasonable" steps to remedy the dangerous conditions does <u>not</u> resume "[u]ntil a reasonable time after the storm has ended".[454] The Landlord may be responsible for resulting damages where its "cleanup efforts make the area more dangerous".[455]

---

448   *See* Rose v. Kulitsa, 946 N.Y.S.2d 69 (App. Term, 1st Dep't 2011).

449   Man Chit Cheng v. Chang, 880 N.Y.S.2d 225 (App. Term, 2d & 11th Jud. Dists. 2008).

450   *2094-2096 Boston Post Rd., LLC,* 2016 WL at 3083340, 2016 N.Y. Misc. LEXIS at 1975; All 4 Sports & Fitness, Inc. v. Hamilton, Kane, Martin Enters., Inc., 22 A.D.3d 512, at 513-14, 802 N.Y.S.2d 470, 471 (App. Div., 2d Dep't 2005) (common area maintenance charges are inextricably intertwined with Landlord's claim for rent). *Cf.* Lucas v. Florent, Inc., 860 N.Y.S.2d 813 (N.Y. Civ. Ct. 2008) (counterclaim for lost business is <u>not</u> inextricably intertwined with claim for unpaid rent).

451   Ferguson v. Antaeus Realty Corp., 94 A.D.3d 806, at 806-07, 941 N.Y.S.2d 870 (App. Div., 2d Dep't 2012) (civil action against Landlord for personal injuries dismissed where the assailant did <u>not</u> gain entry "[t]hrough a negligently maintained entrance") (citation omitted).

452   *Id.*

453   *See* Weinberger v. 52 Duane Assocs., LLC, Index No. 107132-09, 2011 WL 5059079, 2011 N.Y. Misc. LEXIS 4957 (N.Y. Cnty. Sup. Ct. Oct. 13, 2011), *aff'd*, 102 A.D.3d 618 (App. Div., 1st Dep't 2013).

454   Weinberger v. 52 Duane Assocs., LLC, 102 A.D.3d 618 (App. Div., 1st Dep't 2013).

455   *Weinberger,* 2011 WL at 5059079, 2011 N.Y. Misc. LEXIS at 4957.

C. DISCOVERY

There is no formal discovery in a summary proceeding without a Court Order pursuant to CPLR § 408.[456] As a general matter, the party seeking discovery must demonstrate that (1) the Petitioner established a cause of action or that the Respondent has an affirmative defense; (2) the need to determine information directly related to the cause of action or claim; (3) the requested discovery must be narrowly tailored to clarify disputed facts; (4) prejudice if the discovery is denied; and (5) whether the Court is able to diminish any resulting prejudice.[457]

While discovery is typically requested for documents, records, and an inspection of the premises, a Landlord was permitted to have an independent medical examination performed when the Tenant placed his medical condition at issue.[458] In *Windsor Plaza v. De Pinies*, the discovery dispute involved the Tenant's assertion that he temporarily left the premises due to "health concerns" and the illegal subletting of the apartment.[459]

Discovery relating to the Tenant's cell phone records was permitted in a non-primary residence proceeding.[460] In *7 E. 86th Realty*

---

456 Discovery may be permitted where information sought regarding the use of the premises was "[p]eculiarly within the tenant's knowledge". *See* Quality and Ruskin Assocs. v. London, 800 N.Y.S.2d 259, 261 (App. Term, 2d & 11th Jud. Dists. 2005) (internal citations omitted). In addition, Tenants were granted "limited discovery relating to the apartment improvements that were the basis" of a rent overcharge claim. *See* 2701 Grand Assoc. LLC v. Morel, 31 N.Y.S.3d 924 (App. Term, 1st Dep't 2016).

457 Lonray, Inc. v. Newhouse, 229 A.D.2d 440, 644 N.Y.S.2d 900 (App. Div., 2d Dep't 1996); Zada Assocs. v. Meluccio, 28 N.Y.S.3d 651 (App. Term, 1st Dep't 2015) (discovery regarding unauthorized alterations); 72A Realty Assocs. v. Lucas, 26 N.Y.S.3d 216 (App. Term, 1st Dep't 2015) (discovery regarding rent overcharge counterclaim); New York Univ. v. Farkas, 468 N.Y.S.2d 808 (N.Y. Civ. Ct. 1983). *But see* Inwood Gardens, Inc. v. Udoh, 26 N.Y.S.3d 213 (App. Term, 1st Dep't 2015) (discovery denied where request was "overbroad and burdensome, or sought irrelevant information").

458 Windsor Plaza v. De Pinies, N.Y.L.J., June 5, 2014, at 1, col. 3 (N.Y. Civ. Ct. 2014).

459 *Id.; see* WHGA Renaissance Apts., L.P. v. Jackson, 37 N.Y.S.3d 809 (App. Term, 1st Dep't 2016) (discovery permitted where the Tenant, who was diagnosed with paranoid schizophrenia, placed her mental condition and ability to form the requisite knowledge at issue).

460 7 E. 86th Realty LLC v. Leof, Index No. 60946-15, 2016 WL 3581672, 2016 N.Y. Misc. LEXIS 2428 (N.Y. Civ. Ct. June 30, 2016).

LLC, the Housing Part reasoned that there was ample need to determine the Tenant's physical location during the relevant period and whether "she primarily reside[d] in the Subject Premises".[461]

The parties may agree to voluntarily participate in discovery and exchange documents without Court intervention prior to a hearing. However, counsel should be guided accordingly when seeking information from an unrepresented litigant "without any judicial oversight".[462] In *Missionary Sisters, Inc.*, the Appellate Term admonished counsel for requesting and obtaining documents from an 86-year old unrepresented Tenant without a Court Order.[463]

A party may serve a Notice to Admit pursuant to CPLR § 3123, without leave of Court, provided the notice is served no fewer than three (3) days before the return date. A Notice to Admit, which is intended to eliminate undisputed issues, may not seek information regarding the "ultimate conclusions" or questions "going to the heart of the matter".[464] The Respondent's response must be served no later than one (1) day before the return date.[465]

In addition, the parties may subpoena witnesses and business records. A subpoena seeking the records of a governmental agency, such as a police report or proof of payment to the Petitioner, must be "So Ordered" by the Court and may be provided on one (1) day notice to the agency.[466] The governmental records are generally admissible as evidence without the preparer being called to testify provided a certification or authentication is submitted from the head of the agency.[467]

---

461 *Id.* (the parties stipulated the relevant discovery period).

462 Missionary Sisters, Inc. v. Fauerbach, Index No. 570939-15, 2016 WL 3063436, 2016 N.Y. Misc. LEXIS 1942 (App. Term, 1st Dep't May 31, 2016).

463 *Id.* (the remedy was to suppress the documents without prejudice to filing a formal discovery motion).

464 Hyatt Ave. Assocs., LLC v. Rahman, 17 N.Y.S.3d 579 (App. Term, 2d, 11th & 13th Jud. Dists. 2015) (in a non-primary residence holdover proceeding, seeking an admission on the number of days the Tenant lived in the rent stabilized apartment was inappropriate).

465 CPLR §§ 408, 3123.

466 *Id.* § 2307.

467 *Id.* §§ 2307, 4518. *See generally* New York Cnty. Dist. Attorney's Office v. Rodriguez,

Otherwise, as in any other action, an attorney may issue subpoenas without leave of Court, and a *pro se* litigant must always obtain Court approval.

D. JURY TRIALS

Albeit highly unusual in a summary proceeding, either party may demand that the case be tried before a jury. If the Petitioner requests a jury trial, the demand may be made at any time prior to the hearing provided the applicable jury fee is paid. Otherwise, a jury trial is waived.[468] A Respondent's demand for a jury trial must be made at the time of the Answer.[469]

Since a jury trial must be scheduled in advance, at times it may be used by the Respondent as a negotiating tactic. Although the Court is cognizant of various motivations for the actions taken by either party, the right to a jury trial is both statutory and permissible provided a timely demand is made and the appropriate jury trial fee is paid. The parties should note, however, that a lease provision barring a trial by jury, similar to a lease provision barring counterclaims, will typically be enforced.[470]

536 N.Y.S.2d 933, 937-38 (N.Y. Civ. Ct. 1988); Barcher v. Radovich, 183 A.D.2d 689, at 690-91, 583 N.Y.S.2d 276, 278 (App. Div., 2d Dep't 1992).

468   *See* N.Y. City Civ. Ct. Act § 1303; N.Y. Uniform City Ct. Act § 1303; N.Y. Uniform Dist. Ct. Act § 1303. *See also* N.Y. Uniform Just. Ct. Act § 1303; Mangano v. Ikinko, 958 N.Y.S.2d 308 (Ossining Just. Ct. 2010).

469   *See* N.Y. City Civ. Ct. Act § 1303; Uniform City Ct. Act § 1303; Uniform Dist. Ct. Act § 1303; *see also* Uniform Just. Ct. Act § 1303. *See* Dexter 345 Inc. v. Belem, 964 N.Y.S.2d 58 (App. Term, 1st Dep't 2012) (jury trial request denied); Tanenbaum Assocs., L.L.P. v. Yudenfreund, 831 N.Y.S.2d 363 (App. Term, 2d & 11th Jud. Dists. 2006).

470   Inwood Gardens, Inc. v. Udoh, 26 N.Y.S.3d 213 (App. Term, 1st Dep't 2015); Man Chit Cheng v. Chang, 880 N.Y.S.2d 225 (App. Term, 2d & 11th Jud. Dists. 2008); P & J Hous. Partners, LLC v. Alvarado, 941 N.Y.S.2d 539 (App. Term, 1st Dep't 2011).

AFFIRMATIVE DEFENSES

When considering affirmative defenses, the reader should be mindful that there is no duty to mitigate damages in a Landlord and Tenant dispute. Specifically, the Court of Appeals has held that a Landlord is <u>not</u> obligated to re-let or attempt to re-rent the premises because the rental agreement is "[r]ecognized as a present transfer of an estate in real property".[471] This principle applies to both residential and commercial leases except where the rental agreement provides, or the parties agree, otherwise.[472]

The affirmative defenses identified in this and the following chapter are some of the more frequently raised defenses in summary proceedings. They do <u>not</u> comprise an exhaustive list.

---

471   Holy Props. Ltd., L.P. v. Kenneth Cole Prods., Inc., 87 N.Y.2d 130, at 133, 637 N.Y.S.2d 964, 966 (1995).

472   *See* PHH Mtg. Corp. v. Ferro, Kuba, Mangano, Skylar, Gacovino & Lake, P.C., 113 A.D.3d 831, 979 N.Y.S.2d 536 (App. Div., 2d Dep't 2014) (Landlord not obligated to mitigate damages when the Subtenant holds over); REP A8 LLC v. Aventura Tech., Inc., 68 A.D.3d 1087, at 1089, 893 N.Y.S.2d 83, 86 (App. Div., 2d Dep't 2009) (commercial lease); Gordon v. Eshaghoff, 60 A.D.3d 807, at 808, 876 N.Y.S.2d 433, 434 (App. Div., 2d Dep't 2009) (residential lease). *See also* Johnston v. MGM Emerald Enters., Inc., 69 A.D.3d 674, at 676, 893 N.Y.S.2d 176, 178 (App. Div., 2d Dep't 2010) (unambiguous provision limiting damages enforceable absent "[a] special relationship between the parties, a statutory prohibition, or an overriding public policy").

A. IMPLIED WARRANTY OF HABITABILITY (RESIDENTIAL PROPERTY ONLY)

The warranty of habitability is perhaps the most frequently asserted affirmative defense in <u>residential</u> non-payment proceedings.[473] The defense is <u>not</u> intended to be a complete defense, but rather the Tenant seeks an abatement of all or a portion of the unpaid rent due to defective conditions in the premises. The conditions giving rise to the defense must be continuous, rather than episodic, to be applicable.[474]

The warranty of habitability imposes three (3) requirements regarding the condition of the premises. The premises must be (1) fit for human habitation; (2) fit for the uses reasonably intended by the parties; and (3) may <u>not</u> subject the occupants to conditions that are dangerous, hazardous or detrimental to life or safety.[475] If any of the above conditions are not satisfied, then the Tenant is entitled to an abatement of rent provided the Landlord was given notice of the defective conditions and the problems were not corrected within a reasonable period of time.[476]

A rent abatement will <u>not</u> be given where the Landlord was not made aware of the defective conditions.[477] Moreover, an abatement is improper for the period where the Tenant was uncooperative with the

---

473   RPL § 235-b. The warranty of habitability is <u>not</u> a viable defense in either holdover proceedings or commercial cases. *See* Goethals Mobile Park, Inc. v. Staten Island Meadowbrook Park Civ. Assn., Inc., 208 A.D.2d 896, at 897-98, 618 N.Y.S.2d 409, 411 (App. Div., 2d Dep't 1994) (holdover proceeding); 76th St. Owners' Corp. v. Elshiekh, 910 N.Y.S.2d 765 (N.Y. Civ. Ct. 2010) (holdover proceeding); Azour, LLC v. Tax Sister, Inc., 909 N.Y.S.2d 282, 284 (App. Term, 2d, 11th & 13th Jud. Dists. 2010) (commercial property). For a discussion on an exception to this rule, *see supra*, note 119 and accompanying text.

474   *See generally* Hersh v. One Fifth Ave. Apt. Corp., Index No. 157593-14, 2016 WL 2606745, 2016 N.Y. Misc. LEXIS 1706 (N.Y. Cnty. Sup. Ct. May 5, 2016); Metz v. Duenas, 707 N.Y.S.2d 598, 599-600 (Nassau Cnty. Dist. Ct. 2000).

475   RPL § 235-b. *See generally* Goldhirsch v. St. George Tower and Grill Owners Corp., 142 A.D.3d 1044, 37 N.Y.S.3d 616 (App. Div., 2d Dep't 2016).

476   *See* Gawad v. Aviad, 960 N.Y.S.2d 50 (App. Term, 2d, 11th & 13th Jud. Dists. 2012).

477   72A Realty Assocs., L.P. v. Mercado, 1 N.Y.S.3d 876 (App. Term, 1st Dep't 2014); BRG 321, LLC v. Brown, Index No. 78339-14, 2015 WL 4558727, 2015 N.Y. Misc. LEXIS 2665 (N.Y. Civ. Ct. March 4, 2015).

Landlord's efforts to address the conditions or interfered with the repairs.[478] An abatement was similarly denied where the Tenant vacated the premises prior to the loss of electricity and did not return until after the power was restored.[479]

The defense, which may <u>not</u> be waived in a rental agreement, may only be used for the essential functions of the premises.[480] For example, the defense has been successfully asserted where the Landlord failed to provide heat and hot water;[481] the tap water had an "overpowering odor";[482] the stove emitted a gas smell;[483] mold;[484] bedbugs;[485] second-hand smoke;[486] defective sewer pipes;[487] lack of light and ventilation due to nearby construction;[488] lead-based paint;[489] flooding in the

---

478 *See* LGS Realty Partners LLC v. Kyle, 26 N.Y.S.3d 725 (App. Term, 1st Dep't 2015); Joan A. Bebry, LLC v. Kruglova, 938 N.Y.S.2d 227 (App. Term, 2d, 11th & 13th Jud. Dists. 2011); 150-15 79th Ave. Owners Corp. v. James, 927 N.Y.S.2d 818 (App. Term, 2d, 11th & 13th Jud. Dists. 2011).

479 Adler v. Ogden CAP Props., 126 A.D.3d 544, 2 N.Y.S.3d 902 (App. Div., 1st Dep't 2015).

480 *See generally* Solow v. Wellner, 86 N.Y.2d 582, at 588-89, 635 N.Y.S.2d 132, 134-35 (1995); 65E92, LLC v. Kroell, 7 N.Y.S.3d 245 (N.Y. Civ. Ct. 2015).

481 Salvan v. 127 Mgmt. Corp., 101 A.D.2d 721, 475 N.Y.S.2d 30 (App. Div., 1st Dep't 1984); Leris Realty Corp. v. Robbins, 408 N.Y.S.2d 166, 167-68 (N.Y. Civ. Ct. 1978) (good faith attempt to provide heat and hot water by replacing the boiler did not excuse the breach).

482 Newkirk v. Scala, 90 A.D.3d 1257, 935 N.Y.S.2d 176 (App. Div., 3d Dep't 2011).

483 Jacob v. Sealey, 28 N.Y.S.3d 648 (App. Term, 1st Dep't 2015).

484 Cornell v. 360 W. 51st St. Realty, LLC, 95 A.D.3d 50, 939 N.Y.S.2d 434 (App. Div., 1st Dep't 2012), *rev'd on other grounds*, 22 N.Y.3d 762, 986 N.Y.S.2d 389 (2014).

485 JWD & Sons, Ltd. v. Alexander, 941 N.Y.S.2d 538 (Westchester Cnty. Sup. Ct. 2011); Jefferson House Assocs., LLC v. Boyle, 800 N.Y.S.2d 348 (Ossining Just. Ct. 2005); *Cf.* Gawad v. Aviad, 960 N.Y.S.2d 50 (App. Term, 2d, 11th & 13th Jud. Dists. 2012) (warranty of habitability claim denied where Tenant failed to notify Landlord of the bedbug problem).

486 Reinhard v. Connaught Tower Corp., Index No. 602503-08, 2011 WL 6119800, 2011 N.Y. Misc. LEXIS 5683 (N.Y. Cnty. Sup. Ct. Nov. 30, 2011); Upper E. Lease Assocs., LLC v. Cannon, 924 N.Y.S.2d 312 (Nassau Cnty. Dist. Ct. 2011), *aff'd*, 961 N.Y.S.2d 362 (App. Term, 9th & 10th Jud. Dists. 2012).

487 Gottesman v. The Graham Apts., Inc., 16 N.Y.S.3d 792 (N.Y. Civ. Ct. 2015).

488 Sutton Fifty-Six Co. v. Garrison, 93 A.D.2d 720, 461 N.Y.S.2d 14 (App. Div., 1st Dep't 1983).

489 Chase v. Pistolese, 739 N.Y.S.2d 250, 252-53 (Watertown City Ct. 2002).

apartment;[490] pet odors from a prior Tenant;[491] odor from a dumpster;[492] inoperable air conditioner during the summer;[493] excessive late night noise;[494] and roach and insect infestation.[495]

The defense is <u>not</u> intended for the occasional rodent that appears in the premises or the use of amenities and services such as a door attendant, swimming pool or a gym. The Landlord may be liable under the warranty where the conditions were caused by a third-party; i.e., someone other than the Tenant or his guests.[496] Although the defense may <u>not</u> be waived in a rental agreement, the failure to assert the defense in a summary proceeding precludes the Tenant from raising it on appeal.[497]

The party asserting the defense will typically introduce photographs and other documentary proof to corroborate the claim. After vacating the premises, the Tenant may commence a plenary action for money damages due to the Landlord's breach of the implied warranty of habitability unless the claim was affirmatively asserted as a counterclaim in the summary proceeding.[498]

---

490   Heights 170 LLC v. York, 920 N.Y.S.2d 241 (App. Term, 1ˢᵗ Dep't 2010); McGuinness v. Jakubiak, 431 N.Y.S.2d 755 (Kings Cnty. Sup. Ct. 1980).

491   Tonetti, Jr. v. Penati, 48 A.D.2d 25, 367 N.Y.S.2d 804 (App. Div., 2d Dep't 1975) (dogs); Kekllas v. Saddy, 389 N.Y.S.2d 756 (Nassau Cnty. Dist. Ct. 1976) (cats).

492   Mayourian v. Tanaka, 727 N.Y.S.2d 865 (App. Term, 9ᵗʰ & 10ᵗʰ Jud. Dists. 2001).

493   Whitehouse Estates, Inc. v. Thomson, 386 N.Y.S.2d 733 (N.Y. Civ. Ct. 1976).

494   Nostrand Gardens Co-Op v. Howard, 221 A.D.2d 637, 634 N.Y.S.2d 505 (App. Div., 2d Dep't 1995).

495   Town of Islip Comm. Dev. Agency v. Mulligan, 496 N.Y.S.2d 195, 196-97 (Suffolk Ctny. Dist. Ct. 1985).

496   *Heights 170 LLC*, 920 N.Y.S.2d at 241 (flooding caused by neighboring Tenant).

497   *See* Hickey v. Trahan, 31 N.Y.S.3d 921 (App. Term, 9ᵗʰ & 10ᵗʰ Jud. Dists. 2016).

498   *See* Newkirk v. Scala, 90 A.D.3d 1257, 935 N.Y.S.2d 176 (App. Div., 3d Dep't 2011).

B. ILLEGAL APARTMENTS

Outside New York City, there is generally no prohibition against a Landlord collecting rent for an "illegal" apartment with a few exceptions as discussed below. In other words, a Tenant is <u>not</u> relieved of the obligation to pay rent merely because the Landlord failed to obtain a rental permit or the premises lacked an appropriate certificate of occupancy.

Although illegal apartments may pose safety and health risks, these matters are properly adjudicated by the local governing municipality in a civil and/or criminal action for civil penalties, fines and, in egregious cases, a jail sentence. Landlord and Tenant disputes and code enforcement matters are often interrelated as evidenced by the fact that a fair number of Landlords appearing in the Housing Parts are also defendants in town and municipal matters regarding alleged code violations, including renting without a permit, building without a permit and the lack of a certificate of occupancy. Interestingly, a local village ordinance conditioning the issuance or renewal of a rental permit upon the owner's "forced consent" to a warrantless inspection of the premises has been held unconstitutional.[499]

1. THE SUBJECT PREMISES DOES NOT HAVE A RENTAL PERMIT

In the context of a summary proceeding, where the illegal apartment is either a single-family or a two-family residence, the Landlord may be awarded unpaid rent provided a proper rent demand was made.[500] The

---

499   ATM One, LLC v. Incorporated Vill. of Hempstead, 91 A.D.3d 585, 936 N.Y.S.2d 263 (App. Div., 2d Dep't 2012) (discussing Sokolov v. Village of Freeport, 52 N.Y.2d 341, 438 N.Y.S.2d 257 (1981)). *Cf.* Wisoff v. City of Schenectady, 116 A.D.3d 1187, 984 N.Y.S.2d 207 (App. Div., 3d Dep't 2014) (city ordinance upheld where "consent" or a "valid search warrant" required to conduct an administrative inspection); Pashcow v. Town of Babylon, 53 N.Y.2d 687, 439 N.Y.S.2d 103 (1981) (local ordinance upheld where inspection was <u>not</u> required to obtain rental permit); McLean v. City of Kingston, 57 A.D.3d 1269, 869 N.Y.S.2d 685 (App. Div., 3d Dep't 2008) (ordinance requiring inspection of rental properties every two (2) years upheld because the remedy for noncompliance was to seek a search warrant).

500   *See* Thomas v. Brown, 29 N.Y.S.3d 850 (App. Term, 1st Dep't 2015); Madden v. Juillet, 13 N.Y.S.3d 850 (App. Term, 9th & 10th Jud. Dists. 2015); Pickering v. Chappe, 908 N.Y.S.2d 523, 524-25 (App. Term, 2d, 11th & 13th Jud. Dists. 2010).

same holds true for multiple dwellings, which, according to Multiple Dwelling Law § 4(7), are dwellings comprised of three (3) or more families living independently within towns or municipalities of fewer than 325,000 residents.[501]

Notwithstanding the above, the Landlord may <u>not</u> always be entitled to a money judgment. For instance, unpaid rent may not be awarded where a provision within the local governing body's administrative code makes it unlawful to collect rent for an illegal apartment.[502] In addition, if the illegal apartment is a multiple dwelling within a "city, town or village" that has more than 325,000 residents,[503] then the Landlord is similarly prohibited from recovering rent and/or use and occupancy.[504] The prohibition against recovering rent for illegal rental properties applies to "the entire building, not just in the illegally altered apartments".[505]

Another exception that may bar the award of rent is predicated upon ordinary contract principles such as where the Landlord misrepresents that the apartment is "legal" when the apartment is in fact illegal. Under these circumstances, the Court may grant a possessory judgment but refrain from awarding the unpaid rent.[506]

---

501 N.Y. MULTIPLE DWELLING LAW §§ 3(1),(8); 302(1)(b); 325(2) (McKinney 2009).

502 *See, e.g.*, Village of Southampton, N.Y. Town Code, §§ 270-3, 270-13 (2008). *See* Wowaka & Sons, Inc. v. Pardell, 242 A.D.2d 1, at 6-7, 672 N.Y.S.2d 358, 361 (App. Div., 2d Dep't 1998) (explaining that an illegal contract violating statutory provisions that are merely *malum prohibitum* is enforceable). The Appellate Division, Second Department held that the Southampton Town Code permits a Tenant to assert a private action for damages against a Landlord who rents a residence in violation of the local law. *See* Ader v. Guzman, 135 A.D.3d 671, 23 N.Y.S.3d 292 (App. Div., 2d Dep't 2016). Parenthetically, the same Court held that "absent concealment", the Landlord's real estate agent has no duty "to investigate whether the premises had a valid rental permit". Ader v. Guzman, 135 A.D.3d 668, 22 N.Y.S.3d 576 (App. Div., 2d Dep't 2016); *see* RPL § 443(4)(b) (broker disclosure requirements).

503 MULTIPLE DWELLING LAW §§ 3(1),(8).

504 *See Thomas*, 29 N.Y.S.3d at 850; Sheila Props., Inc. v. A Real Good Plumber, Inc., 59 A.D.3d 424, at 425-26, 874 N.Y.S.2d 145, 147-48 (App. Div., 2d Dep't 2009) (property located in New York City).

505 208 Himrod St., LLC v. Irizarry, 988 N.Y.S.2d 526 (App. Term, 2d, 11th & 13th Jud. Dists. 2014); MULTIPLE DWELLING LAW § 302(1)(b).

506 *See* Leva v. Kramer, 899 N.Y.S.2d 60 (Nassau Cnty. Dist. Ct. 2009).

2. THE SUBJECT PREMISES LACKS A CERTIFICATE OF OCCUPANCY

The failure to obtain a certificate of occupancy does <u>not</u> bar the recovery of rent in a summary proceeding.[507] In fact, excluding the aforementioned exceptions, the Tenant remains liable for the rent for at least as long as she remains in possession regardless of the legal status of the premises.[508] This rule has been reaffirmed by case law that holds a rental agreement involving a single-family dwelling impermissibly used as a two-family dwelling is enforceable notwithstanding the lack of a proper certificate of occupancy.[509]

The reader should be mindful of the Appellate Division, Second Department's decision in *Martin v. Easy Living Homes, Inc.* where the owner was denied use and occupancy for a rental property that lacked a certificate of occupancy. The *Martin* decision is distinguishable from the typical illegal apartment case because the Plaintiff-purchaser was seeking specific performance of the sale and the parties did <u>not</u> have a Landlord and Tenant relationship. Moreover, the entire structure lacked a certificate of occupancy, as opposed to just the occupied portion, due to the builder's failure to complete construction.[510]

Interestingly, the lack of a certificate of occupancy is <u>not</u> grounds for the Tenant to recover the security deposit.[511] However, if the Tenant vacates the premises after discovering the unlawful status of the property, then the Tenant may recover the security deposit in a plenary action.[512]

---

507   Casilia v. Webster, LLC, 140 A.D.3d 530, 32 N.Y.S.3d 494 (App. Term, 1st Dep't 2016); *Madden*, 13 N.Y.S.3d at 850; Corbin v. Briley, 747 N.Y.S.2d 134 (App. Term, 9th & 10th Jud. Dists. 2002).

508   *See generally* Phillips & Huyler Assocs. v. Flynn, 225 A.D.2d 475, 640 N.Y.S.2d 26 (App. Div., 1st Dep't 1996) (suggesting a different result had evidence of the Landlord's misrepresentation been presented); Municipal Metallic Bed Mfg. Corp. v. Dobbs, 253 N.Y. 313 (1930).

509   *See, e.g.*, Pickering v. Chappe, 908 N.Y.S.2d 523 (App. Term, 2d, 11th & 13th Jud. Dists. 2010); *Corbin*, 747 N.Y.S.2d at 134; Corsini v. Gottschalk, N.Y.L.J., Dec. 20, 1999, at 32 (App. Term, 9th & 10th Jud. Dists. 1999).

510   Martin v. Easy Living Homes, Inc., 15 A.D.3d 360, at 361, 790 N.Y.S.2d 467, 468-69 (App. Div., 2d Dep't 2005).

511   *See Pickering*, 908 N.Y.S.2d at 523; Schweighofer v. Straub, 885 N.Y.S.2d 713 (App. Term, 9th & 10th Jud. Dists. 2009).

512   *Ader*, 135 A.D.3d at 671, 23 N.Y.S.3d at 292; Sethi v. Naman, 890 N.Y.S.2d 371 (App.

C. ACCEPTANCE OF RENT FOLLOWING TERMINATION OR EXPIRATION OF THE LEASE

Whether the Landlord may accept rent following the expiration or termination of the rental agreement depends on the parties' intent and the timing of the payments relative to the summary proceeding. As discussed below, the acceptance of payment is limited.

1. ACCEPTANCE OF ANOTHER MONTH'S RENT PRIOR TO THE COMMENCEMENT OF A SUMMARY PROCEEDING

The Landlord may continue to accept rent payments until the termination date set forth in the termination notice.[513] However, the acceptance of rent following the lease termination, but prior to the commencement of a summary proceeding, re-establishes the tenancy on a month-to-month basis. As a result, the termination notice is voided and the summary proceeding would be dismissed.[514] It has been held that a holdover proceeding could continue where the Landlord accepted, and inadvertently deposited the payment, but returned same within a reasonable period of time.[515]

Another interesting situation involved the Landlord's oral demand for payment following the termination date set forth in the Thirty-Day Notice, but prior to the commencement of the holdover proceeding. The Tenant, who was current on rent payments through the termination date, responded that he was "away" and would pay the next month's rent in approximately ten (10) days. The Landlord, believing the Tenant

Term, 9ᵗʰ & 10ᵗʰ Jud. Dists. 2009). *See* Security Deposit *infra*, Chapter 14.

513 ATM Four, LLC v. Miller, 961 N.Y.S.2d 356 (Nassau Cnty. Dist. Ct. 2012). *See* Top Value Homes, Inc. v. Continental Petroleum Corp., 784 N.Y.S.2d 924 (Nassau Cnty. Dist. Ct. 2004). *See also* ROBERT F. DOLAN, RASCH'S LANDLORD AND TENANT INCLUDING SUMMARY PROCEEDINGS § 30:16, at 429-30 (4ᵗʰ ed. 2010).

514 *See* RPL § 232-c. *See also* Vita v. Dol-Fan, III, Inc., 852 N.Y.S.2d 589, 590-91 (App. Term, 9ᵗʰ & 10ᵗʰ Jud. Dists. 2007); *Top Value Homes, Inc.*, 784 N.Y.S.2d at 924.

515 Macleay Woods Hous. Co., Inc. v. Franks, 851 N.Y.S.2d 58 (New Rochelle City Ct. 2007) (payment returned approximately fourteen (14) days after receipt did not warrant dismissal). *Cf.* East Bay Assocs. v. Johnson, N.Y.L.J., March 28, 2000, at 28, col. 6 (App. Term, 9ᵗʰ & 10ᵗʰ Jud. Dists. 2000) (checks held for seven (7) weeks and three (3) weeks, respectively, warranted dismissal).

was merely seeking to delay vacating the premises, commenced a holdover proceeding. Several days later, the Tenant presented, and the Landlord accepted, payment of the current month's rent.

In an unreported decision, the Landlord prevailed because there was nothing improper with merely demanding the payment of rent or use and occupancy for another term prior to the commencement of the summary proceeding provided the Landlord did not intend to reinstate the tenancy.[516] However, if the payment had been made when demanded or the parties reached another agreement, neither of which was demonstrated by the credible evidence, then the termination notice would have been vitiated and the action dismissed.

2. ACCEPTANCE OF ANOTHER MONTH'S RENT AFTER THE COMMENCEMENT OF A SUMMARY PROCEEDING

The general rule is that the acceptance of payment following commencement of a holdover proceeding is permitted without voiding the termination notice or creating a new tenancy. This is because the payment, absent an intent to enter into a new Landlord and Tenant relationship, is considered use and occupancy (as opposed to rent) which the Landlord may accept at any time.[517]

There is a split in the jurisdictions regarding the narrow issue of when a summary proceeding is commenced. The differing views are evident in the situation where the Landlord accepts payment for a period after the summary proceeding was filed, but prior to service of the Notice of Petition and Petition. The majority of jurisdictions have adopted the view that commencement occurs at filing, and, therefore, any payments received thereafter are deemed use and occupancy, and the proceeding may continue.[518]

The Appellate Term for the Second, Eleventh and Thirteenth Judicial

---

516 See generally DOLAN, *supra* note 513, § 30:16, at 429-30 (whether a rent demand made following expiration of the notice to quit constitutes a waiver is "a question of intention").

517 See RPAPL § 711(1).

518 See, e.g., ABN Assocs., LLC v. Citizens Advice Bureau, Inc., 910 N.Y.S.2d 760 (App. Term, 1st Dep't 2010).

Districts has taken the opposite approach. In 92 *Bergenbrooklyn, LLC,* the Court reasoned that the proceeding commences upon "service" (not filing) because only then is there certainty that the Respondent is on notice of the summary proceeding.[519] Thus, the Court concluded that the Landlord's acceptance of payment prior to "service" vitiated the termination notice, and, as a result, dismissed the proceeding.[520]

3. ACCEPTANCE OF ARREARS FOLLOWING ISSUANCE OF THE JUDGMENT

Another frequently encountered situation is the Landlord's acceptance of rent for a month <u>prior</u> to the issuance of the judgment. It is well-established that rent arrears may be accepted post-judgment, and absent a clear intent to revive the tenancy, the acceptance of the payment neither reinstates the Landlord and Tenant relationship nor constitutes a basis to vacate the judgment or warrant of eviction.[521] This rule applies to both residential and commercial leaseholds.

4. ACCEPTANCE OF RENT FOR A MONTH SUBSEQUENT TO ISSUANCE OF THE JUDGMENT (FUTURE RENT)

Whether the Landlord may accept rent for a term <u>following</u> the issuance of the judgment depends on the type of leasehold. This situation typically arises where the judgment is issued in November, for example, and the Landlord accepts December's rent the following month.

In a residential case, the acceptance of rent for a period following issuance of the judgment vitiates the judgment and warrant where the parties acted with the intent to reinstate the tenancy.[522] Although the

---

519 92 Bergenbrooklyn, LLC v. Cisarano, 21 N.Y.S.3d 810 (App. Term, 2d, 11th & 13th Jud. Dists. 2015).

520 *Id.* For a discussion on the appropriate precedent where there is a split in the Judicial Departments, *see supra,* Chapter 6 subdiv. B.

521 Fisk Bldg. Assocs. LLC v. Shimazaki II, Inc., 76 A.D.3d 468, 907 N.Y.S.2d 2 (App. Div., 1st Dep't 2010); J.A.R. Mgmt. Corp. v. Foster, 442 N.Y.S.2d 723, 724 (App. Term, 2d & 11th Jud. Dists. 1980); 284-285 Centr. Owners Corp. v. Alexandre, 836 N.Y.S.2d 495 (Nassau Cnty. Dist. Ct. 2007).

522 DiGiglio v. Tepedino, 173 A.D.2d 763, 571 N.Y.S.2d 301 (App. Div., 2d Dep't 1991); Lake

money judgment would remain unaffected, the Landlord would have to commence another summary proceeding on proper notice to regain possession.[523] The Appellate Term for the Second, Eleventh and Thirteenth Judicial Districts has held that where the parties stipulated that the Landlord is entitled to a judgment of possession with a stay on execution for as long as the Tenant pays the arrears, and further that all future payments would first be applied to the current month's rent (as opposed to use and occupancy), the Landlord may accept post-judgment payments without vitiating the judgment.[524] This result appears to be case specific.

The parties will typically include language in the Stipulation of Settlement that payments made following "issuance" of the judgment are deemed use and occupancy, as opposed to rent, and the parties do not intend to revive the tenancy. This negates having to potentially vacate the judgment and warrant because the Landlord may accept use and occupancy at any time without reviving the tenancy.

If the case involves a commercial property, then the Landlord may accept and, in fact, the corporate Tenant has an obligation to pay rent for the time it remains in possession following the issuance of the judgment. The Landlord's judgment and warrant would stand following payment except where the parties intended to revive the tenancy.[525]

Park 135 Crossways Park Dr., LLC v. Wheatley Capital Inc., 958 N.Y.S.2d 61 (Nassau Cnty. Dist. Ct. 2010).

523   DiGiglio, 173 A.D.2d at 763, 571 N.Y.S.2d at 301; Corrado v. Harris, 822 N.Y.S.2d 365, 366 (App. Term, 9th & 10th Jud. Dists. 2006).

524   368 Chauncey Ave. Trust v. Whitaker, 911 N.Y.S.2d 696 (App. Term, 2d, 11th & 13th Jud. Dists. 2010).

525   Crystal Run Newco, LLC v. United Pet Supply, Inc., 70 A.D.3d 1418, 896 N.Y.S.2d 271 (App. Div., 4th Dep't 2010); First Citizens Nat'l Bank v. Koronowski, 46 A.D.3d 1474, at 1475, 848 N.Y.S.2d 494, 495 (App. Div., 4th Dep't 2007).

D. THE TENANT IS NO LONGER IN POSSESSION OF THE SUBJECT PREMISES

1. THE TENANT VACATES PRIOR TO COMMENCEMENT OF A SUMMARY PROCEEDING

Where the Tenant vacates the premises and the Landlord accepts surrender of possession <u>prior</u> to the commencement of a summary proceeding, the Petition must be dismissed because a summary proceeding may <u>not</u> be maintained where "possession" is not at issue.[526] Whether the Tenant is in possession is a factual issue.[527] A critical factor in determining if a surrender occurred is whether the Tenant has any dominion or control over the premises. If the Tenant leaves behind its possessions, absent a waiver, a summary proceeding may continue.

Where the Tenant abandons the premises without a surrender, the Housing Part similarly lacks jurisdiction over the summary proceeding. Since there is no privity of estate between the parties due to the abandonment, the Landlord may instead pursue its remedies based on contract principles in a plenary action but "[m]ay not seek [same in] the speedier summary proceeding in the landlord-tenant court".[528]

A surrender by operation of law, also referred to as an implicit surrender, occurs where the parties act in a manner (without an express agreement) inconsistent with a Landlord and Tenant relationship which "[i]ndicates their intent to deem the lease terminated".[529] The Tenant's return of the keys in and of itself does <u>not</u> constitute a surren-

---

526 *See* Clark v. Singletary, 31 N.Y.S.3d 920 (App. Term, 9th & 10th Jud. Dists. 2016); O'Connell v. Singletary, 926 N.Y.S.2d 345 (App. Term, 9th & 10th Jud. Dists. 2011); Phoenix Indus., Inc. v. Ultimate Sports, LLC, 859 N.Y.S.2d 906 (App. Term, 9th & 10th Jud. Dists. 2008).

527 *See* Riverside Research Inst. v. KMGA, Inc., 68 N.Y.2d 689, at 692, 506 N.Y.S.2d 302, 304 (1986); PK Rest., LLC v. Lifshutz, 138 A.D.3d 434, 30 N.Y.S.3d 13 (App. Div., 1st Dep't 2016); South Ferry Bldg. Co. v. 44 Wall St. Fund, Inc., 535 N.Y.S.2d 685 (N.Y. Civ. Ct. 1988).

528 *South Ferry Bldg. Co.*, 535 N.Y.S.2d at 688.

529 Fragomeni v. AIM Servs., Inc., 135 A.D.3d 1272, 23 N.Y.S.3d 496 (App. Div., 3d Dep't 2016); Ford Coyle Props., Inc. v. 3029 Ave. V Realty, LLC, 63 A.D.3d 782, 881 N.Y.S.2d 146, 147 (App. Div., 2d Dep't 2009).

der by operation of law.[530]

A surrender of possession bars the award of rent for any month subsequent to the surrender in a summary proceeding.[531] In other words, when the Tenant vacates the premises before the rental agreement expires and the Landlord re-enters the property and changes the locks, the Landlord is prohibited from commencing a summary proceeding. The proper course of action for the Landlord is a plenary action for money damages.[532]

2. THE TENANT VACATES AFTER COMMENCEMENT OF A SUMMARY PROCEEDING

The Landlord may continue to pursue its claims in a summary proceeding where the Tenant vacates the premises after the proceeding was commenced.[533] However, the Landlord and Tenant relationship is considered terminated as of the date the Tenant vacated, and, as a result, the money judgment may not include rent or use and occupancy for a period following the surrender.[534] An exception to this rule is where the rental agreement contains a survival clause that provides the Tenant's obligations continue following the termination of the lease, which the Landlord may pursue in a plenary action.

---

530 *Ford Coyle Props., Inc., LLC*, 63 A.D.3d at 782, 881 N.Y.S.2d at 147.

531 *See generally* 4400 Equities, Inc. v. Dhinsa, 52 A.D.3d 654, 862 N.Y.S.2d 597 (App. Div., 2d Dep't 2008); Deer Hills Hardware, Inc. v. Conlin Realty Corp., 292 A.D.2d 565, 739 N.Y.S.2d 597 (App. Div., 2d Dep't 2002); *see also* Priegue v. Paulus, 988 N.Y.S.2d 525 (App. Term, 9th & 10th Jud. Dists. 2014) (occupants liable for rent obligations where they failed to inform the Landlord they had vacated the premises and returned the keys).

532 *See* 44th St. Photo, Inc. v. Abrams, Index No. 2733-14, 2016 WL 2584842, 2016 N.Y. Misc. LEXIS 1646 (App. Term, 9th & 10th Jud. Dists. April 25, 2016); Flatbush Patio LLC v. Gause, 836 N.Y.S.2d 485 n.1 (N.Y. Civ. Ct. 2006); *South Ferry Bldg. Co.*, 535 N.Y.S.2d at 687-88.

533 1129 N. Blvd., LLC v. Astra Group, Inc., 992 N.Y.S.2d 159 (App. Term, 9th & 10th Jud. Dists. 2014); Bahamonde v. Grabel, 939 N.Y.S.2d 226 (App. Term, 9th & 10th Jud. Dists. 2011).

534 *See* Patchogue Assocs. v. Sears, Roebuck and Co., 951 N.Y.S.2d 314 (App. Term, 9th & 10th Jud. Dists. 2012); Cornwell v. Sanford, 222 N.Y. 248 (1918). *See generally* MH Residential 1, LLC v. Barrett, 78 A.D.3d 99, at 103, 908 N.Y.S.2d 6, 9 (App. Div., 1st Dep't 2010) (commenting that "[w]here a summary proceeding to recover possession of real property has been instituted, the landlord-tenant relationship may only be terminated by actual surrender of the premises or by issuance of a warrant of eviction").

E. THE PETITION ASSERTS BOTH
NON-PAYMENT AND HOLDOVER CLAIMS

As a general matter, the Landlord may <u>not</u> assert both non-payment and holdover claims in the Petition. The exception to this rule appears to be where the rental agreement includes a provision that the lease is terminated upon the non-payment of rent, in which case the inconsistent claims may be asserted in the alternative.[535]

Interestingly, the Second Department's Appellate Term for the Ninth and Tenth Judicial Districts previously held in *Seaton* that the inconsistent claims were <u>not</u> permitted.[536] Although both the holdover and non-payment claims were eventually dismissed, the Court concluded that where a Landlord commences a summary proceeding alleging both holdover and non-payment claims, "only the nonpayment claim is maintainable".[537]

The Appellate Term has since clarified that the mere filing of a non-payment proceeding does <u>not</u> automatically nullify an existing holdover proceeding.[538] Although dual proceedings are not simultaneously permitted, the Court permitted the holdover proceeding to continue because the non-payment proceeding was "immediately" discontinued (two (2) days later).[539]

---

535   Jacobson v. Raff, 927 N.Y.S.2d 816 (App. Term, 9th & 10th Jud. Dists. 2011) (holding "[u]nder certain circumstances, inconsistent causes of action for nonpayment of rent and holding over after the termination of a tenancy may be pleaded in the alternative"); *see* Kern v. Guller, 40 A.D.3d 1231, at 1232, 835 N.Y.S.2d 764, 765 (App. Div., 3d Dep't 2007) (holding that pleading non-payment and holdover claims in the alternative was permissible pursuant to CPLR § 3014 where the parties' month-to-month tenancy was terminated); Azour, LLC v. Tax Sister, Inc., 909 N.Y.S.2d 282 (App. Term, 2d, 11th & 13th Jud. Dists. 2010) (permitting joint trial of a non-payment proceeding and a subsequent holdover proceeding following termination of the tenancy).

536   *See* Seaton v. Chavez, 816 N.Y.S.2d 701 (App. Term, 9th & 10th Jud. Dists. 2006).

537   *Id.* Parenthetically, the same Court subsequently held that a non-payment proceeding was barred by a previously commenced ejectment proceeding because the "ejectment action is deemed a [re-entry] by [the] landlord into possession" and an election to terminate the lease. *See* Jefferson Vall. Mall Ltd. P'ship v. Franchise Acquisition Group, Inc., 874 N.Y.S.2d 667, 668 (App. Term, 9th & 10th Jud. Dists. 2008).

538   72nd St. Assocs., LLC v. Persson, 13 N.Y.S.3d 853 (App. Term, 1st Dep't 2015).

539   *Id.*

In *145 E. 16th St. LLC v. Spencer*, the Appellate Term held that the commencement of two (2) non-payment proceedings while the dismissal of Landlord's holdover proceeding was pending appeal did <u>not</u> vitiate the holdover proceeding's predicate notice or demonstrate an intent to create a new Landlord and Tenant relationship.[540] The controversy arose when the holdover proceeding was reinstated. The Court rejected the Tenant's assertion that the non-payment proceedings, which were subsequently discontinued or dismissed without prejudice, required dismissal of the holdover proceeding.[541]

F. ACTUAL AND CONSTRUCTIVE EVICTIONS

1. CONSTRUCTIVE EVICTION

A constructive eviction occurs where the Landlord commits a wrongful act or an omission that substantially denies the Tenant's "beneficial use and enjoyment" of all or a portion of the premises.[542] For example, where the Landlord fails to repair a perpetually leaking roof, a constructive eviction would result if the Tenant is unable to perform its operations in the premises due to the non-repair.

To assert the defense, the Tenant must vacate the portions of the premises claimed to have been denied within a reasonable period of time.[543] The Tenant need not abandon the entire premises, only those affected areas.[544] If the Tenant continues to use the portion of the prem-

---

540 145 E. 16th St. LLC v. Spencer, 13 N.Y.S.3d 851 (App. Term, 1st Dep't 2015).

541 *Id.* The Court emphasized that the non-payment proceedings were commenced <u>after</u> the holdover proceeding was dismissed. *Id.*

542 *See generally* Barash v. Pennsylvania Term. Real Estate Corp., 26 N.Y.2d 77, 308 N.Y.S.2d 649 (1970) (dismissing action where plaintiff-Tenant failed to make a *prima facie* case for either a constructive or actual eviction).

543 *See* 7001 E. 71st St., LLC v. Millenium Health Servs., 138 A.D.3d 573, 28 N.Y.S.3d 604 (App. Div., 1st Dep't 2016); 36 Main Realty Corp. v. Wang Law Office, PLLC, 19 N.Y.S.3d 654 (App. Term, 2d, 11th & 13th Jud. Dists. 2015); Zurel U.S.A., Inc. v. Magnum Realty Corp., 279 A.D.2d 520, at 521, 719 N.Y.S.2d 276 (App. Div., 2d Dep't 2001) (a reasonable time for a commercial tenant to vacate may be three (3) to four (4) months).

544 *See* Minjak Co. v. Randolph, 140 A.D.2d 245, 528 N.Y.S.2d 554 (App. Div., 1st Dep't

ises at issue, even if the usage is greatly diminished, then the defense of constructive eviction is <u>not</u> available.[545]

A Subtenant may <u>not</u> assert a constructive eviction claim against the Landlord because a Landlord and Tenant relationship is a necessary element.[546] Of note, a commercial Tenant that remains in possession must continue to pay rent even where the Landlord fails to provide essential services.[547]

A Tenant that has been constructively evicted is entitled to an abatement of rent (not an entire suspension of rent).[548] Although expert testimony is <u>not</u> required in a residential case, expert testimony is required in a commercial case to determine the reasonable diminution of the rental value.[549]

A constructive eviction claim does <u>not</u> arise where the rental agreement (1) authorizes the Landlord to enter the premises to make repairs and alterations, and further (2) precludes a rent abatement on that basis.[550] In fact, "[a]lterations to leased premises, made with the consent of the tenant, do not amount to an eviction, no matter how extensive or the degree of interference with the tenant's occupancy".[551]

1988); N.N. Int'l (USA) Corp. v. Gladden Props. LLC, Index No. 103909-09, 2016 WL 3747428, 2016 N.Y. Misc. LEXIS 2546 (N.Y. Cnty. Sup. Ct. May 31, 2016).

545   *See* Arpino v. Cicciaro, 967 N.Y.S.2d 865 (App. Term, 9th & 10th Jud. Dists. 2012) (holding where commercial workshop area "ha[d] been used for its intended purposes, albeit for a drastically reduced amount of time each day during the colder months of the year, there has been no abandonment"); Garry v. Ryan & Henderson, P.C., 36 N.Y.S.3d 364 (Nassau Cnty. Dist. Ct. 2016).

546   *7001 E. 71st St., LLC,* 138 A.D.3d at 573, 28 N.Y.S.3d at 604.

547   Thor 725 8th Ave. LLC v. Goonetilleke, 4968-CV-14, 2015 WL 906002, 2015 U.S. Dist. LEXIS 25696 (S.D.N.Y. March 3, 2015) (Landlord's posting of "Retail Space Available" signs and allowing prospective lessees to view the premises did not constitute a constructive eviction).

548   *See Minjack Co.,* 140 A.D.2d at 245, 528 N.Y.S.2d at 554; 174 Mott Group, LLC v. Lucky 168 Rest. Corp., 856 N.Y.S.2d 500 (N.Y. Civ. Ct. 2008).

549   *See* Arbern Realty Co. v. Clay Craft Planters Co., Inc., 727 N.Y.S.2d 236, 237 (App. Term, 9th & 10th Jud. Dists. 2001); New York City Economic Dev. Corp. v. Harborside Mini Storage, Inc., 819 N.Y.S.2d 211 (N.Y. Civ. Ct. 2006).

550   APF 286 Mad LLC v. RIS Real Props., Inc., 13 N.Y.S.3d 849 (App. Term, 1st Dep't 2015).

551   *Id.*; 737 Park Ave. Acquisition LLC v. Robert B. Jetter, M.D., PLLC, 7 N.Y.S.3d 245 (App. Term, 1st Dep't 2014) (same).

2. ACTUAL EVICTION

An actual eviction occurs where the Tenant is wrongfully ousted from physical possession of all or a portion of the premises, such as where the Landlord changes the locks or bars the Tenant from entering. Expert testimony is <u>not</u> required to establish the defense.[552] The remedy for the unlawful eviction is the complete suspension of rent even where the wrongful act only denied the Tenant's use and enjoyment of a portion of the premises.[553]

A "trivial" intrusion or interference with the Tenant's use and enjoyment of commercial premises is <u>not</u> an eviction, and, as a result, the Tenant is <u>not</u> entitled to an abatement of rent.[554] In *Eastside Exh. Corp. v. 210 E. 86th St. Corp.*, the Court of Appeals held that the Landlord's taking of a mere twelve (12) square feet of non-essential lobby space within the 15,000 to 19,000 square foot movie theater was a "*de minimis* taking*" that not only failed to justify a full abatement of the rent, but further precluded injunctive and monetary relief.[555] Whether the taking is *de minimis* is determined on a case-by-case basis. The Appellate Term for the Second, Eleventh and Thirteenth Judicial Districts has extended the "*de minimis* taking" rule to residential leaseholds.[556]

Where the Tenant elects to withhold rent following a partial actual eviction, the Tenant may <u>not</u> assert a claim for damages against the

---

552   *See* 487 Elmwood, Inc. v. Hassett, 107 A.D.2d 285, at 289, 486 N.Y.S.2d 113, 117 (App. Div., 4th Dep't 1985) (expert testimony is required, however, to establish damages resulting from an actual eviction).

553   *See* Frame v. Horizons Wine & Cheese, Ltd., 95 A.D.2d 514, at 518, 467 N.Y.S.2d 630, 633 (App. Div., 2d Dep't 1983) (where there is a partial actual eviction, the Landlord may <u>not</u> recover use and occupancy for the remaining portion of the premises occupied by the Tenant) (*citing* Barash v. Pennsylvania Term. Real Estate Corp., 26 N.Y.2d 77, 308 N.Y.S.2d 649 (1970)).

554   *See* Eastside Exh. Corp. v. 210 E. 86th St. Corp., 18 N.Y.3d 617, 942 N.Y.S.2d 19 (2012).

555   *Id.*

556   *See* Paskov v. Kreshitchki, 954 N.Y.S.2d 760 (App. Term, 2d, 11th & 13th Jud. Dists. 2012); *cf.* Goldstone v. Gracie Terr. Apt. Corp., 110 A.D.3d 101, 970 N.Y.S.2d 783 (App. Div., 1st Dep't 2013) (denying Tenant's motion for a preliminary injunction because the minimal taking failed to result in irreparable harm).

Landlord.[557] However, if the Tenant opts to pursue a claim for damages due to the actual eviction, then the Tenant waives the right to raise the unlawful eviction as a defense in a non-payment proceeding.[558]

3. SELF-HELP BY THE LANDLORD PROHIBITED (TREBLE DAMAGES)

In New York, only the Sheriff or Marshal may perform or authorize an eviction pursuant to an Order of the Court. Accordingly, the Landlord may not resort to self-help relief such as turning off the utilities, padlocking the entrance, changing the locks and/or removing the Tenant's possessions.[559]

A wrongfully ousted Tenant may commence a proceeding in the Housing Part by Order to Show Cause to be restored to the premises and, if necessary, direct the Sheriff or Marshal to remove and change the locks.[560] Although the Housing Part may direct the restoration of the Tenant, who would be the Petitioner in the action, the Court may not award money damages.[561] The Tenant would, however, be entitled to treble damages in a subsequent plenary action (not the special proceeding).[562] No predicate notice is required prior to commencing the proceeding, but the current occupant must be named as a Respondent.[563]

The statute of limitations for an unlawful eviction claim is one (1)

---

557   Schwartz v. Hotel Owners Corp., 132 A.D.3d 541, 20 N.Y.S.3d 341 (App. Div., 1st Dep't 2015); *Frame*, 95 A.D.2d at 514, 467 N.Y.S.2d at 633.

558   *Frame*, 95 A.D.2d at 514, 467 N.Y.S.2d at 633.

559   Clinkscale v. Sampson, 48 A.D.3d 730, 853 N.Y.S.2d 572 (App. Div., 2d Dep't 2008); Coleman v. Murray, 934 N.Y.S.2d 33 (Suffolk Cnty. Dist. Ct. 2011).

560   RPAPL § 713(10).

561   Eze v. Spring Creek Gardens, 85 A.D.3d 1102, 925 N.Y.S.2d 888 (App. Div., 2d Dep't 2011); Rostant v. Swersky, 79 A.D.3d 456, at 457, 912 N.Y.S.2d 200, 201-02 (App. Div., 1st Dep't 2010); Cudar v. O'Shea, 951 N.Y.S.2d 312 (App. Term, 2d, 11th & 13th Jud. Dists. 2012); Viglietta v. Lavoie, 932 N.Y.S.2d 307 (App. Term, 9th & 10th Jud. Dists. 2011).

562   RPAPL § 853. *See* Hood v. Koziej, 140 A.D.3d 563, 37 N.Y.S.3d 68 (App. Div., 1st Dep't 2016); *Clinkscale*, 48 A.D.3d at 731, 853 N.Y.S.2d at 573.

563   Bay Ridge Chicken Grill, Inc. v. Cirrus Data Int'l, LLC, 26 N.Y.S.3d 723 (App. Term, 2d, 11th & 13th Jud. Dists. 2015) (proceeding dismissed where Tenant-Petitioner failed to name current occupant as a party in the proceeding).

year which "[b]egins to run when 'it is reasonably certain that the tenant has been unequivocally removed with at least the implicit denial of any return' ".[564] A special proceeding to be restored to possession is improper where the individual claiming the unlawful eviction was not in "actual possession" or "constructive possession" at the time of the unlawful entry.[565] In fact, where the occupant abandoned the premises, there can be no liability for wrongful eviction or trespass.[566]

When the Landlord is awarded a possessory judgment and a warrant of eviction from the Court but nonetheless elects to utilize self-help, the Tenant's recourse is to commence a new proceeding to be restored to the premises in the Housing Part or other court of competent jurisdiction. The Tenant may <u>not</u> seek such relief by way of Order to Show Cause in the Landlord's summary proceeding.[567] For example, in *Triangle Props. #14, LLC*, the Tenant's motion to be restored to possession following the Landlord's use of self-help was denied because the Tenants "[w]ere not removed pursuant to a judgment or order of the court,...[and as a result] the court was without authority, in [a] nonpayment proceeding commenced by landlord, to direct [the] landlord to restore [the tenants] to possession".[568]

On the other hand, a Respondent evicted by the Sheriff or Marshal may move to be restored to the property in the Landlord's summary proceeding. Standing to commence the proceeding is <u>not</u> contingent on the number of consecutive days the wrongfully displaced occupant was in possession.[569]

---

564   PK Rest., LLC v. Lifshutz, 138 A.D.3d 434, 30 N.Y.S.3d 13 (App. Div., 1st Dep't 2016); *see* Kolomensky v. Wiener, 135 A.D.2d 505, 522 N.Y.S.2d 156 (App. Div., 2d Dep't 1987).

565   *Viglietta*, 932 N.Y.S.2d at 307 (noting the Petitioner previously commenced a civil action for title in Supreme Court).

566   *See* Ovcharenko v. 65th Booth Assocs., 131 A.D.3d 1144, 16 N.Y.S.3d 763 (App. Div., 2d Dep't 2015) (summary judgment denied where there was a question of fact whether the Tenant abandoned the premises); Salem v. U.S. Bank Nat'l Assoc., 82 A.D.3d 865, 918 N.Y.S.2d 532 (App. Div., 2d Dep't 2011).

567   Triangle Props. # 14, LLC v. Beauty Salon Depot/Beauty U.S.A., 920 N.Y.S.2d 245 (App. Term, 9th & 10th Jud. Dists. 2010).

568   *Id.*

569   Goncalves v. Soho Vill. Realty, Inc., 9 N.Y.S.3d 522 (App. Term, 1st Dep't 2015).

In a commercial case, the Landlord may avail itself of a lease provision authorizing re-entry based upon a breach by the Tenant provided the re-entry is done in a reasonable manner and without force.[570] In *Martinez v. Ulloa*, the Appellate Term dismissed the Tenant's special proceeding to be restored to possession absent sufficient evidence that the Landlord violated the lease or that the re-entry was completed in an unreasonable and/or forceful manner. However, in that case, the Tenants were independently returned to possession with the assistance of the Police.[571] As a result, the Court denied the Landlord's cross-motion for another judgment of possession because the Landlord originally used self-help without the assistance of the Court and "cannot now complain of being denied the opportunity to short circuit the procedural requirements of a summary proceeding...."[572]

G. BREACH OF THE COVENANT TO REPAIR (COMMERCIAL LEASES ONLY)

Absent a lease provision specifying the circumstances upon which the Tenant may withhold rent, a commercial Tenant must continue to pay rent where the Landlord breaches the rental agreement by failing to make required repairs. In other words, the Landlord's failure to make the repairs is <u>not</u> a defense in a non-payment proceeding.

This is because the covenant to pay rent is independent of the covenant to make repairs as long as the Tenant remains in possession.[573] Any

---

570 *See* Drapaniotis v. 36-08 33ʳᵈ St. Corp., 48 A.D.3d 736, 853 N.Y.S.2d 356 (App. Div., 2d Dep't 2008); Bozewicz v. Nash Metalware Co., 284 A.D.2d 288, 725 N.Y.S.2d 671 (App. Div., 2d Dep't 2001); Jovana Spaghetti House v. Heritage Co. of Massena, 189 A.D.2d 1041, 592 N.Y.S.2d 879 (App. Div., 3d Dep't 1993).

571 Martinez v. Ulloa, 22 N.Y.S.3d 787 (App. Term, 2d, 11ᵗʰ & 13ᵗʰ Jud. Dists. 2015).

572 *Id.*

573 Universal Comms. Network, Inc. v. 229 W. 28ᵗʰ Owner, LLC, 85 A.D.3d 668, 926 N.Y.S.2d 479 (App. Div., 1ˢᵗ Dep't 2011); Westchester Cnty. Indus. Dev. Agency v. Morris Indus. Bldrs., 278 A.D.2d 232, 717 N.Y.S.2d 279 (App. Div., 2d Dep't 2000); 91 E. Main St. Realty Corp. v. Angelic Creations by Lucia, 884 N.Y.S.2d 565, 566 (App. Term, 9ᵗʰ & 10ᵗʰ Jud. Dists. 2009). A lease provision reserving the Landlord's right to enter the premises to make repairs does <u>not</u> necessarily establish a duty to make the repairs. *See* Han v. Kemp, Pin &

damages sustained by the Tenant may be asserted as a counterclaim, if not barred by the rental agreement, or in a plenary action in a court of competent jurisdiction.

H. THE LANDLORD DID NOT OWN THE PREMISES WHEN THE ACTION WAS COMMENCED

Although demonstrating lawful "title" or ownership of the premises is typically an element of the Landlord's case, ownership is <u>not</u> required to maintain a summary proceeding because RPAPL § 721 explicitly permits, *inter alia*, a "landlord or lessor" to bring a summary proceeding without requiring ownership.[574]. It is a fundamental principle of Landlord and Tenant Law that the Housing Part may <u>not</u> determine issues of "title",[575] but rather the Court may adjudicate the issue solely for the purpose of determining which party is entitled to "possession".[576]

Accordingly, the Tenant may assert that the Landlord is <u>not</u> the owner or lacks a superior interest in the premises as an affirmative defense, but the Tenant may <u>not</u> affirmatively claim that it is the "owner" in a summary proceeding.[577] The defense is further limited by the principle of estoppel to deny the Landlord's title which precludes the defense where the Tenant entered into the rental agreement acknowledging, accepting and benefitting from the Landlord's title and the Landlord's

---

Ski, LLC, 142 A.D.3d 688, 36 N.Y.S.3d 883 (App. Div., 2d Dep't 2016) (out-of-possession Landlord generally has no responsibility to maintain commercial premises in a "reasonably safe condition").

574 RPAPL § 721 (listing eleven (11) categories of individuals and entities that may commence a summary proceeding). *See* Tacfield Assocs., LLC v. Davis, 990 N.Y.S.2d 440 (App. Term, 2d, 11th & 13th Jud. Dists. 2014); Mirra v. Pattee, 862 N.Y.S.2d 815 (App. Term, 2d & 11th Jud. Dists. 2008).

575 *See* Chopra v. Prusik, 801 N.Y.S.2d 692, 693 (App. Term, 2d & 11th Jud. Dists. 2005).

576 Nissequogue Boat Club v. State of New York, 14 A.D.3d 542, at 544, 789 N.Y.S.2d 71, 73 (App. Div., 2d Dep't 2005); Yacoob v. Persuad, 950 N.Y.S.2d 611 (App. Term, 2d, 11th & 13th Jud. Dists. 2012); LCD Holding Corp. v. Velez, 980 N.Y.S.2d 276 (N.Y. Civ. Ct. 2013).

577 Jacob Marion, LLC v. El Bey, 36 N.Y.S.3d 47 (App. Term, 2d, 11th & 13th Jud. Dists. 2016) (default judgment vacated where Respondent plausibly asserted she was the lawful owner of the premises); Muzio v. Rogers, 867 N.Y.S.2d 376 (App. Term, 9th & 10th Jud. Dists. 2008).

permission to grant possession.[578] In other words, absent a showing that the Landlord's title was transferred <u>after</u> entering into the Landlord and Tenant relationship, the Tenant may <u>not</u> challenge the Landlord's right to maintain a summary proceeding where it previously acknowledged that the Landlord had a superior interest in the premises.

Asserting the defense that the Tenant is the "owner" of the subject premises by adverse possession is <u>not</u> without risk. If the Housing Part rules in favor of the Landlord, then the Tenant may be collaterally estopped from raising the issue of title in any other action or forum.[579] However, if the Tenant prevails in the summary proceeding, then the issue of title may be raised again in a subsequent declaratory judgment action in a court of competent jurisdiction.[580] The declaratory action would have to be filed within sixty (60) days of entry of the Housing Part's decision.[581]

---

578 The parties are required to abide by the terms of their negotiated relationship for as long as it continues. *See* ROBERT F. DOLAN, RASCH'S LANDLORD AND TENANT INCLUDING SUMMARY PROCEEDINGS § 5:8, at 253-54 (4th ed. 2010); *Tacfield Assocs., LLC*, 990 N.Y.S.2d at 440. In a post-foreclosure holdover summary proceeding, the defense of lack of title or ownership may be waived where the Tenant had ample opportunity, but failed to raise the defense in the mortgage foreclosure action. *See* M & T Mtg. Corp. v. Larkins, 910 N.Y.S.2d 763 (App. Term, 2d, 11th & 13th Jud. Dists. 2010).

579 *See Nissequogue Boat Club*, 14 A.D.3d at 543-44, 789 N.Y.S.2d at 73.

580 To demonstrate title by adverse possession not founded or based upon a written instrument, the Tenant must establish (1) "acts sufficiently open" to put a reasonable owner on notice or that (2) the subject premises was "protected by a substantial inclosure". *See* RPAPL §§ 521, 522 (as amended in 2008). In addition, the Tenant must establish that the possession was hostile and under a claim of right, actual, open and notorious, exclusive and continuous for at least ten (10) years. Estate of Becker v. Murtagh, 19 N.Y.3d 75, 945 N.Y.S.2d 196 (2012); Scalamander Cove, LLC v. Bachmann, 119 A.D.3d 547, 987 N.Y.S.2d 902 (App. Div., 2d Dep't 2014); Maya's Black Creek, LLC v. Angelo Balbo Realty Corp., 82 A.D.3d 1175, 920 N.Y.S.2d 172 (App. Div., 2d Dep't 2011).

581 RPAPL § 747(2). *See* Haque v. Rob, 83 A.D.3d 895, 920 N.Y.S.2d 707 (App. Div., 2d Dep't 2011) (*citing* Henry Modell & Co. v. Minister, Elders & Deacons of the Ref. Prot. Dutch Church of City of N.Y., 68 N.Y.2d 456, at 462-63, 510 N.Y.S.2d 63, 66-67 (1986)).

I. THE LANDLORD IS DIVESTED OF OWNERSHIP DURING THE SUMMARY PROCEEDING

Unless the Court otherwise directs, CPLR § 1018 authorizes the continuation of a summary proceeding where the Landlord sells or otherwise transfers ownership of the premises during the pendency of the proceeding.[582] Ideally, the parties would bring the transfer to the attention of the Court such that a substitution may occur without disruption. Regardless, in *Tabak v. Steele*, the Appellate Term for the First Department held that the Landlord could continue to pursue monetary relief during the pendency of the appeal without substituting the transferee because the "delay did not affect the continued progress of the proceeding".[583] Significantly, the controversy was limited to the monetary dispute, and the judgment was binding on the transferee.[584]

However, some have taken the approach that where possession is sought, such as in a summary proceeding, the transferring Landlord may seek unpaid rent and "added" rent in the summary proceeding until title was transferred, but it may not be awarded a judgment of possession or a warrant of eviction. The rationale is that due to the transfer, the Landlord lacks the capacity to enforce a warrant of eviction, and, as a result, it should not be holding the warrant for an indefinite period without any guarantee the appropriate party will be substituted.

Another option is for the Housing Part to transfer the summary proceeding to the Civil Part of the Court, assign a new index number and convert the matter into a plenary action for money damages.[585] The Petition would be deemed the Complaint, and the Tenant would be given no fewer than twenty (20) days to formally interpose an Answer. The monetary relief would be limited to use and occupancy and other claims until the Landlord was divested of ownership. Finally, the trans-

---

582 CPLR § 1018; *see generally* Tabak v. Steele, 901 N.Y.S.2d 903 (App. Term, 1st Dep't 2009); Buywise Holding, LLC v. Harris, 31 A.D.3d 681, 821 N.Y.S.2d 213 (App. Div., 2d Dep't 2006).

583 *Tabak*, 901 N.Y.S.2d at 903.

584 *Id.*; Bova v. Vinciguerra, 139 A.D.2d 797, 526 N.Y.S.2d 671 (App. Div., 3d Dep't 1988).

585 East Bronx Props., Inc. v. James, 103 N.Y.S.2d 535 (N.Y. Mun. Ct. 1951).

fer would be without prejudice to the transferee commencing its own proceeding for possession provided the claim was neither waived nor abandoned.

There is a caveat to proceeding in this manner. Since the local Court's ability to award a money judgment in a plenary action is limited to the maximum jurisdictional dollar amount of the Court, the Court lacks subject matter jurisdiction over the dispute where the claim exceeds the threshold.

Moreover, the Court is without authority to reduce or modify the claim on its own.[586] If the claim is voluntarily reduced to within the Court's jurisdictional dollar limit, then the Landlord may not seek the balance in another forum because "claim-splitting" is not permitted.[587] On the other hand, if the Landlord refuses to reduce the claim to within the dollar jurisdictional limit of the Court, then the case will be dismissed because the dollar amount was not reduced "by motion or stipulation".[588]

In deciding whether to reduce the amount of the claim, the Landlord need not concern itself with the applicable statute of limitations. This is because when an action is dismissed due to a lack of subject matter

---

586 Although there is no dollar restriction on the amount of rent the Housing Part may award in a summary proceeding, the Court's monetary jurisdictional limitation is applicable to plenary actions. *See* Eastrich No. 80 Corp. v. Patrolmen's Benev. Assoc., 688 N.Y.S.2d 409 (App. Term, 1st Dep't 1999); Campbell v. Fairfield Pres. Assocs., 798 N.Y.S.2d 707 (App. Term, 2d & 11th Jud. Dists. 2004). The monetary threshold of civil actions is $25,000 in the New York City Civil Courts; $15,000 in the District Courts and City Courts Outside of New York City; and $3,000 in the Justice Courts. N.Y. City Civ. Ct. Act § 202 (McKinney 2009); N.Y. Uniform City Ct. Act § 202 (McKinney 2009); N.Y. Uniform Dist. Ct. Act § 202 (McKinney 2009); N.Y. Uniform Just. Ct. Act § 202 (McKinney 2009).

587 *See generally* Bay Crest Assoc. v. Paar, 4 N.Y.S.3d 812 (App. Term, 9th & 10th Jud. Dists. 2015) (holding that plaintiff's claims for annual assessments and attorney's fees "were part of a single cause of action", and, as a result, subject to the $15,000 monetary jurisdictional limit of plenary actions in the District Court); Rocco v. Badalamente, 867 N.Y.S.2d 20 (App. Term, 9th & 10th Jud. Dists. 2008) (the claim-splitting doctrine "[r]equires a plaintiff to join all installments due under a single contract [such as rent] at the time suit is commenced") (internal citations omitted).

588 Boland v. Miller, 867 N.Y.S.2d 15 (App. Term, 9th & 10th Jud. Dists. 2008). *But see* Eastrich No. 80 Corp., 688 N.Y.S.2d at 409 (pursuant to Article VI, § 19(f) of the New York State Constitution, the New York City Courts may transfer cases that they do not have subject matter jurisdiction over to the Supreme Court). Article VI, § 19(I) of the New York State Constitution prohibits the District Courts, City Courts outside of New York City and Justice Courts from exercising the same transfer authority.

jurisdiction, the Landlord has an additional six (6) months to commence a plenary action in a court of competent jurisdiction even where the statute of limitations has since expired.[589]

J. SUCCESSOR LANDLORDS

A successor Landlord acquires the premises subject to the terms and conditions of the existing tenancy, including any waiver of rights, where the successor Landlord has actual or constructive knowledge of the leasehold.[590] The Tenant's possession of the premises at the time of the transfer constitutes, at minimum, constructive notice.[591] The successor Landlord will be bound by an oral waiver of a lease provision made prior to the transfer of ownership.[592]

The introduction of an Assignment of the Rents may be required to obtain a money judgment for unpaid rent prior to the transfer. With the possible exception where there is a waiver of rights, the Tenant generally need not be concerned that the new Landlord will unilaterally implement different terms than those agreed to by the former Landlord. For example, in *Magal Props. LLC v. Gritsyk*, the Appellate Term held that the successor Landlord was bound by an agreement made sixteen (16) years earlier authorizing certain alterations.[593]

Pursuant to General Obligations Law § 7-108, a successor Landlord is deemed to have knowledge of the security deposit tendered to the former Landlord where the premises is a residential dwelling containing six (6) or more units. The successor Landlord is further responsible

---

589   CPLR § 205(a). *See* Parker v. Mack, 61 N.Y.2d 114, at 118, 472 N.Y.S.2d 882, 884 (1984); *Campbell*, 798 N.Y.S.2d at 707.

590   *See generally* Stoneybrook Realty, L.L.C. v. Cremktco, Inc., 675 N.Y.S.2d 749, 751 (App. Term, 9th & 10th Jud. Dists. 1998).

591   Stracham v. Bresnick, 76 A.D.3d 1009, at 1010-11, 908 N.Y.S.2d 95, 97 (App. Div., 2d Dep't 2010).

592   *See* 5 Sunset Park Holdings, LLC v. Brito, 950 N.Y.S.2d 491 (App. Term, 2d, 11th & 13th Jud. Dists. 2012) (former Landlord orally waived requirement of obtaining written consent prior to alterations).

593   Magal Props. LLC v. Gritsyk, 28 N.Y.S.3d 649 (App. Term, 1st Dep't 2015) (dismissing holdover proceeding).

for appropriately applying and/or returning the security deposit.[594]

K. AUTOMATIC LEASE RENEWAL PROVISION

Pursuant to General Obligations Law § 5-905, a lease provision that states the rental agreement automatically renews upon expiration is <u>not</u> enforceable unless the Landlord provides the Tenant a written reminder of the renewal provision <u>prior</u> to the expiration of the lease. The failure to provide written notice "renders the automatic renewal clause…unenforceable as against public policy of this State".[595]

Where notice is <u>not</u> provided, the Tenant has the option of remaining in possession or vacating the premises because the "[L]andlord places himself in the position, when he does not give notice…of abiding by the Tenant's choice of what [the Tenant] wishes to do".[596] If the Tenant elects to stay, then a month-to-month tenancy is created upon the Landlord's acceptance of the rent payment.[597]

L. FAILURE TO EXERCISE OPTION TO RENEW COMMERCIAL LEASE

A commercial Tenant's failure to timely exercise a lease renewal provision may be forgiven, in equity, where the failure (1) was due to "inadvertence", "negligence" or "honest mistake"; (2) would result in forfeiture by the Tenant; and (3) there was no prejudice to the Landlord.[598] It has been held that "forfeiture" results where the Tenant, in good faith and with the intention of renewing the lease, makes

---

594   *See* Battle v. Smith, 950 N.Y.S.2d 721 (App. Term, 9th & 10th Jud. Dists. 2012).

595   Hain v. Zwitzer, 875 N.Y.S.2d 820 (Rochester City Ct. 2008); Malone Assocs. v. Grand Union Co., 249 A.D.2d 830, at 831, 671 N.Y.S.2d 861, 862 (App. Div., 3d Dep't 1998); J.H. Holding Co. v. Wooten, 291 N.Y. 427, 430 (1943) (RPL § 230 "was enacted solely for the protection of the tenant"). *Cf.* Stop & Shop Supermkt. Co., LLC v. Goldsmith, Index No. 3052-CV-10, 2013 WL 3179501, 2013 U.S. Dist. LEXIS 90820 (S.D.N.Y. June 24, 2013). RPL § 230 was substantially transferred into General Obligations Law § 5-905, which became law, effective September 27, 1964.

596   Mobil Oil Corp. v. Lione, 322 N.Y.S.2d 82, 86 (Suffolk Cnty. Dist. Ct. 1971).

597   *Id.* at 84-85. *See* RPL §§ 232-a (within New York City), 232-b (outside New York City).

598   J.N.A. Realty Corp. v. Cross Bay Chelsea, Inc., 42 N.Y.2d 392, 397 N.Y.S.2d 958 (1977).

substantial improvements to the premises that will cause a "substantial loss" if the lease is not renewed.[599]

In *135 E. 57th St. LLC v. Daffy's Inc.*, the Appellate Division, First Department excused the untimely lease renewal where the delay was due to an inadvertent calendaring error, the Tenant acted in good faith and there was no discernible prejudice.[600] On the other hand, the Tenant's failure to deliver the renewal notice to Landlord's attorney by certified mail, as required by the lease, may not be excused.[601] In *2039 Jericho Turnpike Corp.*, the Appellate Division, Second Department reasoned that since there was no credible evidence suggesting that a renewal notice had been provided, it could not reasonably conclude that the Landlord waived the requirements of the agreement's renewal notice provision.[602]

A similar outcome was reached with respect to an out of possession Tenant.[603] In *Baygold Assocs.*, the Tenant failed to establish that forfeiture would result because it could not demonstrate that the improvements made more than two (2) decades earlier were completed with the intent of renewing the lease.[604] Although the occupants clearly sustained damages, the Court of Appeals concluded that "[t]he forfeiture rule was crafted to protect tenants in possession who make improvements of a 'substantial character' with an eye toward renewing a lease, not to protect the revenue stream of an out-of-possession tenant…."[605]

---

599   *Id.*

600   *See* 135 E. 57th St. LLC v. Daffy's Inc., 91 A.D.3d 1, 934 N.Y.S.2d 112 (App. Div., 1st Dep't 2011).

601   2039 Jericho Turnpike Corp. v. Caglayan, 64 A.D.3d 609, 882 N.Y.S.2d 311 (App. Div., 2d Dep't 2009).

602   *Id.*, 64 A.D.3d at 609-10, 882 N.Y.S.2d at 312-13.

603   Baygold Assocs., Inc. v. Congregation Yetev Lev of Monsey, Inc., 19 N.Y.3d 223, 947 N.Y.S.2d 794 (2012).

604   *Id.*

605   *Id.*

M. BANKRUPTCY

A summary proceeding commenced <u>after</u> the Tenant files for bankruptcy protection is improper, and will be dismissed even where the Landlord had no notice of the bankruptcy petition.[606] However, where the summary proceeding precedes the bankruptcy filing, the proceeding will be stayed pursuant to 11 U. S. C. § 362(a).

An exception exists (i.e., the stay does <u>not</u> apply and the eviction may occur) pursuant to 11 U.S.C. § 362(b)(22) where the bankruptcy filing occurs <u>after</u> the judgment of possession and warrant of eviction have been issued.[607] Interestingly, there is an exception to the inapplicability of the stay exception (i.e., the stay applies and the eviction may <u>not</u> occur) where the Tenant had the right to cure the default and deposited with the Bankruptcy Court the past due rent for the 30-day period following the bankruptcy petition.[608]

In the event the Tenant files for bankruptcy during the summary proceeding (prior to the issuance of the judgment) and a Subtenant is named as a co-Respondent, the proceeding will be stayed against the Tenant and either stayed or, if proper, dismissed against the Subtenant because the Landlord may <u>not</u> proceed directly against a Subtenant.[609] The Landlord may seek an Order from the Bankruptcy Court lifting the stay if the property is separate from the estate.

A discharge in bankruptcy eliminates the Tenant's personal liability for rent arrears and other monetary debts under the rental agreement. As a result, the Landlord would be permitted to seek an eviction

---

606   Carr v. McGriff, 8 A.D.3d 420, 781 N.Y.S.2d 34 (App. Div., 2d Dep't 2004); Chen v. Dickerson, 847 N.Y.S.2d 334, 336 (App. Term, 9th & 10th Jud. Dists. 2007) (automatic bankruptcy stay prohibits "commencement and continuation" of an action against the debtor arising prior to the bankruptcy proceeding); Kocher v. Smith, 980 N.Y.S.2d 252 (Poughkeepsie City Ct. 2014).

607   North Tower Phase III Assoc. v. Petrov, 930 N.Y.S.2d 175 (N.Y. Civ. Ct. 2011); Santodonato v. Voelker, 881 N.Y.S.2d 366 (Nassau Cnty. Dist. Ct. 2009).

608   11 U.S.C. § 362(l)(1); *North Tower Phase III Assoc.*, 930 N.Y.S.2d at 175.

609   *See generally* Tefft v. Apex Pawnbroking & Jewelry Co., Inc., 75 A.D.2d 891, 428 N.Y.S.2d 52, 53 (App. Div., 2d Dep't 1980) ("[a] subtenant incurs no liability directly to a paramount lessor for performance of covenants contained in the original lease").

in a summary proceeding notwithstanding the bankruptcy filing, but the Landlord may <u>not</u> collect unpaid rent or other monetary relief.[610] In other words, following the bankruptcy discharge or other Order lifting the stay, the Landlord may "[p]ursue any remedy to which it is entitled under state law for breach of the tenant's obligation to pay rent, <u>except</u> a remedy against the debtor personally to collect the money due".[611]

N. LIFE TENANT

A Life Tenant is entitled to possession of the premises for the duration of his or her life. It is well-established that the "[s]ubstance of a life estate consists in the life tenant's right to exclude all others from the possession of the subject property for the duration of his or her own life".[612]

A life estate may be created by trust, deed or will, and is terminated in the following ways: (1) upon the death of the life tenant; (2) the surrender or forfeiture of the premises by the life tenant; or (3) a provision within the instrument that created the life estate.[613] A summary proceeding may involve disputes concerning the termination of a life estate. For example, in *Kurek v. Luszcyk*, the Petitioner alleged that the parties executed a "clarification" document following the creation of the life estate whereby the life tenant agreed to pay monthly rent. The Appellate Term affirmed the dismissal of the non-payment proceeding because the original conveyance was "clear and unambiguous" and, as such, gave no credence to the purported obligations described within the clarifying document.[614]

---

610   *See* Cey Realty Assocs., LLC v. Pettway, 29 N.Y.S.3d 846 (App. Term, 1st Dep't 2015) (permanently staying execution of warrant of eviction where the Tenant paid, and the Landlord accepted, rent arrears following the bankruptcy); 428 E. 66th St. LLC v. Meirowitz, 824 N.Y.S.2d 762 (App. Term, 1st Dep't 2006).

611   Dulac v. Dabrowski, 4 A.D.3d 308, 774 N.Y.S.2d 487 (App. Div., 1st Dep't 2004) (the underlying debt "is not extinguished" when the debtor's debts are personally discharged) (emphasis added).

612   Torre v. Giorgio, 51 A.D.3d 1010, 858 N.Y.S.2d 765 (App. Div., 2d Dep't 2008).

613   Kurek v. Luszcyk, 28 N.Y.S.3d 550 (App. Term, 2d, 11th & 13th Jud. Dists. 2015) (*citing* 56 N.Y. Jur 2d, Estates, Powers, and Restraints on Alienation, §§ 36, 40).

614   *Id.*

O. RECORDING OF THE LEASE

Rental agreements of three (3) or more years may be recorded pursuant to Real Property Law § 291. However, the failure to record such a lease only voids the lease as against a bona fide subsequent purchaser for value who recorded first.[615] Accordingly, where a Landlord is a bona fide purchaser for value, the Tenant may <u>not</u> use the non-recording of the rental agreement with the prior owner as a defense for early termination or the non-payment of rent because the lease is unenforceable against the Landlord.[616]

---

615 *See* RPL §§ 290-91; Hi-Rise Laundry Equip. Corp. v. Matrix Props., Inc., 96 A.D.2d 930, 466 N.Y.S.2d 375 (App. Div., 2d Dep't 1983); RR Reo II, LLC v. Omeje, 939 N.Y.S.2d 743 (App. Term, 2d, 11th & 13th Jud. Dists. 2011); Levy v. Pedersen, 983 N.Y.S.2d 204 (Nassau Cnty. Dist. Ct. 2013).

616 Jackson v. Robergeau, 781 N.Y.S.2d 625 (App. Term, 2d & 11th Jud. Dists. 2003); 1644 Broadway LLC v. Jimenez, 933 N.Y.S.2d 645 (N.Y. Civ. Ct. 2014).

CHAPTER 9

ADDITIONAL
AFFIRMATIVE DEFENSES

Additional affirmative defenses are discussed in this chapter. Once again, the list is not exhaustive but rather identifies some of the defenses frequently raised in summary proceedings.

A. PREMISES RENDERED UNTENANTABLE DUE TO FIRE OR THE ELEMENTS

Where the property is destroyed or otherwise rendered unfit for occupancy due to no fault of the Tenant or the Tenant's guests, the Tenant may, without notice, surrender possession and terminate the rental agreement.[617] The exception to this rule is where the lease provides for another remedy, in which case, the negotiated lease provision would prevail.

When RPL § 227 is invoked, the Tenant's obligation to pay further rent is terminated and any advanced payments must be "adjusted to the date of [the] surrender".[618] This provision is commonly utilized where the property is damaged by fire, but there is no preclusion for other uncontrollable natural disasters such as hurricanes and storms. For example, RPL§ 227 was applicable to Tenants victimized by Super Storm Sandy, which in October of 2012, resulted in the displacement of thousands of New Yorkers. If the damage caused by a natural disaster does

---

617 RPL § 227.

618 *Id.*; *cf.* Goldhirsch v. St. George Tower and Grill Owners Corp., 142 A.D.3d 1044, 37 N.Y.S.3d 616 (App. Div., 2d Dep't 2016) (enforcing lease provision providing for a proportional rent abatement where a fire renders the premises "partly or wholly untenantable").

not render the premises uninhabitable or the Tenant does not vacate the premises, then a residential Tenant may still be entitled to an abatement of rent based upon the warranty of habitability.[619]

B. THE TENANT MADE MORTGAGE PAYMENTS ON BEHALF OF THE LANDLORD

A summary proceeding may not be utilized to re-gain possession where the occupant's payments were monthly mortgage installments, as opposed to rent.[620] Although the Landlord may charge rent in an amount equal to the mortgage obligations, and further apply rent payments towards the mortgage, the defense typically arises where the Tenant directly pays the lender on behalf of the Landlord. The defense is further frequently asserted in connection with the anticipated sale of the premises to the occupant.

A Tenant is not entitled to a credit for mortgage payments made on behalf of the Landlord. In *Amherst Med. Park, Inc. v. Amherst Orthopaedics, P.C.*, the Appellate Division, Fourth Department held that notwithstanding the parties' agreement, a commercial Tenant could not offset the mortgage payments purportedly made by the Tenant's guarantor.[621]

In addition, the occupant's failure to obtain a mortgage commitment for the purchase of the premises, even if agreed, may not be the basis for a summary proceeding.[622] Rather, the owner would have to commence a

---

619   Park W. Mgmt. Corp. v. Mitchell, 47 N.Y.2d 316, 418 N.Y.S.2d 310 (1979); NYCHA Coney Is. Homes v. Ramos, 971 N.Y.S.2d 422 (N.Y. Civ. Ct. 2013). *But see* Adler v. Ogden CAP Props., 126 A.D.3d 544, 2 N.Y.S.3d 902 (App. Div., 1st Dep't 2015) (defense not available where Tenants "left their apartments before they lost electricity and they did not return until after the electricity had been restored"). *See* Affirmative Defenses *supra*, Chapter 8 subdiv. A.

620   *See* Tello v. Dylag, 15 N.Y.S.3d 715 (App. Term, 9th & 10th Jud. Dists. 2015); Cazares v. Aguilar, 950 N.Y.S.2d 721 (Nassau Cnty. Dist. Ct. 2012); ROBERT F. DOLAN, RASCH'S LANDLORD AND TENANT INCLUDING SUMMARY PROCEEDINGS § 38:15, at 584-86 (4th ed. 2010).

621   Amherst Med. Park, Inc. v. Amherst Orthopedics, P.C., 31 A.D.3d 1131, at 1133, 818 N.Y.S.2d 884, 885 (App. Div., 4th Dep't 2006).

622   Cat Hollow Estates, Inc. v. Savoia, 46 A.D.3d 1293, at 1294, 849 N.Y.S.2d 111, 112, (App. Div., 3d Dep't 2007).

plenary or a declaratory action in a court of competent jurisdiction.

C. THE PARTIES ENTERED INTO A PURCHASE AGREEMENT DURING THE LEASEHOLD (MERGER)

A Landlord and Tenant relationship is terminated when the parties enter into a contract of sale. This is because the anticipated sale of the property transforms the relationship from a tenancy into that of vendor and vendee in possession.[623]

As a result, even if the sale is <u>not</u> consummated, the Landlord may not evict the former-Tenant (vendee) in a summary proceeding following expiration of the rental agreement.[624] Exceptions to this rule may exist where the contract was not executed, the parties elected to rescind the contract and re-establish the tenancy or where an intent to continue the tenancy may be inferred from the parties' conduct.[625] Another exception falls within the ambit of RPAPL § 713(9) which authorizes a summary proceeding where the proposed purchaser remains in possession after defaulting on contract terms that were "necessarily to be performed within ninety days".[626] Parenthetically, a summary proceeding is improper where the parties enter into a joint venture to sell the premises.[627]

---

623   Barbarita v. Shilling, 111 A.D.2d 200, at 201-02, 489 N.Y.S.2d 86, 87 (App. Div., 2d Dep't 1985); Koppelman v. Barrett, Jr., 17 N.Y.S.3d 584 (App. Term, 9th & 10th Jud. Dists. 2015).

624   Kaygreen Realty Co., LLC v. IG Second Generation Partners, L.P., Index Nos. 10073-08, 3992-07, 2010 WL 1846713, 2010 N.Y. Misc. LEXIS 1887 (Queens Cnty. Sup. Ct. April 9, 2010), aff'd as modified, 78 A.D.3d 1010, at 1015-16, 912 N.Y.S.2d 246 (App. Div., 2d Dep't 2010).

625   Hadlick, Jr. v. DiGiantommaso, 154 A.D.2d 338, 545 N.Y.S.2d 816 (App. Div., 2d Dep't 1989); Kaygreen Realty Co., LLC, 2010 WL at 1846713, 2010 N.Y. Misc. LEXIS at 1887, aff'd as modified, 78 A.D.3d at 1015-16, 912 N.Y.S.2d at 246.

626   Jacobs v. Andolina, 123 A.D.2d 835, at 836-37, 507 N.Y.S.2d 450, 452-53 (App. Div., 2d Dep't 1986); see Koppelman, 17 N.Y.S.3d at 584; Gorbrook Assocs., Inc. v. Silverstein, 966 N.Y.S.2d 346 (App. Term, 9th & 10th Jud. Dists. 2012) (whether the contract of sale could be completed within 90 days is an issue of fact).

627   See Tello v. Dylag, 15 N.Y.S.3d 715 (App. Term, 9th & 10th Jud. Dists. 2015).

D. MUTUAL MISTAKE/FRUSTRATION OF PURPOSE (RESCISSION OF LEASE)

The defense of mutual mistake is an equitable defense that allows for the rescission of a rental agreement where a substantial mistake on the part of both parties existed at the time the rental agreement was executed.[628] Rescission may result where the mistake "was so substantial that there was no 'true meeting of the parties' minds' ".[629] For example, if the parties agree that the premises are to be used as a restaurant, but, unbeknownst to either side, the parcel may not be re-zoned for this purpose, then the lease may not be enforceable.[630] Similarly, a zoning law change after entering into the rental agreement may result in rescission if the "[r]easonable expectations of the parties…[are] frustrated due to circumstances beyond the control of the parties".[631] The reader should bear in mind that a party's failure "to take advantage of 'easily accessible' means of ascertaining" the correct information may result in the denial of rescission.[632]

---

628   *See* Dandey Realty Corp. v. Nick's Hideaway, Inc., 886 N.Y.S.2d 549, 550 (App. Term, 9th & 10th Jud. Dists. 2009) (commercial lease rescinded due to mistaken belief the premises could be used as a restaurant).

629   Lakshmi Grocery & Gas, Inc. v. GRJH, Inc., 138 A.D.3d 1290, 30 N.Y.S.3d 743 (App. Div., 3d Dep't 2016) (commercial lease rescinded where Landlord's representative "provided the wrong sales figures").

630   *Dandey Realty Corp.*, 886 N.Y.S.2d at 549.

631   Burnside 711, LLC v. Nassau Regional Off-Track Betting Corp., 67 A.D.3d 718, at 720, 888 N.Y.S.2d 212, 213-14 (App. Div., 2d Dep't 2009) (premises re-zoned prior to taking possession or paying rent).

632   *Lakshmi Grocery & Gas, Inc.*, 138 A.D.3d at 1290, 30 N.Y.S.3d at 743; *cf.* 1357 Tarrytown Rd. Auto, LLC v. Granite Props., LLC, 142 A.D.3d 976, 37 N.Y.S.3d 341 (App. Div., 2d Dep't 2016) (rescission denied where commercial lease was subject to "any restrictions of local law, zoning or ordinance" and the Landlord "made no representation concerning the suitability of the premises for the [Tenant's] intended business").

E. LEASE TERMINATION AND FORFEITURE CLAUSE FOR A BREACH OTHER THAN THE NON-PAYMENT OF RENT

In order for a lease forfeiture provision to be upheld, the Court must make an independent determination that the provision is reasonable and a "material breach" had occurred. The following factors are typically considered: (1) the Landlord reserved the right to declare the forfeiture; (2) a clear and unambiguous "material breach" of a substantial lease obligation; (3) the Landlord's prompt exercising of its rights; and (4) a determination that enforcement of the lease provision would <u>not</u> be unconscionable.[633] The Court applies the doctrine of substantial performance in determining whether a breach was "material".[634]

It has been held that the Tenant's failure to provide a copy of a renter's insurance policy is <u>not</u> a material breach.[635] However, the failure to maintain a continuous insurance policy, when required to do so, may be sufficient to terminate the tenancy.[636] This is the case even where the insurance was subsequently obtained because the replacement policy "[d]oes not protect [the Landlord] against the unknown universe of any claims arising during the period of no insurance coverage".[637]

The Housing Part held in *Rubinstein Bros.* that the Landlord could <u>not</u> terminate the tenancy where the rental agreement authorized the Landlord to purchase the required insurance at the Tenant's expense.[638]

---

633   Helsam Realty Co., Inc. v. H.J.A. Holding Corp, 781 N.Y.S.2d 554, 557 (App. Term, 2d & 11th Jud. Dists. 2004) (*citing* ROBERT F. DOLAN, RASCH'S LANDLORD AND TENANT INCLUDING SUMMARY PROCEEDINGS § 23:39, at 202-05 (4th ed. 2010)); *cf.* Freund & Freund & Co., Inc., v. Biscuits & Baths Tribeca, LLC, 889 N.Y.S.2d 505 (N.Y. Civ. Ct. 2009).

634   DOLAN, *supra* note 633, § 23:39, at 203-04.

635   Rubinstein Bros. v. Ole of 34th St., Inc., 421 N.Y.S.2d 534, 537 (N.Y. Civ. Ct. 1979).

636   117-119 Leasing Corp. v. Reliable Wool Stock, LLC, 139 A.D.3d 420, 30 N.Y.S.3d 622 (App. Div., 1st Dep't 2016) (the "tenant's failure to obtain insurance was not curable"); JT Queens Carwash, Inc. v. 88-16 N. Blvd., LLC, 101 A.D.3d 1089, 956 N.Y.S.2d 536 (App. Div., 2d Dep't 2012).

637   Kim v. Idylwood, N.Y., LLC, 66 A.D.3d 528, 886 N.Y.S.2d 337 (App. Div., 1st Dep't 2009); *cf.* Metropolitan Transp. Auth. v. Kura River Mgmt., Ltd., 292 A.D.2d 230, 739 N.Y.S.2d 668 (App. Div., 1st Dep't 2002) (lease forfeiture clause <u>not</u> enforceable due to inadequate notice).

638   *Rubinstein Bros.*, 421 N.Y.S.2d at 537. *See* DOLAN, *supra* note 633, § 23:39, at 203.

The trial court reasoned that since there was "another easily spelled out remedy in the lease", including compensation for the additional expense in a plenary action, the drastic remedy of lease termination was inappropriate.[639]

F. TENANTS IN COMMON

A tenant in common shares equal ownership rights in the premises with one (1) or more persons and/or entities. Common examples include married couples who own their home and siblings bequeathed equal ownership in the family residence.

It is well-established that tenants in common have an equal right to possession of the premises, which precludes their removal in a summary proceeding.[640] This is the case even where the tenants in common entered into a separate agreement for the payment of rent or use and occupancy.[641] The proper recourse to recover possession against a tenant in common is to commence an action in partition pursuant to RPAPL § 901.

A tenant in common may not bind a non-consenting tenant in common to a lease with a third party. It has been held, however, that a tenant in common may commence a summary proceeding without the consent or participation of the other.[642] A lessee, such as a family member who enters into possession with the permission of just one (1) tenant in common, may share possession with the non-consenting tenant in common. This is commonly referred to as joint possession.

As stated previously, where there is a breach of the agreement, a non-consenting tenant in common may commence a summary proceeding

---

639   *Rubinstein Bros.,* 421 N.Y.S.2d at 537.

640   *See* Rabin v. Rabin, 13 N.Y.S.3d 852 (App. Term, 9th & 10th Jud. Dists. 2015) (noting the parties may seek relief in the Surrogate's Court where the executor of the Estate was a tenant in common); Lee v. Tabasko, 957 N.Y.S.2d 636 (Nassau Cnty. Dist. Ct. 2010); *see generally* Pivarsky v. Island Hills Golf Club, Inc., Index No. 34488-12, 2013 WL 5823063, 2013 N.Y. Misc. LEXIS 4924 (Suffolk Cnty. Sup. Ct. Oct. 15, 2013).

641   Dolan, *supra* note 633, § 38:21, at 589-90.

642   Bernadotte v. Woolford, 33 N.Y.S.3d 877 (Nassau Cnty. Dist. Ct. 2016).

without the other co-tenant's consent. However, the ultimate relief available in the summary proceeding is the termination of the lessee's "exclusive occupancy". As a result, rather than the removal of the lessee, a non-consenting tenant in common may achieve joint possession with the lessee. Parenthetically, the summary proceeding will be dismissed where the petitioning tenant in common is already in possession and/ or sharing the premises with the lessee.[643]

G. LACHES (STALE RENT)

The defense of laches is an equitable defense based upon the principle of fairness.[644] To establish the defense, the Tenant must demonstrate that (1) the Landlord has a valid claim, such as the non-payment of rent; (2) the Landlord delayed in asserting its rights; (3) a lack of knowledge or notice the Landlord would assert its rights; and (4) injury or prejudice to the Tenant if the relief is granted, including the Tenant's inability to pay because the Tenant reasonably believed the Landlord would not attempt to collect the rent.[645]

The defense of laches is available only in residential cases.[646] Where the defense is successfully asserted, the Landlord may be awarded a money judgment for unpaid rent, but the Tenant may remain in

---

643 *Id.*

644 Similar to other equitable defenses, the defense of laches may not be available in either a plenary or small claims action within a court of limited jurisdiction. Robinson v. Robles, 906 N.Y.S.2d 844, 846-47 (Rochester City Ct. 2010).

645 *See generally* Jean v. Joseph, 117 A.D.3d 989, 986 N.Y.S.2d 547 (App. Div., 2d Dep't 2014); Dwyer v. Mazzola, 171 A.D.2d 726, 567 N.Y.S.2d 281 (App. Div., 2d Dep't 1991) ("[m] ere delay alone, without prejudice [or injury] does not constitute laches") (citations omitted); Matter of County of Orange (Al Turi Landfill, Inc.), 75 A.D.3d 224, at 237-39, 903 N.Y.S.2d 60, 69-70 (App. Div., 2d Dep't 2010); Layla Assocs., LLC v. Acosta, 984 N.Y.S.2d 632 (N.Y. Civ. Ct. 2013); Building Mgmt. Co., Inc. v. Bonifacio, 906 N.Y.S.2d 770 (N.Y. Civ. Ct. 2009).

646 UBO Realty Corp. v. Fulton, Index No. 405-92, 1993 N.Y. Misc. LEXIS 665 (App. Term, 1st Dep't 1993) (laches defense not available in a commercial case); Brenner v. General Plumbing Corp., 13 N.Y.S.3d 849 (N.Y. Civ. Ct. 2015) (same); Vinroz, LLC v. Gutierrez, 886 N.Y.S.2d 72 (Nassau Cnty. Dist. Ct. 2009).

possession of the premises.[647] However, where the Landlord asserts an adequate explanation for the delay in filing suit, the Court must determine whether the delay was reasonable under the circumstances.[648]

H. THE TENANT PASSES AWAY DURING THE TENANCY

Unless agreed otherwise, the death of the Tenant prior to the expiration of the rental agreement neither terminates the rental agreement nor alleviates the obligation to pay rent. Instead, the rental agreement passes onto the estate of the decedent, and the executor, administrator or other legal representative of the estate may maintain the premises until the expiration of the lease or such other time as it may be properly terminated or cancelled. In other words, the estate is substituted for the decedent as a party to the rental agreement, and the benefits and obligations thereunder may be enforced.[649]

As a practical matter, a successor Tenant is not liable for the predecessor's arrears (unless obligated pursuant to an agreement) because the successor was not a party when the arrears accrued. Since "a successor in interest is not a tenant until he becomes a party to a lease... and because [the] tenant did not become a party until after the arrears sought had accrued, a nonpayment proceeding does not lie" for the predecessor's arrears.[650]

The Landlord must name the estate of the decedent (as opposed to

---

647   City of New York v. Betancourt, 362 N.Y.S.2d 728, 729-30 (App Term, 1st Dep't 1974); Haberman v. Singer, 3 A.D.3d 188, 771 N.Y.S.2d 505 (App. Div., 1st Dep't 2004); Anderson Ave. Assocs., L.P. v. Garcia, 21 N.Y.S.3d 606 (N.Y. Civ. Ct. 2015); *Building Mgmt. Co., Inc.,* 906 N.Y.S.2d at 770. Although there is no predetermined period of time, it has been held that where more than three months' rent is sought, a presumption that the rent is stale is created, which shifts "[t]o [the] Landlord the burden of establishing diligence in bringing the proceeding". *See* STP Assoc., LLC v. Holacek, 885 N.Y.S.2d 713 (Nassau Cnty. Dist. Ct. 2009).

648   *See Building Mgmt. Co., Inc.,* 906 N.Y.S.2d at 770.

649   *See* De Christoforo v. Shore Ridge Assocs., 116 A.D.2d 123, at 126, 500 N.Y.S.2d 528, 530 (App. Div., 2d Dep't 1986).

650   East Harlem Pilot Block Bldg. IV HDFC, Inc. v. Diaz, 9 N.Y.S.3d 592 (App. Term, 1st Dep't 2015).

the decedent) in a summary proceeding and serve all notices upon the estate in the same fashion it would the Tenant. The proceeding must be brought against the executor or administrator in her representative capacity because an estate is not a legal entity.[651] If an administrator or executor has not been designated, the Landlord may petition the Surrogate's Court for the appointment of an administrator.[652]

With respect to non-payment proceedings, RPAPL § 711(2) provides that where "no representative or person has taken possession of the premises and no administrator or executor has been appointed, the proceeding may be commenced after three months from the date of death of the tenant by joining the surviving spouse or if there is none, then one of the surviving issue or if there is none, then any one of the distributees".[653] The burden is on the Landlord to demonstrate that an administrator or executor was not duly appointed.[654] The three (3) month statutory stay period pursuant to RPAPL § 711(2) does not apply to a "[h]oldover proceeding where a tenant or undertenant is deceased".[655]

On the other hand, if the lease expired prior to the Tenant's death, then the decedent's estate is not a necessary party and need not be named in the summary proceeding.[656] This is because the "[p]ossessory claim of the estate lapsed upon termination of decedent's lease".[657]

---

651 Visutton Assocs. v. Fastman, 991 N.Y.S.2d 240 (App. Term, 2d, 11th & 13th Jud. Dists. 2014).

652 Westway Plaza Assocs. v. Doe, 179 A.D.2d 408, at 409-10, 578 N.Y.S.2d 166, 167 (App. Div., 1st Dep't 1992).

653 RPAPL § 711(2). See 50 Riverside Tenants Corp. v. Morales, 975 N.Y.S.2d 365 (App. Term, 1st Dep't 2013); Poulakas v. Ortiz, 885 N.Y.S.2d 865, 870 (N.Y. Civ. Ct. 2009) (the Legislature did not intend RPAPL § 711(2) to be available only where the premises was vacant).

654 See Mandalay Leasing L.P. v. Gibson, Index No. 65186-02, 2003 WL 1085914, 2003 N.Y. Misc. LEXIS 157 (N.Y. Civ. Ct. Feb. 28, 2003).

655 Fang v. DaSilva, 927 N.Y.S.2d 816 (App. Term, 2d, 11th & 13th Jud. Dists. 2011).

656 See Marine Terr. Assocs. v. Kesoglides, 884 N.Y.S.2d 552 (App. Term, 2d, 11th & 13th Jud. Dists. 2009); Ryerson Towers, Inc. v. Estate of Laura Brown, 612 N.Y.S.2d 99 (App. Term, 2d & 11th Jud. Dists. 1994).

657 Ellis v. Disch, 851 N.Y.S.2d 57 (App. Term, 1st Dep't 2007); see also Marine Terr. Assocs., 884 N.Y.S.2d at 553.

Accordingly, where the Tenant's death occurs after the termination of the rental agreement but prior to the commencement of the summary proceeding, the proceeding will be dismissed against the decedent due to the lack of jurisdiction over the decedent or decedent's estate.[658]

I. NON-DELIVERED WRITTEN LEASE

A written rental agreement is <u>not</u> valid until an executed copy is delivered and accepted by both parties.[659] Where the executed agreement is <u>not</u> provided to one (1) of the parties and the Tenant does <u>not</u> take possession of the premises, the agreement is unenforceable.[660]

If the Tenant takes possession without receiving a copy of the executed lease, the lease may be enforced on a month-to-month basis.[661] It has been held that the act of signing the rental agreement "in the presence of both parties" is adequate delivery, particularly where the Tenant has paid a month's rent.[662]

---

658 *Fang*, 927 N.Y.S.2d at 816. If the tenant had an existing lease at the time of death, then the proper party would be the decedent's estate provided there was grounds for a summary proceeding. Otherwise, in the absence of a designee or representative on behalf of the estate, the lender may seek the appointment of an administrator in Surrogate's Court. *See Westway Plaza Assocs.*, 578 N.Y.S.2d at 167.

659   219 Broadway Corp. v. Alexander's, Inc., 46 N.Y.2d 506, at 511-12, 414 N.Y.S.2d 889, 891-92 (1979).

660   *See generally* Dlugosz v. O'Brien, 36 A.D.3d 1035, at 1036-37, 828 N.Y.S.2d 628, 629-30 (App. Div., 3d Dep't 2007) (execution and delivery of lease is required); 709 Rte. 52, Inc. v. DelCastillo, 910 N.Y.S.2d 408 (App. Term, 9th & 10th Jud. Dists. 2010) (signed but undelivered lease unenforceable where the Tenant did not receive the keys or take possession); Setauket Props. Corp. v. Open Doors Mgmt., Inc., Index No. 28294-09, 2010 WL 3235411, 2010 N.Y. Misc. LEXIS 3765 (Suffolk Cnty. Sup. Ct. Aug. 5, 2010).

661   RPL §§ 232-a (within New York City), 232-b (outside New York City).

662   Storico Dev., LLC v. Batlle, 9 A.D.3d 908, at 909, 780 N.Y.S.2d 696, 697 (App. Div., 4th Dep't 2004); Levinson v. Bailey, Index No. 115438-10, 2012 WL 2648276, 2012 N.Y. Misc. LEXIS 3110 (N.Y. Cnty. Sup. Ct. June 15, 2012).

J. RENT RECEIPTS (RESIDENTIAL LEASE)

For residential properties, the Landlord has a duty to provide a receipt when the Tenant pays the rent by any means other than personal check.[663] The receipt must be signed by the person who received the payment, identify the premises, and list the date, dollar amount and period for which the payment was made.[664] If the rent is tendered by personal check, then upon written request, a receipt must be provided.[665]

The statute does <u>not</u> impose a penalty for non-compliance. In *Robinson v. Robles*, the Rochester City Court opted not to penalize the Landlord for failing to provide rent receipts.[666] Similarly, in *Reed v. Ragsdale*, absent a "clear" violation of the law, the Landlord was entitled to an award for the unpaid rent.[667]

However, in both *Brinkman v. Cahill* and *Palmieri v. Hernandez*, the Courts held that any "doubt [regarding compliance] should be resolved in favor of the tenant".[668] Another trial court suggested that there should be a rebuttable presumption that the rent was paid when the Landlord fails to provide rent receipts.[669]

K. CONDOMINIUMS (NON-OCCUPYING OWNER)

The New York Condominium Act provides that where a non-occupying Landlord-owner fails to pay the condominium's monthly association fees, including maintenance, common charges, assessments and late fees, within sixty (60) days of the allowable grace period set forth in the condominium rules, the condominium's managing board may demand that the Tenant pays all future rent to the condominium

---

663   RPL § 235-e.

664   *Id.* § 235-e(a).

665   *Id.* § 235-e(b).

666   Robinson v. Robles, 906 N.Y.S.2d 844 (Rochester City Ct. 2010).

667   Reed v. Ragsdale, 695 N.Y.S.2d 240 (Newark Just. Ct. 1999).

668   Brinkman v. Cahill, 543 N.Y.S.2d 636, 637 (Arcadia Just. Ct. 1989); Palmieri v. Hernandez, 485 N.Y.S.2d 915, 916 (Mt. Vernon City Ct. 1984).

669   Gummerson v. Strecker, 806 N.Y.S.2d 445 (Auburn City Ct. 2005).

association until paid in-full.[670] The payments "relieve" the Tenant of rent obligations to the Landlord and constitute an absolute defense in a non-payment proceeding.[671] If the Tenant fails to comply with the condominium's demand, then the condominium association may seek to evict the Tenant.[672]

Disputes regarding payment may be commenced as a special proceeding in the Housing Part or a declaratory judgment action in Supreme Court. The non-occupying owner is entitled to a meeting with the condominium's managing board within thirty (30) days of providing written notice that he or she is disputing the claim.[673]

The condominium association <u>must</u> provide written notice to both the non-occupying owner and the Tenant within three (3) business days of the final payment.[674] Parenthetically, the laws governing rent stabilized properties are <u>not</u> applicable to condominium and cooperative apartments.[675]

L. RETALIATORY EVICTION

The Landlord may <u>not</u> serve a notice to quit, substantially alter the terms of a rental agreement or commence a proceeding in retaliation for any of the following protected acts: (1) a complaint made in good faith to a governmental agency regarding the Landlord's alleged violation of a health or safety law, regulation, code or ordinance; (2) action taken to enforce the Tenant's rights pursuant to the rental agreement; or (3) the Tenant's participation in a Tenant's or resident's association.[676]

---

670 RPL §§ 339-kk(b),[c].

671 *Id.* § 339-kk(e).

672 *See* The Bd. of Mgrs. of 222 Riverside Dr. Condominium v. Holland, Index No. 103410-12, 2014 WL 1620931, 2014 N.Y. Misc. LEXIS 1814 (N.Y. Cnty. Sup. Ct. April 17, 2014).

673 RPL § 339-kk[c].

674 *Id.*

675 *See* The Bd. of Mgrs. of 222 Riverside Dr. Condominium, 2014 WL at 1620931, 2014 N.Y. Misc. LEXIS at 1814.

676 RPL § 223-b. *Cf.* Loscalzo v. Rodriguez, 13 N.Y.S.3d 850 (App. Term, 9th & 10th Jud. Dists. 2015) (retaliatory eviction <u>not</u> applicable where the Tenant's claims "did not involve

In addition, the Landlord may <u>not</u> refuse to renew an existing lease or offer a new lease for less than one (1) year in retaliation of the above conduct.[677]

The defense of retaliatory eviction may be asserted in a holdover proceeding involving residential premises excluding owner-occupied dwellings with fewer than four (4) units.[678] The rationale for excluding smaller owner-occupied dwellings is the concern that the public interest may <u>not</u> be served by "keeping together in one house [the] landlord and the tenant who is suing" on the grounds of retaliatory eviction.[679] Other remedies may be available to the Tenant in a court of competent jurisdiction.

The defense is <u>not</u> applicable in a non-payment proceeding.[680] An exception to this rule is where the Landlord's non-payment claim is frivolous or otherwise a pretext for commencing an unlawful proceeding. In addition, the defense may <u>not</u> be asserted where the summary proceeding is based upon a breach by the Tenant or the Tenant's guests, or where the tenancy was terminated pursuant to the terms of the lease as a result of a bona fide transfer of ownership.[681]

The Tenant must affirmatively assert the defense or it is deemed waived, and, even where applicable, the defense does <u>not</u> alleviate the requirement to pay rent. The Tenant may also assert the claim of retaliatory eviction as a counterclaim pursuant to RPL § 223-b(3).[682]

A lease provision charging the Tenant a fee for making a bona fide

---

an alleged violation by landlord of a health or safety law or regulation, or the enforcement of a right under the rental agreement").

677   *See* RPL § 223-b(2).

678   *Id.* § 223-b(6). *See* Sills v. Dellavalle, 9 A.D.3d 561, at 561-62, 780 N.Y.S.2d 193, 194-95 (App. Div., 3d Dep't 2004). A retaliatory eviction claim may not be raised in a summary proceeding involving commercial property. *See* Tirse v. Andrews, 128 A.D.3d 1112, 8 N.Y.S.3d 711 (App. Div., 3d Dep't 2015).

679   Weil v. Kaplan, 670 N.Y.S.2d 666, 668 (App. Term, 9th & 10th Jud. Dists. 1997).

680   Chelsea Ridge NY, LLC v. Clarke, 983 N.Y.S.2d 201 (App. Term, 9th & 10th Jud. Dists. 2013); 390 W. End Assocs. v. Raiff, 636 N.Y.S.2d 965, 967 (App. Term, 1st Dep't 1995).

681   RPL § 223-b(6).

682   601 W. 160 Realty Corp. v. Henry, 731 N.Y.S.2d 581 (App. Term, 2d & 11th Jud. Dists. 2001).

complaint against the Landlord is unenforceable.[683] Real Property Law § 223-b(5) creates a rebuttable presumption that the Landlord acted in an unlawful manner when a summary proceeding is commenced within six (6) months of the Tenant exercising a protected right or receiving a judgment in its favor in a prior eviction proceeding.[684] A retaliatory eviction claim may subject the Landlord to civil damages and additional liability, including injunctive and other equitable remedies, in a court of competent jurisdiction.

The statute of limitations for a retaliatory eviction claim is one (1) year following the unlawful eviction.[685] Where the Tenant enters into a Stipulation of Settlement consenting to a judgment of possession, the claim is waived because the Tenant "[c]onceded the validity of the proceeding on which the final judgment was based".[686]

M. NEW YORK SOLDIERS' AND SAILORS' CIVIL RELIEF ACT

A Landlord may <u>not</u> evict "a person in military service or the spouse, children, or other dependents of a person in military service" from a residential property except with leave of Court.[687] The law is intended to ease some of the burdens that have been placed on the men and women of all branches of our military, including reservists and members of organized State militias, who have put their lives on hold to defend our nation.[688]

---

683   RPL § 223-b(5-a).

684   Orange Falls, LLC v. Forrest, 37 N.Y.S.3d 207 (Glens Falls City Ct. 2016). *But see* Gordon v. 476 Broadway Realty Corp., 129 A.D.3d 547, 12 N.Y.S.3d 37 (App. Div., 1ˢᵗ Dep't 2015) (termination of tenancy due to lease violation does not give rise to the presumption of retaliation).

685   CPLR § 215(7). *See* Munoz v. 221 W. 16ᵗʰ Realty LLC, 24 A.D.3d 112, 804 N.Y.S.2d 248 (App. Div., 1st Dep't 2005).

686   *Cf.* Witters v. Yatrakis, 867 N.Y.S.2d 21 (App. Term, 2d & 11ᵗʰ Jud. Dists. 2008). Although the Tenant preserved the right to pursue a retaliatory eviction claim in the stipulation, the proceeding was dismissed due to the failure to state a claim upon which relief may be granted. *Id.*

687   N.Y. MILITARY LAW § 309(1) (McKinney 2003).

688   *Id.* § 300.

The statute provides that the Court may stay the proceeding for a maximum of six (6) months or make any "other order as may be just" where it is shown the military service "materially affected" the ability to pay rent.[689] The protections afforded under the law are <u>not</u> intended as a defense for the non-payment of rent due to reasons other than military service.

Although Military Law § 309(2) applies to the non-payment of rent, it has been held that the general stay provision of Military Law § 304 is applicable to holdover proceedings.[690] A person who "knowingly takes part" or "attempts" to take part in the eviction of a member of the military without leave of Court may be guilty of a misdemeanor, which is punishable by a maximum fine of $1,000 and/or one (1) year in jail.[691]

N. SUCCESSION RIGHTS (RENT STABILIZED) (NEW YORK CITY)

In New York City, where the Tenant permanently vacates a rent stabilized apartment, a "family member"[692] who simultaneously resided in the premises with the Tenant as his or her primary residence for at least the immediate past two (2) years may be named the Tenant on the renewal lease.[693] The term "family member" has been expanded beyond traditional family relationships to include any person who resided in the premises with the Tenant as a primary residence and demonstrates an "emotional and financial commitment, and interdependence between [them]".[694]

---

689 *Id.* § 309(2).

690 New York City Hous. Auth. v. Kostyan, Index No. 67740-07, 2007 N.Y. Misc. LEXIS 8785 (N.Y. Civ. Ct. Dec. 18, 2007) (granting 90-day stay where the Tenant's failure to appear was due to active military duty).

691 N.Y. MILITARY LAW § 309(3).

692 The Rent Stabilization Code's definition of a "family member" includes, but is not limited to, the Tenant's spouse, son, daughter, stepson, stepdaughter, father, mother, stepfather, stepmother, brother, sister, grandfather, grandmother, grandson, granddaughter, father-in-law, mother-in-law, son-in-law or daughter-in-law. *See* RSC [9 N.Y.C.R.R.] § 2520.6(o)(1).

693 *Id.* [9 N.Y.C.R.R.] § 2523.5(b)(1).

694 *Id.* [9 N.Y.C.R.R.] § 2520.6(o)(2).

Where the Tenant is either a senior citizen (age 62 or older)[695] or a "disabled person",[696] succession rights may apply provided the family member resided with the Tenant for no less than one (1) year immediately prior to the vacating.[697] The factors commonly considered for non-traditional family members include (1) longevity of the relationship; (2) sharing or relying upon one another to pay expenses and common necessities; (3) intermingling of finances and accounts; (4) engaging in family activities and functions; (5) formalizing legal documents and responsibilities; (6) holding themselves out to be family members; (7) caring for one another; and (8) any other behavior evincing the "intention of creating a long-term, emotionally-committed relationship".[698] Although there is no determinative factor, an intimate relationship is neither required nor considered.[699]

The time period for computing compliance with the residency requirement is <u>not</u> interrupted when the family member "temporarily" relocates due to (1) active military duty; (2) enrollment as a full-time student; (3) pursuant to Court Order unrelated to the lease; (4) employment requirements; (5) hospitalization; or (6) other reasonable grounds.[700] In *Limani Realty, LLC v. Zayfert*, succession rights were denied where the Tenant's adult son temporarily relocated to attend school as a "part-time" student during the two-year look-back period.[701]

---

695   *Id.* [9 N.Y.C.R.R.] § 2520.6(p).

696   The term "disabled person" is defined as "a person who has an impairment which results from anatomical, physiological or psychological conditions, other than addiction to alcohol, gambling, or any controlled substance, which are demonstrable by medically acceptable clinical and laboratory diagnostic techniques, and which are expected to be permanent and which prevent such person from engaging in any substantial gainful employment". *See id.* [9 N.Y.C.R.R.] § 2520.6(q).

697   *Id.* [9 N.Y.C.R.R.] § 2523.5(b)(1).

698   *Id.* [9 N.Y.C.R.R.] § 2520.6(o)(2).

699   *See id.; see, e.g.,* Naroznik v. Prockett, 15 N.Y.S.3d 713 (App. Term, 2d, 11th & 13th Jud. Dists. 2015).

700   RSC [9 N.Y.C.R.R.] § 2523.5(b)(2).

701   Limani Realty, LLC v. Zayfert, 970 N.Y.S.2d 345 (App. Term, 2d, 11th & 13th Jud. Dists. 2012) (evidence failed to demonstrate that the premises was used as the adult son's primary residence "from the time he reached majority until the end of the look-back period").

On the other hand, the Appellate Division, First Department granted succession rights where the family member and Tenant resided together for eight (8) years prior to the Tenant's passing during which they shared household expenses, traveled together, celebrated birthdays and holidays in one another's company, and the Tenant's hospital records listed the occupant as her "partner".[702] A similar outcome was reached where the Tenant and family member lived together for approximately twenty-five (25) years, and the family member was the Tenant's sole care giver.[703] The Court noted that the Tenant and occupant had become life partners two (2) years prior to the Tenant's passing.[704]

In *Hitchcock Plaza Inc. v. Fortune*, the Tenant's niece was awarded succession rights where she and her uncle shared household expenses, and they traveled and attended religious ceremonies together.[705] The Court concluded that the "modest intermingling of finances" was <u>not</u> sufficient to negate the overall family-like relationship.[706]

---

702 WSC Riverside Dr. Owners LLC v. Williams, 125 A.D.3d 458, 3 N.Y.S.3d 342 (App. Div., 1st Dep't 2015); *see* 585 W. 204th LLC v. Peralta, Index No. 570094-16, 2016 WL 5419636, 2016 N.Y. Misc. LEXIS 3419 (App. Term, 1st Dep't Sept. 28, 2016) (Tenant's adult son established succession rights where he resided in the rent controlled apartment from birth, including the two-year period immediately preceding his mother's death); Infinity Corp. v. Danko, 9 N.Y.S.3d 593 (App. Term, 1st Dep't 2015) (succession rights granted where the occupant and Tenant "enjoyed a family-type relationship" for nearly 20 years).

703 *Naroznik*, 15 N.Y.S.3d at 713.

704 *Id.*, 15 N.Y.S.3d at 713. Nieces and nephews are <u>not</u> included in the list of traditional family members. *See* RSC [9 N.Y.C.R.R.] § 2520.6(o).

705 Hitchcock Plaza, Inc. v. Fortune, 15 N.Y.S.3d 711 (App. Term, 1st Dep't 2015).

706 *Id.*; *see* PACST 1244-46, 1356, LLC v. Swinton, 31 N.Y.S.3d 923 (App. Term, 2d, 11th & 13th Jud. Dists. 2016) (great-niece qualified for succession rights after establishing "the requisite emotional and financial commitment and interdependence between her and tenant").

O. NO PET RULE (NEW YORK CITY—MULTIPLE DWELLINGS)

In New York City multiple dwellings, which are three (3) or more families living independently within a building, a lease provision barring household pets is unenforceable and waived where the Tenant harbored a pet "openly and notoriously" for at least three (3) months with no adverse action taken by the Landlord.[707] For the pet waiver to be invoked, the Landlord <u>must</u> have "knowledge" (actual or constructive) of the Tenant's harboring of the pet.[708]

P. WAIVABLE DEFENSES

As a practical matter, the failure to assert a non-jurisdictional affirmative defense in the Answer or a pre-Answer motion to dismiss results in waiver of the defense.[709] For example, the lack of personal jurisdiction due to improper service;[710] the Petitioner's lack of standing to commence the summary proceeding;[711] and the failure to verify the Petition[712] are waived when not timely asserted. The lack of subject matter jurisdiction may <u>not</u> be waived under any circumstance.[713]

---

707 Administrative Code of the City of New York § 27-2009.1(b).

708 *Id.*; 149th St., LLC v. Rodriguez, 31 N.Y.S.3d 922 (App. Term, 2d, 11th & 13th Jud. Dists. 2016) (knowledge of pet is imputed to the Landlord where the Landlord's agents and/or employees are aware of the Tenant's dog); 184 W. 10th St. Corp. v. Marvits, 59 A.D.3d 287, 874 N.Y.S.2d 403 (App. Div., 1st Dep't 2009) (Tenant's cats).

709 Hickey v. Trahan, 31 N.Y.S.3d 921 (App. Term, 9th & 10th Jud. Dists. 2016); Otufale v. Whetstone, 906 N.Y.S.2d 781 (App. Term, 1st Dep't 2010).

710 Iodice v. Academics R Us, Inc., 26 N.Y.S.3d 724 (App. Term, 1st Dep't 2015) (defense waived when not asserted in the Answer, and Tenant may <u>not</u> assert the defense for the first time in an Amended Answer); *Otufale*, 906 N.Y.S.2d at 781; Citi Land Servs., LLC v. McDowell, 926 N.Y.S.2d 343 (App. Term, 2d & 11th & 13th Jud. Dists. 2011) (lack of personal jurisdiction due to improper service waived when not asserted in the Answer); Forest Hills S. Owners, Inc. v. Ishida, 943 N.Y.S.2d 791 (App. Term, 2d, 11th & 13th Jud. Dists. 2011) (improper service of the rent demand). *See also* CPLR § 3211(e) (listing circumstances where the defense of lack of personal jurisdiction is waived).

711 Chen v. Ray, 26 N.Y.S.3d 212 (App. Term, 1st Dep't 2015).

712 *See* Morse v. Brozzo, 94 A.D.3d 1184, 942 N.Y.S.2d 246 (App. Div., 3d Dep't 2012).

713 Certain statutory provisions, such as service of a notice terminating the tenancy pursuant to the New York City Rent Stabilization Code, may <u>not</u> be waived even with consent.

Notwithstanding a non-waiver provision within the rental agreement, the Landlord's acceptance of rent with knowledge of the Tenant's breach may constitute a waiver of the Landlord's right to terminate the tenancy.[714] This is because the "[k]nowing acceptance of rent without any effort to terminate the lease justifies the inference that the landlord has elected to hold the tenant to the lease", and therefore waive the violation.[715] Whether a waiver has occurred is an issue of fact.[716]

See, e.g., Kings Hwy. Realty Corp. v. Riley, 950 N.Y.S.2d 723 (App. Term, 2d, 11th & 13th Jud. Dists. 2012).

714   I & T Petroleum Inc. v. Lascalia, 880 N.Y.S.2d 873 (Nassau Cnty. Sup. Ct. 2009) (Landlord may accept rent and waive the remedies for the violation, including termination of the lease). *See also* Dice v. Inwood Hills Condominium, 237 A.D.2d 403, 655 N.Y.S.2d 562 (App. Div., 2d Dep't 1997) ("[t]he existence of a non-waiver clause does not in itself preclude waiver of a contract clause").

715   Jefpaul Garage Corp. v. Presbyterian Hosp., 61 N.Y.2d 442, at 448, 474 N.Y.S.2d 458, 461 (1984); Lee v. Wright, 108 A.D.2d 678, at 680, 485 N.Y.S.2d 543, 544 (App. Div., 1st Dep't 1985).

716   Fundamental Portfolio Advisors, Inc. v. Tocqueville Asset Mgmt., L.P., 7 N.Y.3d 96, at 104-05, 817 N.Y.S.2d 606 (2006).

SOCIAL SERVICES LAW ("SPIEGEL LAW")— PUBLIC ASSISTANCE

In New York, eligible individuals of limited financial means may receive federal public assistance in the form of supplemental security income.[717] When the federal program took effect in 1974, New York discontinued its public assistance program, titled "Aid to Aged, Blind and Disabled", and adopted a new Title 6 of Article 5 of the Social Services Law ("SSL"), titled "Additional State Payments for Eligible Aged, Blind and Disabled Persons".[718]

As a result, the State "established a state-wide program of additional state payments" for qualifying individuals.[719] To be eligible for the additional state payments, an individual must be over the age of sixty-five (65), blind or disabled, satisfy the residency and citizenry requirements and have countable income and/or resources at or below mandatory minimum monthly standards.[720]

---

717 *See* N.Y. Soc. Servs. Law § 211 (2003). The rules and regulations pertaining to federal supplemental security income may be found at 42 U.S.C. § 1381, Pub. Law No. 92-603, 86 Stat. 1465 (1972).

718 SSL §§ 207-212; *see generally* Khrapunskiy v. Doar, 12 N.Y.3d 478, 881 N.Y.S.2d 377 (2009). Additional provisions governing the amount of monthly grants and allowances are codified at SSL § 131-a, which is commonly referred to as the "safety net assistance" provision. *Khrapunskiy*, 12 N.Y.3d at 478, 881 N.Y.S.2d at 377.

719 SSL § 207.

720 *Id.* § 209.

A. VIOLATIONS AND UNSAFE BUILDING CONDITIONS

New York State public assistance payments, which include an allowance for shelter costs, may be made directly to the Landlord.[721] Social Services Law § 143-b was enacted in 1962 to counteract the unscrupulous practice of some Landlords who received rent payments on behalf of public assistance recipients, but failed to provide the required services and/or offer a safe environment in which to live.

Social Services Law § 143-b(5) provides a defense in non-payment proceedings where the building has "existing violations...which relate to conditions [that] are dangerous, hazardous or detrimental to life or health".[722] Where the local health or building department notifies the Department of Social Services of the unsafe conditions, the agency may issue a notice withholding shelter payments. The notice to withhold payments is a complete defense, subject to a determination by the Court, in a non-payment proceeding because neither a possessory judgment nor a money judgment may be issued for any period in which the dangerous or hazardous conditions existed.[723]

The defense may be asserted after the Department of Social Services or other governmental agency withholds rent payments.[724] The defense is not applicable in holdover proceedings.[725]

---

721 *Id.* § 143-b(1).

722 *Id.* § 143-b(5)(a).

723 *Id.* § 143-b(5)(b).

724 Notre Dame Leasing, LLC v. Rosario, 308 A.D.2d 164, 761 N.Y.S.2d 292 (App. Div., 2d Dep't 2003), *aff'd*, 2 N.Y.3d 459, 779 N.Y.S.2d 801 (2004); Fifty-Seven Assocs., L.P. v. Feinman, 924 N.Y.S.2d 309 (App. Term, 1st Dep't 2011) (Spiegel defense refuted where Tenant did not provide Landlord access to correct housing code violations).

725 Valentine v. Maybank, 501 N.Y.S.2d 553, 554 (Suffolk Cnty. Dist. Ct. 1986).

B. ADULT HOME OPERATORS

Certified adult home operators may terminate an Adult Care Admission Agreement with a supplemental security income recipient in limited circumstances, such as the failure to pay "authorized charges, expenses and other assessments." RPAPL § 713-a and SSL § 461-h(15) provide that authorized adult home operators and their residents are <u>not</u> governed by conventional Landlord and Tenant relationships. As a result, an adult home seeking to terminate a resident's Admission Agreement neither commences a non-payment nor a holdover proceeding.[726] Instead, the adult home operator may commence a special proceeding in the Housing Part where grounds for termination are established.[727]

The New York State Admission Agreement generally requires that an adult home operator accepts supplemental security income benefits in full satisfaction of the services provided. Although the resident may receive further financial assistance in the form of a personal needs allowance ("PNA"), the adult home operator may <u>not</u> accept these monies under any circumstance.[728]

If the adult home operator prevails against a supplemental security income recipient, the adult home operator must assist the resident in finding a new residence. As such, instead of an eviction, the resident may continue to reside in the adult home until another suitable residence is located.[729]

---

726 RPAPL § 713-a; SSL § 461-h(15).

727 RPAPL § 713-a; SSL § 461-g; *see* Oceanview Manor Home for Adults v. Vargas, 32 N.Y.S.3d 863 (N.Y. Civ. Ct. 2016). Parenthetically, the Appellate Division, First Department dismissed as moot a preemptive declaratory judgment action against an adult home operator because "due process is insured to a resident of this type of home before their admission agreement may be involuntarily terminated". Campbell v. Blum, 91 A.D.2d 937, 457 N.Y.S.2d 816 (App. Div., 1st Dep't 1983).

728 SSL § 131-o(2); Dworkin v. Dombrowski, 308 A.D.2d 88, at 96, 761 N.Y.S.2d 245, 251 (App. Div., 2d Dep't 2003) (SSL § 131-o(2) prohibits an adult facility "from contracting with [SSI recipients] ... as to give rise to an obligation on their part to expend part or all of their personal allowance to pay for services or supplies").

729 P & A Reckless v. Howard, 16 N.Y.S.3d 895 (App. Term, 9th & 10th Jud. Dists. 2015) (the "requirement [that the home assists in finding a new home] may provide a basis to stay

The Admission Agreement also typically provides that upon thirty (30) days written notice, the resident may be required to pay additional charges "due to the [adult home's] increased cost of maintenance and operation". In *Lockwood v. DeLeon*, an adult home operator sought to terminate a supplemental security income recipient's Admission Agreement due to her failure to pay increased maintenance and operation costs. Although there was unchallenged testimony from a qualified State employee, the proceeding was dismissed because the adult home failed to substantiate a basis for the rate increase. The adult home's accountant acknowledged that since "maintenance and operation" costs are <u>not</u> normally defined accounting terms, the adult home lumped "maintenance and operation" costs with its other expenses, including those for non-chargeable "supplies and services".[730]

execution of the warrant").

730 *See* Lockwood v. DeLeon, Index No. BALT 654-09 (Suffolk Cnty. Dist. Ct. Nov. 17, 2009) (unreported decision).

CHAPTER 11

COURTROOM PROCEDURE
AND PROTOCOL

Individuals may represent themselves in a summary proceeding. However, appearing without counsel is discouraged and often disadvantageous. A person holding a Power of Attorney is prohibited from commencing a summary proceeding or representing another individual because that would constitute the unauthorized practice of law.[731] A Power of Attorney may, however, permit the holder to sign and/or verify documents on behalf of the party.

The Appellate Term for the Second, Eleventh and Thirteenth Judicial Districts has held that partnerships and limited partnerships must appear by counsel.[732] Corporations and limited liability companies must also appear by counsel.[733] An agent of a corporate Landlord, unless a

---

731   Whitehead v. Town House Equities, Ltd., 8 A.D.3d 369, 777 N.Y.S.2d 917 (App. Div., 2d Dep't 2004); Pinpoint Techs. 3, LLC v. Mogilevsky, 15 N.Y.S.3d 714 (App. Term, 2d, 11th & 13th Jud. Dists. 2015) (breach of contract claim); 91 E. Main St. Realty Corp. v. Angelic Creations by Lucia, 884 N.Y.S.2d 565, 567 (App. Term, 9th & 10th Jud. Dists. 2009); *see also* Ontario Heights Homeowners Assoc. v. Town of Oswego Planning Bd., 77 A.D.3d 1465, at 1466, 908 N.Y.S.2d 514, 515 (App. Div., 4th Dep't 2010) (party who is not an attorney may not represent co-Petitioners).

732   Ernest & Maryanna Jeremias Family P'ship, L.P. v. Sadykov, 11 N.Y.S.3d 792 (App. Term, 2d, 11th & 13th Jud. Dists. 2015) (holding that as a matter of "policy and uniformity", since partnerships and limited partnerships were "largely subsumed within the definition of voluntary associations when Civil Practice Act § 236 was enacted", these entities need counsel). *Cf.* Net Leased Real Estate Props., Operating P'ship v. Air Chef, Inc., Index No. 652704-13, 2014 WL 2859262, 2014 N.Y. Misc. LEXIS 2793 (N.Y. Cnty. Sup. Ct. June 20, 2014) ("[a] partnership that is not a registered limited liability partnership may appear *pro se* in a civil action").

733   CPLR § 321. *See* Michael Reilly Design, Inc. v. Houraney, 40 A.D.3d 592, at 593-94, 835 N.Y.S.2d 640, 641 (App. Div., 2d Dep't 2007).

duly admitted attorney, may <u>not</u> commence a summary proceeding on behalf of the corporate entity.[734]

A. NASSAU SUFFOLK LAW SERVICES COMMITTEE, INC.

The Nassau Suffolk Law Services Committee, Inc. ("Committee") staffs some of the Housing Parts on Long Island with attorneys who represent Respondents of limited financial means. The Committee, which is not affiliated with the Court, will represent a Petitioner on rare occasions, such as when the owner has a mental health illness. The Court has no input regarding the parties the Committee represents, and it does not assign counsel in civil cases. The Court may, however, appoint a *guardian ad litem* should the need arise.[735] In some locations throughout New York, the Legal Aid Society represents individuals of limited financial means in summary proceedings.

B. CALL OF THE CALENDAR

It cannot be overstated that there is no formula for handling a Housing Part calendar. This Chapter is intended to provide an overview of the procedures and offer a perspective as to what an individual may expect. The descriptions should <u>not</u> in any way be construed as a

---

734   *See* Inland Diversified Real Estate Serv., LLC v. Keiko New York, Inc., 36 N.Y.S.3d 407 (App. Term, 9th & 10th Jud. Dists. 2016).

735   *See* WHGA Renaissance Apts., L.P. v. Jackson, 37 N.Y.S.3d 809 (App. Term, 1st Dep't 2016) (*guardian ad litem* appointed where Tenant suffered from paranoid schizophrenia and was "incapable of adequately defending her rights"); Jamsol Realty, LLC v. German, 997 N.Y.S.2d 891 (App. Term, 2d, 11th & 13th Jud. Dists. 2014) ("[u]pon being advised ... that tenant was an adult incapable of protecting her own rights, it was the duty of the court to determine if this were the case and, if so, to appoint a *guardian ad litem*") (emphasis added) (citations omitted); *see also* All Peoples Hempstead of 309 HDFC v. Milsap, 5 N.Y.S.3d 327 (App. Term, 1st Dep't 2014) (denying Tenant's post-judgment motion to remove the *guardian ad litem* "in the absence of just cause or any showing that the guardian did not fulfill her responsibilities"); Pacific Park LLC v. M.W., Index No. 72501-16, 2016 WL 4945137, 2016 N.Y. Misc. LEXIS 3268 (N.Y. Civ. Ct. Sept. 7, 2016) (denying, without prejudice, motion of non-party Department of Social Services for appointment of a *guardian ad litem* where the motion papers were unable to be personally delivered to Respondent who was hospitalized for schizophrenia).

comment or opinion on any courtroom procedure.

During the first call of the Calendar, which begins at approximately 9:30 a.m., Stipulations of Settlements are heard first, followed by attorney applications for adjournments.[736] The remainder of the Calendar is then called. The parties are routinely directed to conference their case prior to the second call of the Calendar, which does not begin before 10:30 a.m.

Adjournment requests are entertained during first call from both counsel and *pro se* litigants. Each side in a summary proceeding is ordinarily permitted one (1), one (1) week adjournment which will be granted with a "final marking" against the requesting party. Notwithstanding RPAPL § 745(1), which limits adjournments in a summary proceeding outside New York City to ten (10) days, the Court retains "[i]nherent authority to grant a continuance" of longer duration.[737] Accordingly, upon a showing of exigent circumstances or scheduling conflicts, or with the consent of the parties, an adjournment of a longer duration may be granted.

RPAPL § 745(2) sets forth the rules regarding adjournments within New York City. Where the Respondent is granted two (2) adjournments or thirty (30) days passes from the first Court appearance, whichever is sooner (not including the days the matter was adjourned at the Petitioner's request), the Court, upon request, must direct the Respondent to deposit the rent and use and occupancy that accrued following service of the Notice of Petition and Petition.[738]

---

736   For a detailed discussion on Stipulations of Settlement, *see infra*, Chapter 12.

737   Paladino v. Sotille, 835 N.Y.S.2d 799, 801 (App. Term, 9th & 10th Jud. Dists. 2007). *Cf.* Sutton v. Mitrany, 30 A.D.3d 678, 816 N.Y.S.2d 575 (App. Div., 3d Dep't 2006) (trial court did not abuse its discretion in denying Respondent's third request for an adjournment at the hearing where the attorney's affidavit of engagement did not comply with 22 N.Y.C.R.R. § 125.1(e)(1) and no explanation was offered for the delay in making the request).

738   RPAPL § 745(2)(a); *see* Myrtle Venture Five, LLC v. Eye Care Optical of NY, Inc., 11 N.Y.S.3d 796 (App. Term, 2d, 11th & 13th Jud. Dists. 2015) (Court improperly directed the deposit of use and occupancy where 30 days, not including consent adjournments, had not elapsed following service). Any portion of the rent or use and occupancy paid with a government housing subsidy may not be included within the deposit. *See* RPAPL § 745(2) (b). A deposit is not required where the Respondent demonstrates that the Petitioner is not a proper party, or asserts any of the following defenses; actual eviction, actual partial

When the Tenant does <u>not</u> appear at first call, the Landlord will typically be informed of any defects in service. Notwithstanding the defective and/or inadequate proof of service, the Landlord may be inclined to wait until second call in the event the Tenant appears and waives the service deficiencies. Otherwise, the summary proceeding will be dismissed, without prejudice, which means the Landlord may commence a new proceeding (after serving another predicate notice), and the parties often return to Court within a few weeks.

If the Respondent appears without objection, the defense of lack of personal jurisdiction is waived. Not surprisingly, some Tenants wish to proceed despite the defective service to avoid having to return to Court, and further because they may be able to negotiate a more favorable resolution when the Landlord is faced with an outright dismissal.

On the other hand, the Petitioner may withdraw the case prior to dismissal. The withdrawal is typically without prejudice to commencing another summary proceeding after serving a new predicate notice.[739] If a request is made to discontinue the action "with prejudice" (i.e., precluding another proceeding for the same period), then the Tenant must demonstrate prejudice to a substantial right or other special circumstances.[740]

The second call of the Calendar initially mirrors the first call. Stipulations of Settlement are considered first followed by attorney applications for adjournments. Thereafter, attorney applications for default judgments are entertained where the pleadings are facially

---

eviction or constructive eviction, a defense pursuant to SSL § 143-b (section entitled, "Avoidance of Abuses in Connection With Rent Checks"), or that the Court lacks jurisdiction. See RPAPL § 745(2)(a).

739 See generally Elnazer v. Quoquoi, 17 N.Y.S.3d 267 (App. Term, 2d, 11th & 13th Jud. Dists. 2015) (withdrawal of the Petition is the procedural equivalent to a discontinuance without prejudice).

740 See New York Mortgage Trust, Inc. v. Dasdemir, 116 A.D.3d 679, 985 N.Y.S.2d 86 (App. Div., 2d Dep't 2014); Blackwell v. Mikevin Mgmt. III, LLC, 88 A.D.3d 836, 931 N.Y.S.2d 116 (App. Div., 2d Dep't 2011); Expedite Video Conf. Servs., Inc. v. Botello, 67 A.D.3d 961, 890 N.Y.S.2d 82 (App. Div., 2d Dep't 2009); Eugenia VI Venture Holdings, Ltd. v. MapleWood Equity Partners, L.P., 38 A.D.3d 264, 832 N.Y.S.2d 155 (App. Div., 1st Dep't 2007).

sufficient and proper service is alleged.[741] In many of the local courts, applications for default judgments may <u>not</u> be considered until at least one (1) hour <u>after</u> the proceeding is initially called, or at least 10:30 a.m.[742]

The remainder of the Calendar is then called a second time. Oral argument on Orders to Show Cause, which are usually submitted by Respondents seeking to vacate a default judgment and/or requesting additional time to remain in the premises, and motions to dismiss are then heard, followed by hearings.

C. HEARINGS

1. ROLE OF THE COURT

The overwhelming majority of summary proceedings are resolved prior to a hearing. However, in those instances where an amicable resolution is <u>not</u> attainable, the Petitioner must prove its case at a hearing, in which sworn testimony is taken, by a fair preponderance of the evidence.[743] Represented and *pro se* litigants are held to the same standards.[744] In rendering its determination, whether orally on the record or in a written decision, the Court must state the "ultimate or essential facts relied upon in reaching its decision".[745]

---

741 Martine Assocs., LLC v. Minck, 785 N.Y.S.2d 648, 649 (App. Term, 9th & 10th Jud. Dists. 2004).

742 *See* Uniform Civil Rules for the District Court § 212.42(a); Uniform Civil Rules for the City Courts Outside the City of New York § 210.42(a).

743 *See* Mautner-Glick Corp. v. Glazer, 31 N.Y.S.3d 922 (App. Term, 1st Dep't 2016); Tello v. Dylag, 15 N.Y.S.3d 715 (App. Term, 9th & 10th Jud. Dists. 2015); Chelsea Ridge NY, LLC v. Clarke, 983 N.Y.S.2d 201 (App. Term, 9th & 10th Jud. Dists. 2013).

744 Boltz v. Ascolesi, 847 N.Y.S.2d 895 (App. Term, 2d & 11th Jud. Dists. 2007) (*pro se* litigants are "[n]ot entitled to any greater rights than any other party, and cannot get concessions at the expense of another party's rights") (citations omitted).

745 CPLR § 4213(b); *see* 129th St. Cluster Assocs. v. Levy, 26 N.Y.S.3d 214 (App. Term, 1st Dep't 2015) (appeal held in abeyance and the proceeding remanded to the Housing Part for a decision in compliance with CPLR § 4213(b)); RBD Realty Consultants, Inc. v. Espinal, 949 N.Y.S.2d 565 (App. Term, 1st Dep't 2012) (proceeding returned to the Housing Part for a new hearing due to the Court's "cryptic decision" which failed to provide any insight, explanation or rationale for its decision).

During the hearing, the Court accepts (or rejects) evidence and assesses witness credibility.[746] The Court has no obligation to explain the burden of proof or the admissibility of evidence to a *pro se* litigant.[747] However, in its discretion, the Court may provide a *pro se* litigant "some latitude" with respect to protocol and procedure.[748] In addition, the Court may take an active role at the hearing, particularly, but not exclusively, where one (1) or more of the parties are unrepresented, by eliciting and clarifying the testimony of the witnesses "where [it is] proper or necessary…to facilitate or expedite the orderly progress of the trial".[749]

Where the Court reaches a conclusion <u>not</u> supported by the evidence or contrary to law, an Appellate Court may reverse the decision and either rule in favor of the opposing party or remit the matter to the Housing Part for a new hearing before the same or a different judge.[750] For example, a final judgment of possession was vacated where the Housing Part only accepted evidence from the Tenant, thereby shifting the burden of proof.[751] The Appellate Term concluded that it was reversible error to award a possessory judgment where the Landlord was not required to prove its case.[752]

The Housing Part may <u>not</u> *sua sponte* dismiss a summary proceeding due to the Landlord's failure to serve a predicate notice.[753] The

---

746 *See* T & S Realty Corp. v. Lee, 28 N.Y.S.3d 651 (App. Term, 1st Dep't 2015); Sajo Realty Corp. v. Antoine, 18 N.Y.S.3d 581 (App. Term, 2d, 11th & 13th Jud. Dists. 2015).

747 Limani Realty, LLC v. Zayfert, 970 N.Y.S.2d 345 (App. Term, 2d, 11th & 13th Jud. Dists. 2012).

748 *Id.*

749 Accardi v. City of New York, 121 A.D.2d 489, at 491, 503 N.Y.S.2d 818, 820 (App. Div., 2d Dep't 1986) (*quoting* People v. Ellis, 62 A.D.2d 469, at 470, 404 N.Y.S.2d 862, 863 (App. Div., 1st Dep't 1978)); Carlson, Sr. v. Porter, 53 A.D.3d 1129, at 1132, 861 N.Y.S.2d 907, 910 (App. Div., 4th Dep't 2008); Tonkin v. Lofthouse, 34 A.D.3d 1309, 823 N.Y.S.2d 716 (App. Div., 4th Dep't 2006); Kalikow Family P'ship, LP v. Seidemann, 18 N.Y.S.3d 579 (App. Term, 2d, 11th & 13th Jud. Dists. 2015).

750 *See* New York City Hous. Auth. v. Martinez, 26 N.Y.S.3d 725 (App. Tern, 1st Dep't 2015).

751 1764 Majors Path Corp. v. Petrinolis, 36 N.Y.S.3d 408 (App. Term, 9th & 10th Jud. Dists. 2016).

752 *Id.*

753 *See* 80th Inc. v. Witter, 22 N.Y.S.3d 137 (App. Term, 1st Dep't 2015) (holding that "Courts are 'not in the business of blindsiding litigants, who expect us to decide their [cases] on rationales advanced by the parties, not arguments their adversaries never

Appellate Term held in *80th Inc. v. Witter* that the Housing Part was obligated to give the Landlord an opportunity to address the deficiency prior to dismissing the proceeding where the Tenant failed to raise the omission as a defense.[754] Of note, the defense is waived when the parties resolve the proceeding by Stipulation of Settlement.[755]

Provided counsel is present, the Landlord's failure to appear at the hearing does <u>not</u> necessitate a dismissal of the proceeding. Petitioner's counsel may attempt to make a *prima facie* case exclusively through the testimony of the Respondent and other witnesses as well as the documentary exhibits. However, as a practical matter, the Landlord would be bound by the Tenant's testimony that "all of the rent was paid". Likewise, Respondent's counsel may cross-examine Petitioner and call additional witnesses when the Tenant is not present.

With regard to "last minute" adjournment requests, the decision to grant an adjournment is left to the sound discretion of the Court albeit with limitations. For example, denying the adjournment was improper where Tenant's counsel was "engaged" in another Court.[756] However, the denial was upheld where the Tenant sought to retain new counsel during the hearing,[757] and when the Tenant's previous delays resulted in a mistrial.[758]

---

made'") (citation omitted).

754 *Id.*

755 Ng v. Chalasani, 36 N.Y.S.3d 408 (App. Term, 2d, 11th & 13th Jud. Dists. 2016); Hernco, LLC v. Hernandez, 9 N.Y.S.3d 593 n.1 (App. Term, 2d, 11th & 13th Jud. Dists. 2015); Esplanade Gardens, Inc. v. Simms, Index No. 74586-15, 2016 WL 3152675, 2016 N.Y. Misc. LEXIS 2024 (N.Y. Civ. Ct. June 6, 2016) (*citing* 433 W. Assocs. v. Murdock, 276 A.D.2d 360, 715 N.Y.S.2d 6 (App. Div., 1st Dep't 2000)).

756 1346 Park Pl. HDFC v. Wright, 34 N.Y.S.3d 561 (App. Term, 2d, 11th & 13th Jud. Dists. 2016). After denying the adjournment request, the Housing Part gave the Tenant an ultimatum to either discharge her counsel and proceed with the hearing *pro se* or she would be prohibited from participating. The Tenant elected not to discharge counsel, and at essentially what became a default judgment application, the Landlord was awarded possession. *Id.* The Appellate Term reversed, holding that the adjournment request should have been granted. *Id.*

757 *See* West 88th St., LLC v. Henriquez, 5 N.Y.S.3d 331 (App. Term, 1st Dep't 2014).

758 Chen v. Ray, 26 N.Y.S.3d 212 (App. Term, 1st Dep't 2015).

2. EVIDENTIARY ISSUES

The rules of evidence apply to summary proceedings. The decision to permit a party to re-open its case to correct deficiencies in the evidence is left to the discretion of the Court.[759] The reader should be mindful that "admissibility" is not the same as "reliability". In other words, the mere introduction of testimony or an exhibit does <u>not</u> require the trier of fact to give that evidence any weight whatsoever.

a. HEARSAY

It is well-established that an out-of-court statement of a non-party offered for the truth of the matter asserted is <u>not</u> admissible. However, a hearsay statement offered as evidence of the witness' state of mind, rather than for the truth of the statement itself, may be admissible as an exception to the hearsay rule.[760] This situation arises in a variety of forms. For example, the out-of-court statement of an unavailable non-party witness may be admissible in a non-payment proceeding where the Tenant claims that he was told the apartment was "illegal" or that the property was in foreclosure. If the out-of-court statement was offered to demonstrate the Tenant's thought process or reasoning for not paying the rent, as opposed to the status of the premises or that the rent was not paid, then the statement may be admitted. It is worth repeating that admitting the testimony does <u>not</u> mean the testimony will be deemed credible by the trier of fact.

---

759   *See generally* Hyatt Ave. Assocs., LLC v. Rahman, 17 N.Y.S.3d 579 (App. Term, 2d, 11th & 13th Jud. Dists. 2015).

760   *See* Benitez v. Whitehall Apts. Co., LLC, 862 N.Y.S.2d 813 (N.Y. Cnty. Sup. Ct. 2008) (the out-of-court statement of Landlord's superintendent regarding the building's security cameras was properly considered on a motion for summary judgment because the testimony was introduced to demonstrate the victim's state of mind when entering the elevator), *aff'd*, 56 A.D.3d 273, 866 N.Y.S.2d 668 (App. Div., 1st Dep't 2008).

b. BUSINESS RECORDS

Another common dispute involves the introduction of the rental agreement and payment records. Typically, the Landlord will introduce the lease as a contract between the parties after laying a proper foundation and authenticating the signatures.[761] The rental agreement may otherwise be introduced as a business record exception to the hearsay rule through the testimony of a property manager or other agent sufficiently familiar with the company's business records "[t]o aver that the record is what it purports to be and that it came out of the entity's files".[762]

c. BEST EVIDENCE RULE

Where the original rental agreement is either lost or destroyed, the document may be introduced as a secondary source where (1) an adequate explanation for the non-production is provided; (2) the non-production was <u>not</u> the result of bad faith on the part of the moving party; and (3) the accuracy of the secondary source is demonstrated.[763] The Appellate Division, First Department allowed the introduction of proof of the parties' rental agreement as a secondary source, notwithstanding the absence of an explanation for the failure to produce the original, where the Tenant admitted he owed the rent and his counterclaim was based on that same rental agreement.[764]

A reliable photocopy of a lost or destroyed rental agreement may be introduced pursuant to CPLR § 4539. This provision offers an exception for "[c]opies of documents made by an accurate reproduction process, such as photocopying, provided the documents are those of a business

---

761 *See* Tuscan Realty Corp. v. O'Neill, 731 N.Y.S.2d 830 (App. Term, 2d & 11th Jud. Dists. 2001).

762 APF 286 MAD, LLC v. Chittur & Assocs., P.C., 28 N.Y.S.3d 647 (App. Term, 1st Dep't 2016); DeLeon v. Port Auth. of New York and New Jersey, 306 A.D.2d 146, 761 N.Y.S.2d 54 (App. Div., 1st Dep't 2003). *See also* CPLR § 4518.

763 *See generally* Schozer v. William Penn Life Ins. Co. of New York, 84 N.Y.2d 639, 620 N.Y.S.2d 797 (1994).

764 *See* B.N. Realty Assocs. v. Lichtenstein, 96 A.D.3d 434, at 434-35, 949 N.Y.S.2d 1, 2 (App. Div., 1st Dep't 2012).

and the copying was done in the regular course of business. The proponent is thus exempt from the requirement of producing the original or explaining its absence".[765]

d. PHOTOGRAPHS

Photographs may be utilized to confirm or refute the conditions of the premises.[766] Photographs are sometimes further introduced to demonstrate unauthorized alterations and renovations.[767]

Relevant photographs are admissible provided they "fairly and accurately" depict the condition of the subject matter on the date in question.[768] If the movant asserts that the photographs accurately portray the condition of the premises at the relevant time period, then the Court may admit the photographs regardless of when and by whom they were taken.[769]

e. AUDIO RECORDINGS

In New York, it is lawful to record a conversation, without notice, where at least one (1) party to the conversation consents to the recording.[770] However, to introduce the audio recording at a hearing, a proper foundation must be provided through clear and convincing evidence regarding the relevancy, authenticity, completeness and accuracy of the recording.[771]

---

765 174 LLC v. Roberts, 809 N.Y.S.2d 482 (N.Y. Civ. Ct. 2005). *See also* CPLR § 4539. *Cf.* Ramchandani v. Piran Fashions, Inc., 999 N.Y.S.2d 798 (App. Term, 2d, 11th & 13th Jud. Dists. 2014) (copies of rent checks are not admissible where the copies were not authenticated by competent testimony or supporting affidavit).

766 *See generally West 88th St., LLC*, 5 N.Y.S.3d at 331.

767 Zada Assocs. v. Melucci, 28 N.Y.S.3d 651 (App. Term, 1st Dep't 2015).

768 Read v. Ellenville Nat'l Bank, 20 A.D.3d 408, 799 N.Y.S.2d 78 (App. Div., 2d Dep't 2005); Lott-Coakley v. Ann-Gur Realty Corp., 886 N.Y.S.2d 67 (Bronx Cnty. Sup. Ct. 2009).

769 *But see* Leven v. Tallis Dept. Store, 178 A.D.2d 466, 577 N.Y.S.2d 132 (App. Div., 2d Dep't 1991) (unauthenticated photographs taken two (2) years following the accident improperly admitted into evidence).

770 *See* Penal Law § 250; People v. Lasher, 58 N.Y.2d 962, 460 N.Y.S.2d 522 (1983).

771 *See generally* People v. Ely, 68 N.Y.2d 520, 510 N.Y.S.2d 532 (1986); People v. Hurlbert, Jr., 81 A.D.3d 1430, 916 N.Y.S.2d 713 (App. Div., 4th Dep't 2011); Samra v. Messeca, 17 N.Y.S.3d 385 (App. Term, 1st Dep't 2015) (recorded conversation between Tenant and an agent of Landlord admissible).

If the conversation was recorded without at least one (1) party's consent, or otherwise obtained in an unlawful manner in violation of section 250.05 of the Penal Law (eavesdropping), then the audio recording is inadmissible.[772]

3. MONEY JUDGMENTS

In a non-payment proceeding outside New York City, the Court will typically award a prevailing Petitioner the balance of the month's rent and stay enforcement of the warrant of eviction through at least the end of the month. The money judgment in a non-payment proceeding, by definition, includes both rent arrears and use and occupancy because the issuance of a judgment of possession and warrant of eviction retroactively terminates the tenancy as of the date the summary proceeding was commenced.[773] As a result, rent arrears that accrued during the pendency of the non-payment proceeding constitute use and occupancy, and not rent.[774]

Since the rule against apportionment applies to rent (but not use and occupancy),[775] some have argued that the Court has two (2) options in determining the amount of the money judgment in a non-payment proceeding when the Tenant continues to remain in possession. In addition to the rent arrears that accrued prior to the commencement of the summary proceeding, the Court may award use and occupancy for each day the Tenant remains in possession following the commencement through either (1) the date of the award or (2) a definite date in the future (such as the end of the month) with a stay on enforcement until the same date.

The former is based upon the premise that the Court may <u>not</u> award moneys for items that have not yet accrued, and, further, the Landlord may be made whole by recovering the unpaid proceeds in a subsequent plenary action for use and occupancy.[776] This approach appears to be the more

---

772   CPLR § 4506(1).

773   Priegue v. Paulus, 988 N.Y.S.2d 525 (App. Term, 9th & 10th Jud. Dists. 2014).

774   Madden v. Juliet, 13 N.Y.S.3d 850 (App. Term, 9th & 10th Jud. Dists. 2015).

775   *Priegue*, 988 N.Y.S.2d at 525. For a discussion on the Rule Against Apportionment, *see supra*, Chapter 1 subdiv. (D)(2).

776   *See* Rustagi v. Sanchez, 999 N.Y.S.2d 798 (App. Term, 2d, 11th & 13th Jud. Dists. 2014) ("[i]t is well settled that a landlord may bring a separate action to recover the use and occupancy which accrued after the entry of a final judgment in a summary proceeding") (citations omitted).

precise of the two (2) computations because use and occupancy should only be awarded for the actual number of days the Tenant remains in possession without a valid Landlord and Tenant relationship.[777] In other words, if the Court awards use and occupancy until the end of the month, then the Landlord would obtain a "windfall" if the Tenant vacates the premises prior to the stay date. However, until Appellate Courts weigh-in on this issue, varying results may be achieved. Regardless, unless waived, the Landlord may seek use and occupancy otherwise not previously sought or awarded in a subsequent plenary action.

4. STAYS INVOLVING NEW YORK CITY PROPERTIES

For properties within New York City, there are several stay provisions that warrant consideration. For example, RPAPL § 732(2) provides that where the Respondent appeared at the hearing, the Court may stay issuance of the warrant of eviction up to five (5) days from the date of the determination. Where the Respondent defaults, the stay may not exceed ten (10) days from the date of service.[778]

Further exclusive to residential holdover proceedings within New York City, the Court must stay issuance of the warrant of eviction for ten (10) days "during which the respondent may correct such breach".[779] Where the breach is timely cured, the issuance of the warrant is permanently stayed.[780] The Court may not extend the ten-day period, and the Tenant is not entitled to a stay where the breach is incurable or cannot be corrected within ten (10) days.[781]

---

777   *Priegue*, 988 N.Y.S.2d at 525; *Madden*, 13 N.Y.S.3d at 850.

778   RPAPL § 732(3); 22 N.Y.C.R.R. § 208.42(d).

779   RPAPL § 753(4). *See* Lombard v. Station Sq. Inn Apts. Corp., 94 A.D.3d 717, at 720-21, 942 N.Y.S.2d 116, 121 (App. Div., 2d Dep't 2012) (holding the ten (10) day cure period in New York City only applies to proceedings for possession).

780   *See* 111-35 75th Ave. Owners Corp. v. Hendrix, 21 N.Y.S.3d 808 (App. Term, 2d, 11th & 13th Jud. Dists. 2015) (mere commencement of a proceeding to evict unlawful occupants within (10) ten days is insufficient for a permanent stay).

781   259 W. 12th, LLC v. Grossberg, 89 A.D.3d 585, 933 N.Y.S.2d 256 (App. Div., 1st Dep't 2011); *111-35 75th Ave. Owners Corp.*, 21 N.Y.S.3d at 808. *Cf.* 201 W. 54th St. Buyer LLC v. Rodin, 18 N.Y.S.3d 581 (App. Term, 1st Dep't 2015) (removal of sink and medicine cabinet and replacement of wall could be completed within 10 days).

With regard to non-payment proceedings, RPAPL § 747-a provides that where the Landlord is the prevailing party and the Tenant appeared, the Court "shall <u>not</u> grant a stay of the issuance or execution of any warrant of eviction nor stay re-letting of the premises" after five (5) days following the award unless the Tenant satisfies the judgment or deposits the funds with the Clerk of the Court <u>prior</u> to the execution of the warrant.[782] Although the Housing Parts in New York City apparently retain some discretion with regard to its application, an Appellate Court has held that RPAPL § 747-a is unconstitutional as applied to temporary stay requests in connection with post-judgment motions.[783]

For holdover proceedings, the Court may stay "the issuance of a warrant and also stay any execution to collect the costs of the proceeding" up to six (6) months provided certain statutory conditions are fulfilled, including the payment of use and occupancy in an amount determined by the Court.[784] The stay provision is <u>not</u> applicable where (1) the Landlord's plans for the demolition and reconstruction of a new building were approved by the local governing authority or (2) the Tenant is deemed "objectionable".[785] In *Volunteers of America-Greater New York, Inc. v. Carr*, the Appellate Term held that the Tenant, who was evicted due to objectionable conduct that "substantially interfered with the comfort and safety of other residents", including causing property damage and making threatening comments, was not entitled to a stay for the purpose of curing the breach.[786]

---

782 RPAPL § 747-a (emphasis added).

783 *See* Jones v. Allen, 712 N.Y.S.2d 306, 307-08 (App. Term, 2d & 11th Jud. Dists. 2000); Jacob v. Wagenhoffer, 831 N.Y.S.2d 359 (App. Term, 2d & 11th Jud. Dists. 2006) (holding there is no right to a post-judgment temporary stay pursuant to RPAPL § 747-a).

784 RPAPL §§ 753(1)-(3).

785 *Id.* §§ 753(3),(4).

786 Volunteers of America-Greater New York, Inc. v. Carr, 28 N.Y.S.3d 651 (App. Term, 1st Dep't 2015); Gordon v. 476 Broadway Realty Corp., 129 A.D.3d 547, 12 N.Y.S.3d 37 (App. Div., 1st Dep't 2015).

D. PAROL EVIDENCE

Although parol evidence is a rule of "substantive law", and not a rule of evidence, it is important to note that issues of lease interpretation and contemporaneous agreements are frequently raised in summary proceedings. It is well-established that where a written rental agreement is clear, complete and unambiguous, the Court will <u>not</u> consider any additional or extraneous oral or written statements that may contradict the lease terms.[787] In other words, "[a]bsent fraud or mutual mistake, where the parties have reduced their agreement to an integrated writing, the parol evidence rule operates to exclude evidence of all prior or contemporaneous negotiations between the parties offered to contradict or modify the terms of their writing".[788]

However, where the lease provision is ambiguous or vague, the Court may consider parol evidence to assist in the interpretation of the parties' written agreement.[789] For example, parol evidence was permitted to clarify an ambiguous lease provision regarding "the dollar amount of the monthly payments and the meaning of the term 'six month grace period' ".[790] Any ambiguity in the drafting will be construed against the drafter of the document.[791]

---

787 Madison Ave. Leasehold, LLC v. Madison Bentley Assoc., LLC, 8 N.Y.3d 59, 828 N.Y.S.2d 254 (2006) (parol evidence may not be used to create ambiguity within an otherwise clear and unambiguous rental agreement).

788 Lopez v. Platinum Volkswagen, 26 N.Y.S.3d 214 (App. Term, 9th & 10th Jud. Dists. 2015) (citations omitted).

789 First Am. Commercial Bancorp, Inc. v. Saatchi & Saatchi Rowland, Inc., 55 A.D.3d 1264, 865 N.Y.S.2d 424 (App. Div., 4th Dep't 2008) (parol evidence required to clarify sublease boundaries and description); Great S. Bay Family Med. Practice, LLP v. Raynor, 35 A.D.3d 808, 826 N.Y.S.2d 729 (App. Div., 2d Dep't 2006) (parol evidence permitted for "the interpretation of the handwritten changes" to the lease).

790 See Kasiotis v. Jones, Jr., 5 N.Y.S.3d 328 n.2 (Sullivan Cnty. Ct. 2014) (citation omitted); see also 1626 Second Ave. LLC v. Salsberg, 105 A.D.3d 432, 962 N.Y.S.2d 135 (App. Div., 1st Dep't 2013) (parol evidence permitted to "clarify" lease guaranty).

791 See Goldhirsch v. St. George Tower and Grill Owners Corp., 142 A.D.3d 1044, 37 N.Y.S.3d 616 (App. Div., 2d Dep't 2016); Kasiotis, 5 N.Y.S.3d at 328.

E. APPEALS

A party may appeal an Order of the Court by filing a Notice of Appeal and paying the appropriate fee within thirty (30) days of the Notice of Entry.[792] The party must further serve a copy of the transcript of the minutes on the opposing party and execute a Stipulation of Settlement of the Transcript. If the parties cannot agree on settling the minutes, then the party seeking the appeal must make a motion to Settle the Transcript of Minutes.

1. WHERE TO FILE APPEAL

The appropriate Court to take the appeal depends on the location and origination of the trial court. For example, an appeal of an Order of the District Courts, which are exclusively situated within the Second Judicial Department, and the New York City Civil Courts, are made to the appropriate Appellate Term.[793]

Although the Appellate Division in each of the four (4) Judicial Departments has the authority to establish an Appellate Term for the purpose of hearing appeals, only the First and Second Departments have done so to date. Appeals from the City Courts outside New York City and the Justice Courts are made to the appropriate County Court, except where the Court is located within the First or Second Judicial Departments.[794]

---

792 CPLR § 5513.

793 N.Y. Uniform Dist. Ct. Act § 1701 (McKinney 2009); N.Y. City Civ. Ct. Act § 1701 (McKinney 2009). The Appellate Division, Second Department created the Appellate Term for the purpose of such appeals pursuant to 22 N.Y.C.R.R. § 730.1. The Appellate Division, First Department established an Appellate Term pursuant to 22 N.Y.C.R.R. § 640.1. Parenthetically, if the Appellate Terms in the First and Second Judicial Departments did not exist, then appeals from the New York City Civil Courts would be made in the Appellate Division, First Department (N.Y. City Civ. Ct. Act § 1701) and appeals from the District Court would be made in the County Court (Uniform Dist. Ct. Act § 1701).

794 N.Y. Uniform City Ct. Act § 1701 (McKinney 2009); N.Y. Uniform Just. Ct. Act § 1701 (McKinney 2009).

2. LEGAL STANDARDS

The Appellate Court gives "substantial deference" to the Housing Part, which had the opportunity "[t]o observe and evaluate the testimony and demeanor of the witnesses [that] affords it a better perspective from which to assess their credibility".[795] Typically, the Appellate Court will not overturn the Housing Part's decision "[u]nless such determination could not have been reached under any fair interpretation of the evidence.[796]

An appeal may not be taken from a default judgment entered against a non-appearing Tenant.[797] Instead, the defaulting Tenant may move in the Housing Part to vacate the default, and, if that motion is denied, then appeal from the Order denying the motion to vacate the default judgment. Defenses, such as the warranty of habitability and sufficiency of the rent demand, may not be considered for the first time on appeal. With the exception of the defense of a lack of subject matter jurisdiction, if a defense is not raised in the summary proceeding, then the defense will not be considered on appeal.[798]

Two (2) additional procedural protocols should be considered. First, a non-attorney may not appear on behalf of another occupant at any stage of the proceedings, including the appeal.[799] Second, a final possessory judgment and/or money judgment may be vacated or modified against Tenants that are united in interest, even those that did not pursue an appeal.[800] For example, in *Priege v. Paulus*, the money judgment was reduced against the non-appealing Tenant because the Appellant

---

795 Caring Communities Assocs. HDFC v. Boffa, 31 N.Y.S.3d 920 (App. Term, 2d, 11th & 13th Jud. Dists. 2016); Sajo Realty Corp. v. Antoine, 18 N.Y.S.3d 581 (App. Term, 2d, 11th & 13th Jud. Dists. 2015).

796 Parkchester Preserv. Co. L.P. v. Adams, 28 N.Y.S.3d 649 (App. Term, 1st Dep't 2016); Mautner-Glick Corp. v. Glazer, 31 N.Y.S.3d 922 (App. Term, 1st Dep't 2016) (affirming dismissal of summary proceeding where the process server had "no independent recollection" of the service).

797 1764 Majors Path Corp. v. Petrinolis, 36 N.Y.S.3d 408 (App. Term, 9th & 10th Jud. Dists. 2016).

798 Hickey v. Trahan, 31 N.Y.S.3d 921 (App. Term, 9th & 10th Jud. Dists. 2016).

799 Oakwood Terr. Hous. Corp. v. Monk, 36 N.Y.S.3d 48 n.2 (App. Term, 9th & 10th Jud. Dists. 2016).

800 Priegue v. Paulus, 988 N.Y.S.2d 525 (App. Term, 9th & 10th Jud. Dists. 2014).

and non-appealing Tenant shared a common interest in the leasehold which included identical rights and obligations.[801]

3. STAY PENDING APPEAL

A Respondent seeking to stay enforcement of the money judgment pending an appeal may deposit the amount awarded with the Housing Part. However, depositing the funds does <u>not</u> stay the eviction.[802] A request to stay execution of the warrant of eviction, thereby prohibiting the eviction until after the appeal is decided, must be made to the Appellate Term or other appropriate Appellate Court. The Appellate Court may direct the payment of use and occupancy as a condition for granting a stay.

The appeal <u>may</u> be rendered moot if the Tenant is evicted during its pendency because the determination by the Appellate Court "will not affect the rights of the parties".[803] The same may hold true where the Tenant voluntarily vacates the premises during the appeal.[804]

---

801   *Id.; see also Oakwood Terr. Hous. Corp.*, 36 N.Y.S.3d at 48 (proceeding dismissed against both the appealing Tenant and her non-appealing spouse where Petitioner failed to prove or plead a rent demand was made).

802   CPLR § 5519.

803   Michalak v. Fechtel, 911 N.Y.S.2d 693 (App. Term, 9th & 10th Jud. Dists. 2010).

804   Parkchester Preserv. Co. L.P. v. Adams, 28 N.Y.S.3d 649 (App. Term, 1st Dep't 2016).

CHAPTER 12

STIPULATIONS
OF SETTLEMENT

A Stipulation of Settlement is a binding agreement that will generally be enforced in the event of substantial non-compliance.[805] Where the Tenant consents to the entry of a judgment of possession and a warrant of eviction, often in consideration for additional time to remain in possession of the premises and/or a reduction in rent arrears, a motion to vacate the judgment to assert affirmative defenses will typically be denied.[806] This is the case because, as a practical matter, affirmative defenses are waived as a result of the Stipulation of Settlement.[807]

A hearing is typically required where there are issues of fact concerning compliance and/or enforcement of the stipulation. For example, a hearing would be necessary to determine if the execution of the warrant of eviction should be accelerated where the parties dispute whether the Tenant's "objectionable conduct" violated the terms of the agreement.[808]

Due to the high volume of cases in the Housing Parts, amongst other reasons, the Court generally encourages negotiated resolutions.

---

805   *See* 2345 Crotona Gold, LLC v. Dross, 31 N.Y.S.3d 924 (App. Term, 1st Dep't 2016) (motion to vacate stipulation of settlement denied absent evidence of fraud or mistake, and Tenant's failure to timely dispute the rent increase); Stevenson Commons Assocs., LP v. Bishop, 907 N.Y.S.2d 441 (App. Term, 1st Dep't 2010) (stipulation negotiated by counsel); Option One Mortgage Corp. v. Daddi, 60 A.D.3d 920, 874 N.Y.S.2d 822 (App. Div., 2d Dep't 2009) (Stipulation of Settlement constitutes a waiver of affirmative defenses).

806   *See* Michalak v. Fechtel, 911 N.Y.S.2d 693 (App. Term, 9th & 10th Jud. Dists. 2010).

807   *See* Hernco, LLC v. Hernandez, 9 N.Y.S.3d 593 (App. Term, 2d, 11th & 13th Jud. Dists. 2015); Semen v. Dor, 943 N.Y.S.2d 794 (App. Term, 2d, 11th & 13th Jud. Dists. 2011).

808   *See, e.g.,* Caring Communities Assocs. HDFC v. Boffa, 31 N.Y.S.3d 920 (App. Term, 2d, 11th & 13th Jud. Dists. 2016).

There is an inclination to uphold settlements because "[p]arties to a civil dispute are free to chart their own litigation course…and [it] is essential to the management of court calendars and the integrity of the litigation process".[809] For example, a stipulation to discontinue a non-payment proceeding was upheld where the agreement was entered into voluntarily and no explanation was provided for the lengthy delay in seeking to restore the proceeding to the Court's calendar.[810]

Stipulations have similarly been enforced where a commercial Tenant failed to replace the awning in front of the commercial premises;[811] a Landlord was denied "access" to make repairs;[812] a Tenant repeatedly failed to comply with stipulated payment terms;[813] and a *pro se* Tenant "understood the terms of the stipulation and received ample consideration for his agreement to vacate".[814] In addition, in *332 EDC Realty Corp. v. Barlow*, the Housing Part directed the Landlord to accept the late payment of the negotiated arrears ($13,251) to avoid an unnecessary eviction.[815]

On the other hand, a settlement will <u>not</u> be enforced, even when there is substantial compliance, where it "[w]ould be unjust or inequitable, or

---

809   191 St. Assocs. LLC v. Cruz, 29 N.Y.S.3d 848 (App. Term, 1st Dep't 2016) (citations omitted); Thomas v. Brown, 29 N.Y.S.3d 850 (App. Term, 1st Dep't 2015).

810   Banana Kelly Union HDFC v. Chambers, Index No. 571176-15, 2016 WL 3008270, 2016 N.Y. Misc. LEXIS 1898 (App. Term, 1st Dep't May 25, 2016) (Landlord waited eleven (11) months before moving to revoke the stipulation).

811   *See* Serencha Realty Corp. v. A.M. Two In One, Inc., 31 N.Y.S.3d 924 (App. Term, 1st Dep't 2016); 59-61 E. 3rd St., LLC v. Said, 29 N.Y.S.3d 847 (App. Term, 1st Dep't 2015) (two-attorney stipulation enforced against commercial Tenant where the Landlord was not provided "free and unfettered" access to make the agreed upon renovations).

812   Wira Assocs. v. Easy, 26 N.Y.S.3d 216 (App. Term, 2d, 11th & 13th Jud. Dists. 2015).

813   Mehr Props., LLC v. Fonrose, 29 N.Y.S.3d 847 (App. Term, 2d, 11th & 13th Jud. Dists. 2015) (Tenant's fourth Order to Show Case denied following repeated defaults of the stipulation); Third Lenox Terr. Assocs. v. Johnson, 950 N.Y.S.2d 611 (App. Term, 1st Dep't 2012) (stay denied notwithstanding Landlord's initial failure to enforce the Stipulation of Settlement); BPIV-556 W. 188th St. Owner v. Seka, 939 N.Y.S.2d 739 (App. Term, 1st Dep't 2011); The George Units, LLC v. Galan, 939 N.Y.S.2d 740 (App. Term, 1st Dep't 2011).

814   Skeete v. Bah, 29 N.Y.S.3d 849 (App. Term, 1st Dep't 2015); 35 Jackson House Apts. Corp. v. Yaworski, 29 N.Y.S.3d 850 (App. Term, 2d, 11th & 13th Jud. Dists. 2015) (two-attorney stipulation strictly enforced against Tenant who failed to provide the licenses of repair workers).

815   *See, e.g.*, 332 EDC Realty Corp. v. Barlow, 990 N.Y.S.2d 440 (N.Y. Civ. Ct. 2014).

would permit the other party to gain an unconscionable advantage";[816] the agreement "[w]as entered into inadvisably or…it would be inequitable to hold the parties" to its terms;[817] or where there is "[e]vidence of fraud, overreaching, unconscion[able conduct] or illegality".[818] Enforcement of settlements have been denied where the attorney lacked actual and/or apparent authority to enter into the settlement;[819] the Landlord refused to submit the requisite W-9 Form for payment of the rent arrears;[820] proof was provided that the Department of Social Services approved the payment of arrears;[821] and where the money judgment negotiated by the Landlord's attorney and *pro se* Tenant included impermissible items.[822] Moreover, a stipulation that waives the rights and protections afforded under the Rent Stabilization Code is unenforceable.[823]

The Court is <u>not</u> "necessarily bound by language in the stipulation

---

816   368 Chauncey Ave. Trust v. Whitaker, 911 N.Y.S.2d 696 (App. Term, 2d, 11th & 13th Jud. Dists. 2010).

817   600 Hylan Assocs. v. Polshak, 851 N.Y.S.2d 74 (App. Term, 2d & 11th Jud. Dists. 2007) (granting counsel's motion to vacate Stipulation of Settlement and final judgment against the then unrepresented Tenant where viable laches defense asserted); *see also* 2701 Grand Assoc. LLC v. Morel, 31 N.Y.S.3d 924 (App. Term, 1st Dep't 2016) (vacating Stipulation of Settlement and final judgment for rent-regulated premises where the Tenant, now represented by counsel, asserted rent overcharge claim following an 88% rent increase).

818   *See* Chelsea 19 Assocs. v. James, 67 A.D.3d 601, at 602, 889 N.Y.S.2d 564, 566 (App. Div., 1st Dep't 2009) (Tenant's "loss of possession is not a forfeiture but 'merely the contracted-for consequence' of his non-compliance with the stipulation"); Homecomings Financial Real Estate Holdings, LLC v. Glasco, 943 N.Y.S.2d 792 (App. Term, 9th & 10th Jud. Dists. 2011) (motion to vacate stipulation denied where occupant claimed that she was unaware the "settlement terms were negotiable" and failed to establish a viable defense); Hallock v. State of New York, 64 N.Y.2d 224, at 230, 485 N.Y.S.2d 510, 512-13 (1984).

819   *See* Bank of New York v. Betancourt, 950 N.Y.S.2d 721 (App. Term, 9th & 10th Jud. Dists. 2012). *Cf.* 208 Ave. A Assocs. v. Calanni, 5 N.Y.S.3d 330 (App. Term, 1st Dep't 2014) (judgment enforced where Landlord reasonably relied upon the actual or apparent authority of Tenant's counsel to negotiate settlement).

820   Dino Realty Corp. v. Khan, 3 N.Y.S.3d 259 (App. Term, 2d, 11th & 13th Jud. Dists. 2014).

821   Gerard Ct. Assocs., LLC v. Hamer, 31 N.Y.S.3d 921 (App. Term, 1st Dep't 2016).

822   Nu Horizons Manor v. Adderly, 951 N.Y.S.2d 87 (Suffolk Cnty. Dist. Ct. 2012); *see* Inland Diversified Real Estate Serv., LLC v. Keiko New York, Inc., 36 N.Y.S.3d 407 (App. Term, 9th & 10th Jud. Dists. 2016).

823   RSC [9 N.Y.C.R.R.] § 2520.13; *see* 8 Beach St. Realty Inc. v. Blagg, 20 N.Y.S.3d 291 (App. Term, 1st Dep't 2015).

stating that any default shall be deemed material".[824] In addition, the Court may <u>not</u> unilaterally change the terms of the parties' agreement to make the stipulation enforceable.[825]

Amendments to the Petition should be memorialized in the stipulation or, at minimum, placed on the record. For example, if the Petition alleges rent arrears for the months of January and February, but a settlement is not reached until March, and it is further agreed that March's rent is to be included in the Stipulation of Settlement, then the Petitioner must amend the Petition to include the rent for March. Otherwise, the March portion of the money judgment may <u>not</u> be enforced in the event of a dispute over compliance.[826]

It is prudent to require dispositive Stipulations of Settlement to be in writing. It goes without saying that the parties should carefully draft the stipulation to ensure the document accurately reflects that which was agreed. The Court will typically rely upon an otherwise unambiguous Stipulation of Settlement absent clear evidence that the document does not accurately reflect the parties' agreement.[827] To the extent the Court's pre-printed Settlement Form contradicts the parties' handwritten notations, the handwritten notes typically take precedent.[828]

A. RPAPL § 746–PRO SE SETTLEMENTS

The Legislature passed RPAPL § 746 to reduce ambiguity in settlement agreements involving *pro se* litigants. RPAPL § 746, as amended, effective September 26, 2009, requires the Court to "fully describe the terms of the stipulation" (other than for an adjournment or stay of the proceeding) to a *pro se* litigant. Accordingly, where a *pro se* litigant

---

824   135 Amersfort Assoc., LLC v. Jones, 20 N.Y.S.3d 292 (App. Term, 2d, 11th & 13th Jud. Dists. 2015).

825   *Id.* (error for the Court to unilaterally change due date of rent payments).

826   *See* Nathanson v. Mitchell, 836 N.Y.S.2d 487 (Nassau Cnty. Dist. Ct. 2007).

827   Banos v. Rhea, 25 N.Y.3d 266, 11 N.Y.S.3d 515 (2015); 615 Pelham Realty, Inc. v. Herring, 984 N.Y.S.2d 634 (App. Term, 1st Dep't 2014).

828   *See* Hudson Towers Hous. Co. v. VIP Yacht Cruises, Inc., 63 A.D.3d 413, 881 N.Y.S.2d 46 (App. Div., 1st Dep't 2009).

reaches a settlement, the individual may not simply send written correspondence or submit the Stipulation of Settlement to the Clerk. Instead, the parties must appear, and the Court will affirmatively explain that which was agreed.

If a *pro se* litigant reaches an out-of-court agreement and does not appear before the Court, then it may be proper to adjourn the case to another date. A default judgment will typically <u>not</u> be granted against a non-appearing Respondent without first adjourning the proceeding to another date in light of the proposed stipulation.

If the Respondent fails to appear on the adjourned date, then an application for a default judgment may be entertained and the relief granted will typically mirror the terms of the parties' agreement to the extent the Court has the authority to grant such relief. The parties should be mindful that the money judgment is limited to the amount sought in the Petition, unless previously amended, notwithstanding an agreement to include another month's rent in the proposed stipulation.

RPAPL § 746 does <u>not</u> specify the manner in which the Court must explain the terms of the stipulation to an unrepresented litigant. As such, where extreme circumstances warrant a deviation from Court protocol, such as where the *pro se* litigant is convalescing following a medical procedure or other exigent circumstances are demonstrated, the Court as a practical matter may wish to conduct a telephone conference on the record or implement alternative satisfactory methods to ensure compliance with the statutory requirements. Of course, the *pro se* litigant will have had to sign the Stipulation of Settlement.

The provisions of RPAPL § 746 are <u>not</u> applicable where both parties are represented by counsel. However, it is customary to confirm on the record that the attorneys explained the terms and obligations of the stipulation to their clients.

B. A SPOUSE MAY NOT BIND ANOTHER SPOUSE TO A SETTLEMENT

Where the Tenants are spouses and only one (1) spouse appears in Court, the appearing spouse may <u>not</u> sign on behalf of or bind the non-appearing spouse to a settlement agreement.[829] Provided proper service is alleged, the Court will typically enter a default judgment against the non-appearing spouse similar to the terms agreed to by the appearing spouse.[830] The money judgments may be for different amounts because only the amount sought in the Petition, unless previously amended, may be awarded against a non-appearing Tenant. The Court may require that the Petitioner confirms on the record that as long as the appearing spouse complies with the Stipulation of Settlement, the Petitioner will <u>not</u> seek to enforce the judgment and warrant against the non-appearing spouse. The same applies where the Respondents are not married.

C. LANDLORDS' ACCEPTANCE OF FUTURE RENT

1. STIPULATION CONSENTING TO JUDGMENT AND WARRANT WITH TIME TO PAY

Presume in a non-payment proceeding the parties reach a settlement which includes a final judgment of possession, a money judgment and a warrant of eviction, and the enforcement of the warrant of eviction is stayed for a definite period (e.g., three (3) months) to allow the Tenant to pay the arrears without an eviction. Further presume the

---

829 *See* N.Y. General Obligations Law § 3-305 (McKinney 2001); Pinpoint Techs. 3, LLC v. Mogilevsky, 15 N.Y.S.3d 714 (App. Term, 2d, 11th & 13th Jud. Dists. 2015) (breach of contract). A parent may <u>not</u> appear on behalf of her adult daughter. *See* 2701 Grand Assoc. LLC v. Morel, 31 N.Y.S.3d 924 (App. Term, 1st Dep't 2016).

830 *See 2701 Grand Assoc. LLC*, 31 N.Y.S.3d at 924 (vacating judgment against both co-Tenants, including the non-appearing co-Tenant, where rent overcharge claim asserted); *but see* Linden Lefferts, LLC v. Cox, 924 N.Y.S.2d 724 (App. Term, 2d, 11th & 13th Jud. Dists. 2011) (Subtenant's motion to vacate default granted where his spouse, also a Subtenant, entered into agreement with Landlord and other occupants).

parties agree that the Landlord is entitled to compensation for each additional month the Tenant remains in possession, and one (1) week after entering the agreement, the judgment and warrant of eviction are issued at Petitioner's request with the appropriate stay on execution.

For residential properties, the Petitioner will typically seek to include within the stipulation a provision that the money received for a period <u>following</u> the issuance of the judgment is "use and occupancy" (as opposed to rent) and/or that "future payments are <u>not</u> intended to revive the tenancy". Otherwise, the acceptance of subsequent payments may nullify the judgment of possession and warrant of eviction. The money judgment in favor of the Landlord would, however, remain unaffected.

Of note, in *368 Chauncey Ave. Trust v. Whitaker*, the judgment and warrant were upheld where the stipulation provided that "future payments are first to be applied to the current month's <u>rent</u>".[831] The Appellate Term denied a stay on execution of the warrant because the Tenant failed to substantially comply with the payment of rent arrears.[832] In any event, the appropriate term would have been "use and occupancy" because the payment of "rent" presumes the existence of a Landlord and Tenant relationship that requires vacating the judgment of possession and warrant of eviction due to the new tenancy. Use and occupancy, on the other hand, may be accepted at any time with jeopardizing the judgment and warrant.

For commercial properties, the Landlord's acceptance of rent for a future month following issuance of the judgment is permitted provided the parties did <u>not</u> intend to continue the tenancy. In other words, a commercial Landlord may accept the payment of rent following issuance of the judgment and warrant without vitiating the warrant provided there is no intent to revive the tenancy.[833]

---

831 368 Chauncey Ave. Trust v. Whitaker, 911 N.Y.S.2d 696 (App. Term, 2d, 11th & 13th Jud. Dists. 2010).

832 *Id.*

833 *See* First Citizens Nat'l Bank v. Koronowski, 46 A.D.3d 1474, at 1475, 848 N.Y.S.2d 494, 495 (App. Div., 4th Dep't 2007).

A prevailing Landlord in a non-payment proceeding may refrain from submitting a proposed judgment and warrant for a "reasonable period" of time and continue to accept the payment of rent without jeopardizing the award. However, in Suffolk County, a warrant may not be issued two (2) months following the award unless an adequate explanation for the delay is provided. Moreover, once issued, an inordinate delay prior to its execution may result in a "stale warrant". In some locations, the Sheriff will not enforce a warrant three (3) months following issuance. Upon a satisfactory explanation, however, the Court may issue a duplicate warrant. The parties should familiarize themselves with the local rules and protocols regarding the issuance and enforcement of judgments and warrants.

2. STIPULATION ACKNOWLEDGING RENTAL ARREARS ARE OWED WITHOUT A JUDGMENT

The parties may agree that the Tenant will be given time to pay the arrears <u>prior</u> to the issuance of a judgment. The consideration is typically the immediate issuance of a final judgment of possession and a warrant of eviction, without stay, plus a money judgment for all remaining unpaid rent arrears, if the Tenant fails to make a scheduled payment. To obtain the judgment, the Landlord may submit an *ex parte* (without notice) affidavit of non-compliance.

A finding of non-compliance with the stipulation may only be based upon the Tenant's failure to pay rent arrears. Non-compliance may <u>not</u> be based on the failure to pay a future month's rent.[834] Accordingly, many Landlords include within the stipulation that "all payments going forward will first be applied to the current month's rent with any additional monies thereafter applied to the arrears". This means that the Tenant <u>must</u> be current on both the rent and the rent arrears to be in compliance.[835] Absent such a provision, the monies would first

---

834 Fairgate Assocs., Inc. v. Adams, Index Nos. 37-02 and 570767-01, 2002 WL 1770719, 2002 N.Y. Misc. LEXIS 914 (App. Term, 1st Dep't July 29, 2002).

835 *See* 1215 Realty Assocs., LLC v. Thomas, 934 N.Y.S.2d 35 (App. Term, 2d, 11th & 13th Jud. Dists. 2011) (motion to stay execution of warrant of eviction denied where Tenant failed to pay rent while arrears were outstanding); *368 Chauncey Ave. Trust*, 911 N.Y.S.2d at 696.

be applied towards the arrears which would require the Landlord to commence a new summary proceeding if the Tenant failed to pay a subsequent month's rent.[836]

The parties should note that the failure to include a remedy for a default of the settlement agreement (e.g., the issuance of the final judgment of possession, money judgment and warrant of eviction) leaves the Court without authority to grant such relief even where non-compliance is demonstrated.[837] Of note, the Respondent may be inclined to pay the arrears in full before the next month's rent becomes due because once the arrears are satisfied, the non-payment proceeding is deemed resolved and the tenancy continues provided a judgment of possession and warrant of eviction have not been issued. In other words, if the arrears are paid in full, for example, in February (regardless of whether they are paid early or on schedule), then the failure to pay March's rent would not constitute a default, and the Petitioner would have to commence a new non-payment proceeding.

The above principles are illustrated in the following hypothetical situation. Presume the parties enter into a Stipulation of Settlement on December 15th. It is agreed that the monthly rent is $1,000; $800 in rent arrears are owed; and the arrears will be paid in two (2) equal installments of $400 on December 31st and January 10th. The parties further agree that all monies paid going forward are first to be applied to the current month's rent. Lastly, the January rent of $1,000 is due on January 1st.

If the arrears ($800) are paid before January 1st, then the Tenant is in compliance with the stipulation, and the failure to pay January's rent may not be a basis for granting a judgment or warrant. Instead, the Landlord would have to commence a new proceeding on proper notice for January's rent.

---

836   600 Hylan Assocs. v. Polshak, 851 N.Y.S.2d 74 (App. Term, 2d & 11th Jud. Dists. 2007); Nathanson v. Mitchell, 836 N.Y.S.2d 487 (Nassau Cnty. Dist. Ct. 2007).

837   *See* 133 Plus 24 Sanford Ave. Realty Corp. v. Ni, 7 N.Y.S.3d 819 (App. Term, 2d, 11th & 13th Jud. Dists. 2015); Gloria Homes Apts. LP v. Wilson, 17 N.Y.S.3d 382 (App. Term, 1st Dep't 2015) ("Since the parties' intent is not clear from the face of the stipulation, the hearing court should have made findings on the issue").

However, if the Tenant paid $400 on December 31st and an additional $1,000 on January 10th, and no payments are thereafter tendered, then the Tenant would <u>not</u> be in compliance and a judgment and warrant may be issued. This is because after applying the January 10th payment ($1,000) to the January rent, the Tenant would be delinquent on the second payment of rent arrears ($400).

STAYS AND ORDERS
TO SHOW CAUSE

The Court may, within its discretion, stay enforcement of a warrant of eviction. For "good cause", the Court may further vacate a judgment of possession and warrant of eviction prior to execution pursuant to RPAPL § 749(3). Otherwise, the Housing Part's authority to impose provisional remedies is extremely limited.

A. ORDERS TO SHOW CAUSE (VACATING JUDGMENTS)

1. 72-HOUR WRITTEN NOTICE

Following the expiration of all applicable stays, the Sheriff or Marshal must provide the Respondent with a 72-Hour Written Notice prior to the eviction.[838] The 72-Hour notice period, as amended in 2009, excludes Saturday, Sunday and public holidays.[839] The Sheriff's "failure to properly serve the 72-hour notice does not affect the validity of the final judgment".[840]

After receiving a 72-Hour Notice, a Respondent seeking to vacate a default judgment and/or additional time to remain in possession of the premises may submit an *ex parte* Order to Show Cause. The decision to grant a stay in connection with the Order to Show Cause is governed by

---

838   RPAPL § 749(2).

839   *Id.*

840   Capital 2000, LLC v. Tatum, Index No. 588-15, 2016 WL 4023034, 2016 N.Y. Misc. LEXIS 2751 (App. Term, 2d, 11th & 13th Jud. Dists. July 13, 2016) (emphasis added).

CPLR § 2201, which generally authorizes a stay of proceedings "upon such terms as may be just".

The parties should be mindful that the Court's granting of a stay does <u>not</u> vacate the warrant of eviction. Rather, it delays the eviction for as long as the stay remains in place.[841] Personal appearances are generally required for oral argument on the return date. However, where the Tenant is only seeking to vacate a money judgment, personal appearances may <u>not</u> be required.

The Court may further require the payment of use and occupancy for the additional time the Tenant remains in possession of the premises.[842] If the Court declines to sign a 72-Hour Order to Show Cause brought by a *pro se* Respondent, upon request, in some locations, including the District Courts, the motion papers are sent to the Appellate Court for review.

There is an exception to the 72-Hour Notice requirement where the occupant resides in a manufactured home park. If the park's Owner seeks to evict a mobile home Tenant (who owns the mobile home) due to the non-payment of rent or the eviction poses an immediate threat to the health, safety or welfare of the other Tenants, then the Sheriff must provide the occupant a Thirty-Day Written Notice before performing the eviction.[843] Where the Tenant does <u>not</u> own the mobile home, the Sheriff need only provide a 72-Hour Notice.[844]

Parenthetically, at any time after the Landlord prevails in a summary proceeding, the Clerk may issue the Respondent an "emergency letter". The emergency letter notifies the Department of Social Services, or other applicable governmental agency, that the occupant is in need of assistance finding a new residence and the earliest date an eviction may occur.

---

841 *See, e.g.*, BNS Bldgs., LLC v. Morgan, 847 N.Y.S.2d 900 (App. Term, 2d & 11th Jud. Dists. 2007) (affirming conditional stay upon proof of payment Landlord previously refused); Deutsche Bank Nat'l Trust Co. v. Oliver, 879 N.Y.S.2d 674, 676-77 (Nassau Cnty. Dist. Ct. 2009) (staying execution of warrant where Respondent demonstrated ample explanation for the request, including caring for her 92-year old mother who suffered from dementia).

842 The 6465 Realty Co. v. Tsugiyama, 15 N.Y.S.3d 715 (App. Term, 1st Dep't 2015).

843 RPL §§ 233(d)(2)-(3).

844 *Id.*, at § 233(d)(4).

2. GROUNDS TO VACATE A DEFAULT JUDGMENT
AND TRAVERSE HEARINGS

A Respondent may vacate a default judgment by providing (1) a reasonable excuse for the non-appearance or (2) establishing a lack of jurisdiction.[845] In addition to a stay on the execution of the warrant of eviction, the Respondent will typically seek a dismissal of the proceeding or, in the alternative, a hearing on the merits or a traverse hearing regarding service.

Excusable default may be satisfied by an allegation of illness or automobile breakdown on the hearing date. Plausible explanations further include seeking a stay within hours of the non-appearance where the Tenant missed the hearing due to a governmental agency's inspection of the premises;[846] a spouse failing to provide the papers that were served;[847] the Tenant being incarcerated;[848] the Tenant waiting in the "wrong" room of the Courthouse at the time of the default;[849] and a "detailed and credible excuse of law office failure".[850]

An undisclosed, incredulous "medical reason" may <u>not</u> be an

---

845   CPLR §§ 5015(a)(1),(4). *See* IGS Realty Co., L.P. v. James Catering, Inc., 99 A.D.3d 528, 952 N.Y.S.2d 162 (App. Div., 1st Dep't 2012); 903 Realty, LLC v. Michael, 943 N.Y.S.2d 793 (App. Term, 2d, 11th & 13th Jud. Dists. 2011) (motion to vacate default judgment denied due to inadequate explanation for the non-appearance); *but see* Inwood Gardens, Inc. v. Udoh, 26 N.Y.S.3d 213 (App. Term, 1st Dep't 2015) (motion granted where the non-appearance was "not willful", no prejudice resulted from the delay and a possible meritorious defense was asserted); Freire v. Fajardo, 958 N.Y.S.2d 307 (App. Term, 2d, 11th & 13th Jud. Dists. 2010) (default judgment vacated where the Housing Part implicitly communicated that the equitable defense of constructive ownership could not be asserted in a summary proceeding).

846   Jacob Marion, LLC v. Bey, 36 N.Y.S.3d 47 (App. Term, 2d, 11th & 13th Jud. Dists. 2016).

847   Stepping Stones Assocs. v. Garcia, 971 N.Y.S.2d 75 (App. Term, 9th & 10th Jud. Dists. 2013) (judgment vacated after the arrears were paid notwithstanding the lack of a meritorious defense).

848   46 Downing St. LLC v. Thompson, 998 N.Y.S.2d 306 (App. Term, 1st Dep't 2014).

849   Gates Towers, LLC v. Pfohl, Index No. 922-14, 2016 WL 4023958, 2016 N.Y. Misc. LEXIS 2746 (App. Term, 2d, 11th & 13th Jud. Dists. July 20, 2016).

850   Oakdale Manor Owners, Inc. v. Raimondi, 29 N.Y.S.3d 848 (App. Term, 9th & 10th Jud. Dists. 2015).

adequate excuse.[851] Moreover, an intentional default, such as the Tenant's "refusal to participate . . .[due to] unparticular allegations of 'bad faith on the court'", is similarly inexcusable.[852]

Case law has imposed the additional requirement that the Respondent asserts the possibility of a "meritorious defense".[853] For example, in a non-payment proceeding, potential meritorious defenses include, but are not limited to, the rent was paid, a subsequent agreement was reached with the Landlord or that a Warranty of Habitability claim exists entitling the Tenant to an offset against some or all of the rent. The failure to assert a potential meritorious defense necessitates denial of the motion.[854] The same requirements apply to holdover proceedings.

A lack of jurisdiction is itself a basis to vacate a default judgment.[855] Although the affidavit of service generally establishes the presumption of proper service, where the Respondent raises a sufficient basis to challenge service; i.e., the Respondent asserts more than conclusory denials, the Court may <u>not</u> rely solely on the affidavit of service.[856] However, the conclusory statement "I was never served" is <u>not</u> sufficient to require a

---

851   Dexter 345 Inc. v. Belem, 964 N.Y.S.2d 58 (App. Term, 1st Dep't 2012).

852   *See* Sobro Local Dev. Corp. v. Bey, 7 N.Y.S.3d 245 (App. Term, 1st Dep't 2014).

853   *See, e.g., Jacob Marion, LLC,* 36 N.Y.S.3d at 47; Gist v. Mack, 950 N.Y.S.2d 608 (App. Term, 2d, 11th & 13th Jud. Dists. 2012) (granting motion to vacate default judgment and remitting matter for an inquest); Neck Rd. One Realty, LLC v. Artdent, Inc., 950 N.Y.S.2d 724 (App. Term, 2d, 11th & 13th Jud. Dists. 2012) (motion denied); Cymo Trading Corp. v. Manhattan Inn Hostel, LLC, 943 N.Y.S.2d 791 (App. Term, 1st Dep't 2012) (same); Good Realty, LLC v. Weingarten, 936 N.Y.S.2d 58 (App. Term, 2d, 11th & 13th Jud. Dists. 2011); 160-62 E. 2nd St. H.D.F.C. v. Beaumont, 920 N.Y.S.2d 243 (App. Term, 1st Dep't 2010).

854   *See, e.g.,* Hope Founders v. Williams, Index No. 570350-15, 2016 WL 1843224, 2016 N.Y. Misc. LEXIS 1593 (App. Term, 1st Dep't May 3, 2016).

855   *See* F & Realty Corp. v. 1014 Flatbush Ave., Inc., 969 N.Y.S.2d 802 (App. Term, 2d, 11th & 13th Jud. Dists. 2013) (vacating default judgment and dismissing Petition where Landlord failed to mail a copy of the Notice of Petition and Petition to Tenant's known corporate address following service on a person of suitable age and discretion); RR Reo, II, LLC v. Omeje, 939 N.Y.S.2d 743 (App. Term, 2d, 11th & 13th Jud. Dists. 2011) (vacating default judgment and dismissing Petition due to defective service).

856   In a foreclosure proceeding, the Appellate Division, Second Department accepted the process server's second affidavit of service as *prima facie* evidence of proper service where the original affidavit was insufficient. *See* Deutsche Bank Nat'l Trust Co. v. Quinones, 114 A.D.3d 719, 981 N.Y.S.2d 107 (App. Div., 2d Dep't 2014).

traverse hearing.[857]

On the other hand, a credible statement from the Respondent that he or she "was not at home" when personal service is alleged or the listing of an improper address and/or description of the person allegedly served will usually suffice. A sworn statement from the Tenant that "she was home all day" on the purported date of service but "nobody knocked on her door or otherwise attempted to serve her personally on that date" similarly resulted in a traverse hearing.[858]

It is worth repeating that where the Respondent adequately alleges improper service, the Court <u>must</u> conduct a traverse hearing.[859] The burden is on the proponent of service to establish that process was properly served,[860] and exclusive reliance on the affidavit of service is impermissible.[861] If the traverse is sustained, then the default judgment must be vacated, and the proceeding will be dismissed due to the lack of personal jurisdiction.

A process server in New York City must bring "all records…relating to the matter at issue" to the traverse hearing, including the log book

---

857   *See* Medhat O'Kelly, As Administrator of the Estate of Magdy O'Kelly v. "John Doe", 36 N.Y.S.3d 408 (App. Term, 2d, 11th & 13th Jud. Dists. 2016); LC & Assocs. v. Deans, Index No. 1423-01, 2002 WL 31956037, 2002 N.Y. Misc. LEXIS 1693 (App. Term, 9th & 10th Jud. Dists. Sept. 19, 2002) (movant's conclusory statement "I was not served" is insufficient to vacate judgment).

858   West 97th St. Realty Corp. v. Aptaker, Index No. 78484–15, 2016 WL 344157, 2016 N.Y. Misc. LEXIS 230 (N.Y. Civ. Ct. Jan. 25, 2016).

859   *See* 342 E. 67 Realty LLC v. Jacobs, 106 A.D.3d 610, 966 N.Y.S.2d 46 (App. Div., 1st Dep't 2013); 502 Ave. P Corp. v. AM & R Auto Repair Shop, 29 N.Y.S.3d 847 (App. Term, 2d, 11th & 13th Jud. Dists. 2015).

860   *See, e.g.*, Bruckner by the Bridge, LLC v. Gonzales, 18 N.Y.S.3d 577 (N.Y. Civ. Ct. 2015) (traverse sustained where the process server lacked independent recollection of the service and his Logbook was "unreliable"). At a traverse hearing, the Petitioner bears the burden of demonstrating service was properly effectuated by a preponderance of the evidence. *See* Frankel v. Schilling, 149 A.D.2d 657, at 659, 540 N.Y.S.2d 469, 470-71 (App. Div., 2d Dep't 1989); Forest Hills S. Owners, Inc. v. Ishida, 943 N.Y.S.2d 791 (App. Term, 2d, 11th & 13th Jud. Dists. 2011).

861   *502 Ave. P Corp.*, 29 N.Y.S.3d at 847; *see* 77 Commercial Holding, LLC v. Central Plastic, Inc., 4 N.Y.S.3d 464 (App. Term, 2d, 11th & 13th Jud. Dists. 2014); Bham v. Wilson, 809 N.Y.S.2d 776, 777 (App. Term, 9th & 10th Jud. Dists. 2005).

and license where applicable.[862] However, section 208.1 of the Uniform Rules for the New York City Civil Courts provides that these requirements may be waived where good cause is shown and in the interest of justice.[863]

3. UNDERTAKING AS A CONDITION FOR A STAY

If the Order to Show Cause is signed, the Respondent may be directed to post an undertaking with the Court as a condition for the stay. If the Respondent fails to post the undertaking, the Court must still decide the motion on the merits because a denial on the grounds that the undertaking was <u>not</u> posted constitutes reversible error.[864]

4. DECIDING THE ORDER TO SHOW CAUSE

Since the parties, at times, reach a settlement on the return date of the Order to Show Cause, it is worthwhile to have the parties conference the matter. If a resolution is unobtainable and the motion is granted, then the judgment and warrant of eviction may be vacated and the case dismissed, a hearing may be held on the merits, or a traverse hearing scheduled where service is sufficiently disputed. On other occasions, the judgment of possession and warrant of eviction may stand, but the money judgment will be reduced.

If the motion is denied, then the Court will typically lift the stay and authorize enforcement of the judgment and warrant of eviction. The Court may, in its discretion, further extend the stay notwithstanding

---

862   *See* N.Y. UNIFORM RULES FOR NEW YORK CITY CIVIL COURT [22 N.Y.C.R.R.] § 208.29; AMB Fund III New York III & IV, LLC v. WWTL Logistics, Inc., 942 N.Y.S.2d 307 (App. Term, 2d, 11th & 13th Jud. Dists. 2012). This rule applies to process servers in any city with a minimum of one (1) million residents. *See* GENERAL BUSINESS LAW § 89-cc.

863   *See* N.Y. UNIFORM RULES FOR NEW YORK CITY CIVIL COURT [22 N.Y.C.R.R.] § 208.1; *AMB Fund III New York III & IV, LLC*, 942 N.Y.S.2d at 307. *But see* First Commercial Bank of Memphis, N.A. v. Ndiaye, 733 N.Y.S.2d 562 (Queens Cnty. Sup. Ct. 2001) (action dismissed where good cause was <u>not</u> shown for the process server's failure to comply with the statutory requirements).

864   *See* Parkview Equities, LLC v. Coughlin, 986 N.Y.S.2d 866 (App. Term, 9th & 10th Jud. Dists. 2014); Zabolotny v. Andersen, 859 N.Y.S.2d 907 (App. Term, 9th & 10th Jud. Dists. 2008).

the denial of the motion.[865] Absent a specific ruling to the contrary, the Sheriff must provide another 72 Hour Notice.

B. VACATING THE WARRANT (RPAPL § 749(3))

RPAPL § 749(3) permits the Court to vacate a warrant of eviction for "good cause" even where the Tenant fails to offer a reasonable explanation for the default and/or a meritorious defense.[866] Although this provision is typically asserted in connection with the Respondent's motion to vacate a default judgment, there is no statutory requirement limiting the relief to default situations.[867]

It is noteworthy that the statute refers to vacating the warrant of eviction provided the warrant has <u>not</u> been executed. Case law has held that under "appropriate circumstances", the warrant may be vacated and the Tenant restored to possession <u>following</u> the eviction.[868] For example, the Appellate Term, First Department granted a Tenant's motion to be restored to possession where the Tenant acted in good faith, resumed working and paid all of the arrears, eviction costs and Landlord's attorney's fees.[869]

The "[m]ere payment of rent arrears, in and of itself, does not

---

865   *See* 191 St. Assocs. LLC v. Cruz, 29 N.Y.S.3d 848 (App. Term, 1st Dep't 2016) (extending the stay an additional 60 days following denial of Tenant's motion); Waterside Plaza, LLC v. Bhawnaney, 943 N.Y.S.2d 795 (App. Term, 1st Dep't 2012).

866   *See* Birchwood Ct. Owners, Inc. v. Toner, 37 N.Y.S.3d 206 (App. Term, 9th & 10th Jud. Dists. 2016).

867   *See* RPAPL § 749(3). *Cf.* Landmark Props. v. Olivo, 805 N.Y.S.2d 774, 778 (App. Term, 9th & 10th Jud. Dists. 2005) (holding RPAPL § 749(3) is not applicable in a holdover proceeding because the tenancy was terminated (or never existed) prior to the commencement of the summary proceeding "[a]nd the courts are without power to revive the lease, whether through RPAPL § 749(3) or any other mechanism").

868   *See, e.g.,* In re Lafayette Boynton Hous. Corp. v. Pickett, 135 A.D.3d 518, 23 N.Y.S.3d 204 (App. Div., 1st Dep't 2016) (disabled Tenant paid $14,030.59 and made good faith attempts to secure financial assistance for remaining amounts due) (*citing* Brusco v. Braun, 84 N.Y.2d 674, 621 N.Y.S.2d 291 (1994)); *Birchwood Ct. Owners, Inc.*, 37 N.Y.S.3d at 206 (directing Landlord to restore Tenant to possession provided the arrears and use and occupancy are paid within 20 days).

869   2203 Belmont Realty Corp. v. Gant, 36 N.Y.S.3d 410 (App. Term, 1st Dep't 2016).

constitute [the requisite] good cause to vacate the warrant of eviction after issuance of same".[870] Similarly, it has been held that the "[d]ifficulty in obtaining funds" fails to justify vacating the judgment or warrant.[871] RPAPL § 749(3) motions are determined on a case-by-case basis, but where the motion is granted, the money judgment may stand.[872]

---

870 32-05 Newton Ave. Assocs. v. Hailazopoulos, 645 N.Y.S.2d 260, 261-62 (App. Term, 2d & 11th Jud. Dists. 1996); Sherwood Complex, LLC v. Dunn, 897 N.Y.S.2d 672 (App. Term, 2d, 11th & 13th Jud. Dists. 2009); Freedom Capital, LLC v. Pumilio, 816 N.Y.S.2d 695 (App. Term, 9th & 10th Jud. Dists. 2006).

871 *Waterside Plaza, LLC,* 943 N.Y.S.2d at 795; 601 W. Realty, LLC v. Castro, 938 N.Y.S.2d 230 (App. Term, 1st Dep't 2011) (*citing* Chelsea 19 Assocs. v. James, 67 A.D.3d 601, 889 N.Y.S.2d 564 (App. Div., 1st Dep't 2009)).

872 *See, e.g.,* 16 Apt. Assoc., Inc. v. Lewis, 827 N.Y.S.2d 441, 442-43 (App. Term, 9th & 10th Jud. Dists. 2006); Kew Gardens NY, LLC v. Saltos, 814 N.Y.S.2d 891 (App. Term, 2d & 11th Jud. Dists. 2006).

CHAPTER 14

SECURITY DEPOSIT

The security deposit is not rent, but rather funds the Landlord holds in trust for the Tenant until <u>after</u> the Tenant vacates the premises.[873] If the premises are returned in an acceptable condition, then the Landlord is typically required to return the security deposit.[874] However, upon a default by the Tenant, the Landlord may be permitted to use the security deposit "as a setoff against amounts owed" for damages.[875] Typically, the Landlord will apply the security deposit to make repairs for property damage, other than ordinary wear and tear, caused by the Tenant and/or its guests.[876]

The security deposit may be applied towards rent arrears or in satisfaction of a judgment, but only where the rental agreement so provides and/or with the consent of both parties.[877] It has been held, however, that where the Landlord regained possession and has no claims for damages (excluding the money judgment in the summary proceeding), the security deposit may be used to satisfy the money judgment

---

873   *See generally* Anagen, Inc. v. Damasco, 906 N.Y.S.2d 777 (App. Term, 1st Dep't 2009).

874   Pepe v. Clifford, 28 N.Y.S.3d 650 (App. Term, 9th & 10th Jud. Dists. 2015); Castillo v. Galvano, 18 N.Y.S.3d 577 (App. Term, 9th & 10th Jud. Dists. 2015).

875   Ankhbara v. Sharplis-Espirit, 16 N.Y.S.3d 791 (App. Term, 9th & 10th Jud. Dists. 2015) (directing return of security deposit, less an offset for repairs to the stove and bank charge fee).

876   *See* Vanchev v. Mulligan, Index No. 2350-14, 2016 WL 4021103, 2016 N.Y. Misc. LEXIS 2759 (App. Term, 2d, 11th & 13th Jud. Dists. July 13, 2016).

877   *See generally* 501 Fifth Ave. Co., LLC v. Aslam, 136 A.D.3d 535, 25 N.Y.S.3d 180 (App. Div., 1st Dep't 2016).

because the security is then considered to be a liquidated claim.[878]

The Landlord must provide the Tenant with the name and address of the financial institution where the deposit is maintained and the amount.[879] Generally, absent an agreement to the contrary, the Landlord has no obligation to deposit the security in an interest-bearing account. If, however, a residential building contains "six or more family dwelling units", then pursuant to General Obligations Law § 7-103(2-a), the security must be deposited in an interest-bearing account. This statute has been interpreted to mean that when the Landlord owns six (6) or more of the apartments within a building, the security deposit must accrue interest absent an agreement to the contrary.[880]

The security deposit for a rent-stabilized apartment may not exceed the value of one (1) month's rent, and the deposit must be deposited in an interest-bearing account.[881] The Housing Part may not include an unpaid security deposit within the money judgment even where the parties consent to its inclusion in a Stipulation of Settlement.[882]

After the Tenant surrenders possession, the Tenant may seek to recover an unlawfully withheld security deposit either in a plenary action or a properly asserted counterclaim in the summary proceeding.[883] If successful, the Tenant would be awarded a money judgment for the unreturned security deposit because the Housing Part is unable to direct that the Landlord or its attorneys release funds held in escrow (including a security deposit).[884] The Tenant may similarly be awarded a

---

878   *See* D & B Enters. No. 2 v. Cablam Inc., 729 N.Y.S.2d 239 (App. Term, 9th & 10th Jud. Dists. 2001) (the lease failed to include a survival clause).

879   N.Y. GENERAL OBLIGATIONS LAW § 7-103(2).

880   *See* Pritzker v. Park South Lofts LLC, 920 N.Y.S.2d 243 (N.Y. Cnty. Sup. Ct. 2010); Government of the Rep. of South Africa v. Sonsino, 6554-CV-10, 2011 WL 4357381, 2011 U.S. Dist. LEXIS 105773 (S.D.N.Y. Sept. 16, 2011).

881   *See* RSC [9 N.Y.C.R.R.] § 2525.4.

882   Hines v. Ambrose, 907 N.Y.S.2d 437 (App. Term, 9th & 10th Jud. Dists. 2010).

883   *See generally* Posh NY, Inc. v. Lobern Dev. Co., LLC, 924 N.Y.S.2d 311 (App. Term, 9th & 10th Jud. Dists. 2011). The statute of limitations for the unlawful withholding of a security deposit is six (6) years. *See* Sharaf v. Younger, Index No. 372-15, 2016 WL 4798948, 2016 N.Y. Misc. LEXIS 3235 (App. Term, 2d, 11th & 13th Jud. Dists. Sept. 7, 2016).

884   Deutsch v. G. Shore III Dev. Corp., 875 N.Y.S.2d 819 (App. Term, 9th & 10th Jud.

money judgment for the security deposit where the Tenant vacates the premises after discovering the unlawful status of the property, such as the Landlord's failure to obtain a valid rental permit.[885]

A. LANDLORD'S RETENTION OF THE SECURITY DEPOSIT WHERE THE TENANT DOES NOT TAKE POSSESSION

The Landlord may retain the security deposit where the Tenant failed to provide timely notice that it would <u>not</u> take possession of the premises.[886] However, the deposit must be returned if the property was not in move-in or habitable condition at the time the lease commenced.[887] Moreover, both the security deposit and any rent previously paid may be recovered in a plenary action where the Tenant did <u>not</u> take possession after discovering the Landlord rented the premises to another party.[888]

B. UNLAWFUL CONVERSION/COMMINGLING OF THE SECURITY DEPOSIT

Since the relationship between a Landlord and Tenant was changed by General Obligations Law § 7-103 "from [that of] debtor-creditor, to trustee-cestui que trust", the Landlord holds a security deposit similar to that of a trustee.[889] As a result, the Landlord has a duty to refrain from commingling the security deposit with its own funds even where

Dists. 2008); World Realty Corp. v. Consumer Sales, Inc., 862 N.Y.S.2d 812 (App. Term, 9th & 10th Jud. Dists. 2005).

885   Ader v. Guzman, 135 A.D.3d 671, 23 N.Y.S.3d 292 (App. Div., 2d Dep't 2016); Sethi v. Naman, 890 N.Y.S.2d 371 (App. Term, 9th & 10th Jud. Dists. 2009). *See* Illegal Apartments *supra*, Chapter 8 subdiv. B.

886   *See* Ally v. Latchman, 886 N.Y.S.2d 69 (App. Term, 2d, 11th & 13th Jud. Dists. 2009).

887   Siudym v. Sicherer, 901 N.Y.S.2d 910 (App. Term, 9th & 10th Jud. Dists. 2009); Ilacqua v. Sameyah, 880 N.Y.S.2d 873 (App. Term, 9th & 10th Jud. Dists. 2009).

888   *See* Butten v. Maggio Realty LLC, 7 N.Y.S.3d 240 (App. Div., 1st Dep't 2014).

889   N.Y. GENERAL OBLIGATIONS LAW § 7-103 (McKinney 2001). *See* LeRoy v. Sayers, 217 A.D.2d 63, at 67-68, 635 N.Y.S.2d 217, 220-21 (App. Div., 1st Dep't 1995); Finnerty v. Freeman, 673 N.Y.S.2d 843, 844 (App. Term, 9th & 10th Jud. Dists. 1998).

the Tenant breaches the rental agreement (e.g., failed to pay rent).[890]

The failure to provide the Tenant written notice of the financial institution where the security is deposited, in violation of General Obligations Law § 7-103, permits an inference that the Landlord co-mingled the security deposit with personal funds.[891] If the security deposit is commingled, then the Landlord forfeits the right to avail itself of the funds for any purpose, and the Tenant is entitled to its immediate return.[892] However, if the Landlord re-deposits the co-mingled security into a segregated account <u>prior</u> to the expiration of the rental agreement and/or a demand for the return of the security deposit, then the Landlord revives its right to hold the deposit.[893]

A lease provision permitting the Landlord to commingle the security deposit is null and void.[894] Although a setoff "[a]llows entities that owe each other money to apply their mutual debts against each other, thereby avoiding the absurdity of making A pay B when B owes A",[895]

---

890   *See* Hansen v. Lorenzo, 901 N.Y.S.2d 906 (Suffolk Cnty. Dist. Ct. 2009).

891   Gihon, LLC v. 501 Second St., LLC, 103 A.D.3d 840, 962 N.Y.S.2d 238 (App. Div., 2d Dep't 2013).

892   Solomon v. Ness, 118 A.D.3d 773, 987 N.Y.S.2d 220 (App. Div., 2d Dep't 2014); Paterno v. Carroll, 75 A.D.3d 625, at 628, 905 N.Y.S.2d 653, 655-56 (App. Div., 2d Dep't 2010); Matter of Perfection Tech. Servs. Press, Inc., 22 A.D.2d 352, at 356, 256 N.Y.S.2d 166, 170 (App. Div., 2d Dep't 1965); Dan Klores Assocs. v. Abramoff, 288 A.D.2d 121, at 121-22, 733 N.Y.S.2d 388 (App. Div., 1st Dep't 2001) (a Landlord who commingles the security deposit may not use the deposit to "offset ... justifiable repair costs after the tenant vacates"); Kelligrew v. Lynch, 784 N.Y.S.2d 921 (App. Term, 9th & 10th Jud. Dists. 2004) (the "[t]enant's failure to comply with the terms of a lease is not a defense to a landlord's breach of the duty not to commingle the [security] deposit with personal funds"); Vidipax, LLC v. Brown Bear Realty Corp., 880 N.Y.S.2d 228 (N.Y. Cnty. Sup. Ct. 2009) ("[Where there is] commingling at the time of lease expiration ... [the Landlord] forfeited any right ... to avail himself of the security deposit for any purpose entitling plaintiff to its immediate return notwithstanding that plaintiff may have breached the lease") (internal citations omitted).

893   *See* McMaster v. Pearse, 804 N.Y.S.2d 640, 643 n.2 (N.Y. Civ. Ct. 2005) (*citing* MILTON R. FRIEDMAN, FRIEDMAN ON LEASES § 20.4 [Nature of Security Deposit–Statutes], at 1293 (4th ed. 1997) ("[The] Landlord's right to the security [deposit] is revived if the commingling ceases before tenant brings an action to recover the deposit. But segregation after expiration of the term and [vacating] by tenant is held too late for such revival")).

894   N.Y. GENERAL OBLIGATIONS LAW § 7-103(3); *see Solomon*, 118 A.D.3d at 773, 987 N.Y.S.2d at 220.

895   *See generally* Westinghouse Credit Corp. v. D'Urso, 278 F.3d 138, 149 (2d Cir. 2002) (citations omitted).

the Landlord may <u>not</u> use a commingled security deposit as an offset against unpaid rent because a trustee (Landlord) is prohibited from offsetting an obligation of a trust beneficiary (Tenant).[896] However, "[t]he same logic does not pertain where a tenant seeks to apply the security deposit to reduced amounts found owing to the landlord".[897] In other words, the Tenant may offset the commingled security deposit against the rents owed. If no rent is owed, then the Tenant may be awarded the security deposit as damages in a summary proceeding where the claim was timely asserted as a counterclaim, or, otherwise, the Tenant may commence a plenary action for the return of the deposit.

Where there are multiple Landlords, but only one (1) commingles the security deposit, liability may be awarded against either or both, even the non-commingling Landlord, due to the trustee relationship with the Tenant. This is because a non-converting Landlord is responsible for a partner's violation of the fiduciary relationship.[898] Where there is a conversion of the security deposit, the Tenant is entitled to interest from the earliest date of the conversion.[899]

Finally, a lease provision waiving the Tenant's right to the security deposit is void. For example, a lease provision that provides, "[s]hould the Tenant default under the terms of this lease, Tenant will forfeit [the] security and waive all rights to it", is unenforceable.[900]

---

896 *Matter of Perfection Tech. Servs. Press, Inc.*, 256 N.Y.S.2d at 170; *Westinghouse Credit Corp.*, 278 F.3d at 149. *See generally* Fore Improvement Corp. v. Selig, 278 F.2d 143 (2d Cir. 1960).

897 23 E. 39th St. Mgmt. Corp. v. 23 E. 39th St. Developer, 134 A.D.3d 629, 23 N.Y.S.3d 33 (App. Div., 1st Dep't 2015).

898 *See McMaster*, 804 N.Y.S.2d at 647 ("[t]he obligation [of a landlord relating to security deposits] ... do[es] not permit a cofiduciary to claim exemption from responsibility based upon passivity, ignorance of the law, or even the contrary advice of counsel"); Matter of the Estate of Rothko, 43 N.Y.2d 305, at 320, 401 N.Y.S.2d 449, 455 (1977) (an "executor [fiduciary] who knows that his coexecutor is committing breaches of trust and not only fails to exert efforts directed towards prevention but accedes to them is legally accountable even though he was acting on the advice of counsel").

899 *23 E. 39th St. Mgmt. Corp.*, 134 A.D.3d at 632, 23 N.Y.S.3d at 33; *Vidipax, LLC*, 880 N.Y.S.2d at 228.

900 *Hansen*, 901 N.Y.S.2d at 906. *See* GENERAL OBLIGATIONS LAW § 7-103(3).

APPENDICES

APPENDIX A

FREQUENTLY ASKED QUESTIONS

1. **Does the Housing Part determine the lawful owner of the property in a summary proceeding?**

   No. The Court's authority in a summary proceeding is to determine who has or is entitled to "rightful possession" of the subject premises at a particular time. Although "ownership", or at least a demonstration of a superior possessory interest in the premises, may be an element of the Petitioner's case, the Court lacks the authority to make a determination regarding the lawful owner or the holder of the title. Instead, the Court may adjudicate the issue of title for the limited purpose of determining the right to possession, but the ruling is <u>not</u> binding and does not preclude a subsequent determination on ownership in a court of competent jurisdiction (e.g., New York State Supreme Court). An exception to this rule is where the Tenant asserts the defense of title by adverse possession. In that case, if the Landlord prevails in the summary proceeding, the Tenant may be barred from raising the issue in another forum. However, if the Tenant successfully asserts the defense in the summary proceeding, then there is no collateral estoppel and the issue may be raised again in another court proceeding (*see* Chapters 1 and 8(H)).

2. **What are the common types of Landlord and Tenant summary proceedings?**

   There are Landlord and Tenant summary proceedings to recover possession of real property and special proceedings to remedy conditions dangerous to life, health or safety. Summary proceedings to recover possession of real property pursuant to the RPAPL are by far the more common of the proceedings, and they include non-payment and holdover proceedings. Both non-payment and holdover summary proceedings seek to recover the possession of real property. The distinction rests with the parties' relationship. A non-payment proceeding presupposes the existence of a Landlord and Tenant relationship and a default in the payment of rent. A holdover proceeding presupposes that a Landlord and Tenant relationship was either terminated or expired at the time the summary proceeding was commenced, or such a relationship never existed (*see* Chapter 2).

3. If the Landlord is successful in a summary proceeding, what will the Court award?

Regardless of the type of summary proceeding, the Landlord seeks a judgment of possession (lawful possession of the property) and a warrant of eviction. The warrant of eviction is the instrument that permits the eviction if the Tenant does not voluntarily vacate the premises. In a non-payment proceeding, the issuance of the judgment of possession and warrant of eviction terminates the tenancy. The Landlord may further seek a money judgment for unpaid rent and any reasonable item identified as "additional" rent within a written lease (e.g., reasonable attorney's fees, utilities bills etc.). In a holdover proceeding, the Landlord may seek the same monetary relief, plus use and occupancy for the fair and reasonable value of the Tenant's occupation of the premises in the absence of a Landlord and Tenant relationship (*see* Chapters 1 and 2).

4. Is there a dollar limit on the amount of rent or use and occupancy the Landlord may be awarded in the Housing Part?

No. Unlike the civil part of the Court that may have a maximum dollar jurisdictional limit, there is no dollar limit on the amount of rent and/or use and occupancy awarded in a summary proceeding (*see* Chapter 1).

5. **If the Tenant or the Tenant's guests caused damage to the property, may the Housing Part award the Landlord damages?**

No. Although the destruction of the premises by the Tenant may be grounds to terminate the rental agreement, the Housing Part has no authority to award the Landlord damages. The Landlord may, however, seek monetary damages in a plenary action in the civil part of the Court or other court of competent jurisdiction absent a waiver (*see* Chapter 1).

6. **What happens if the Landlord is unsuccessful on her claims?**

In a summary proceeding, the Landlord has the burden of proving her case by a fair preponderance of the evidence. Otherwise, the matter will be dismissed. If the dismissal is based upon a determination on the merits (e.g., following a hearing), then the case will be dismissed "with prejudice". The Landlord would then be prohibited from bringing another proceeding for the same term, but may commence a new action for a future breach after serving a new predicate notice. If the case is dismissed due to improper service (e.g., the Notice of Petition and/or Petition were not served properly and/or in a timely manner) or the Landlord chooses to withdraw the proceeding prior to a decision on the merits, then the case will typically be dismissed "without prejudice", which means another proceeding for the same term may be commenced after another predicate notice is served (*see* Chapters 2, 3 and 6).

7. **Does the Landlord have to name all of the Tenants identified in the lease in a summary proceeding?**

Yes. The Landlord's failure to name all of the Tenants in a summary proceeding warrants dismissal. This is the case because each Tenant is both a "proper" and a "necessary" party to the proceeding. The decision to name a Subtenant is left to the discretion of the Landlord. A Subtenant is considered a "proper" but <u>not</u> a "necessary" party, and therefore does not have to be named. However, a Subtenant not named in a summary proceeding will <u>not</u> be included on the judgment of possession or warrant of eviction. It has been held that the spouse and adult children of a Tenant need not be named or served in a summary proceeding unless they have an "independent possessory right" to the subject premises (*see* Chapter 4).

8. May a Landlord enforce a lease guaranty in a summary proceeding?

No. The Landlord may not sue the Guarantor for money damages in a summary proceeding. In fact, the Guarantor may not be named in the Petition unless the Guarantor has an "independent possessory right" to the premises. The Landlord may commence a plenary action in a court of competent jurisdiction to enforce the Guaranty (*see* Chapter 4).

9. What happens if the Tenant does not appear in Court?

The Landlord will generally be awarded a judgment of possession, a money judgment for unpaid rent and/or use and occupancy in addition to reasonable "additional" rent items pursuant to a written lease, and a warrant of eviction provided the pleadings are facially sufficient and proper service is alleged. If rent for a new period becomes due on or before the hearing date, the Landlord may not amend the Petition for a higher dollar amount when the Tenant is not present (*see* Chapter 5).

10. When does the Notice of Petition and Petition have to be served? Who may serve the papers?

Other than non-payment proceedings in New York City, service must generally be completed no fewer than five (5) days but not more than twelve (12) days prior to the hearing date. This is referred to as the "5 and 12 Rule". In New York, there are three (3) ways to serve process—personal delivery, suitable age and discretion, and conspicuous place service ("nail and mail"). The Court does not count the "day of reckoning" (i.e., the date service is completed) when computing whether service was timely. However, the day the proceeding is to be heard is counted. Where the last day for service falls on a Saturday, Sunday or public holiday, the time to complete service is extended to the next business day. Service may not be made on Sunday or other religious observance day. Any non-party individual over the age of 18 years of age may serve the Notice of Petition and Petition. In New York City, a process server is required to maintain and bring a log book to the traverse hearing (hearing on service), although this requirement may be waived for good cause and in the interest of justice (*see* Chapters 6 and 13).

11. Is the Tenant required to serve and file an Answer to the Petition?

The Tenant may (not required) formally respond to the Petition on or before the initial Court date (i.e., return date), either orally or in writing, by denying all or a portion of the allegations and asserting affirmative defenses. The Answer, unlike the Petition, need <u>not</u> be verified when in writing, and its purpose is to frame the issues before the Court, preserve the right of appeal and maintain the ability to assert related claims in another action. The failure to submit an Answer does <u>not</u> preclude the Tenant from asserting defenses at the hearing. There are two (2) notable exceptions. First, where the Petition is served between eight (8) and twelve (12) days before the return date, the Petitioner may require that an Answer is served at least three (3) days prior to the hearing. The second exception applies to non-payment proceedings in New York City where the Tenant must answer the Petition within five (5) days of service (*see* Chapter 7).

12. May the Tenant file counterclaims for damages against the Landlord?

Yes. The Tenant may file counterclaims for an unlimited dollar amount in a summary proceeding with the exception of the Justice Courts, where counterclaims are limited to a maximum of $3,000. The Housing Part may, within its discretion, dismiss a counterclaim without prejudice to commencement of a plenary action where the counterclaim is insufficiently plead, unclear and/or otherwise not properly before the Housing Part. A lease provision prohibiting counterclaims is generally enforceable provided the counterclaims are not "inextricably intertwined" with the Petitioner's underlying claim (*see* Chapter 7).

13. Are there jury trials in a summary proceeding?

Yes. Although infrequently requested, the Landlord may demand a jury trial provided the jury fee is paid prior to the hearing. The Respondent may similarly demand a jury trial provided the jury fee is paid at either the time of the Answer or the return date of the Notice of Petition and Petition. Otherwise, a jury trial is deemed waived (check the Court's rules regarding jury trials). Generally, a lease provision barring a trial by jury will be enforced (*see* Chapter 7).

14. Since the Housing Part is <u>not</u> a Court of equity, are there any affirmative defenses that may not be asserted in a summary proceeding?

No. A Respondent may assert any affirmative defense whether based in law and/or equity in a summary proceeding (*see* Chapters 8 and 9).

15. Is the Tenant required to pay rent for an "illegal" apartment?

Depends, but in most circumstances the answer is Yes. Outside New York City, there is generally no bar prohibiting a Landlord from collecting or being awarded rent and/or use and occupancy for an illegal apartment. However, if the local governing administrative body passes a law or resolution making it unlawful to collect rent on a property that lacks a rental permit or a proper certificate of occupancy, then the unpaid rent or use and occupancy will <u>not</u> be awarded. Moreover, if the illegal apartment is a multiple dwelling in a town or municipality of more than 325,000 people, then unpaid rent and use and occupancy will similarly not be awarded to the Landlord (*see* Chapter 8).

16. Is an attorney required to represent the Landlord and Tenant in a summary proceeding?

An individual may choose to represent him- or herself, but it is not recommended because summary proceedings are highly specialized and strict compliance with the applicable laws is required. A duly authorized agent (i.e., counsel) may commence a summary proceeding on behalf of the Landlord. However, a Power of Attorney does <u>not</u>

constitute a duly authorized representative. Both corporations and limited liability companies must be represented by counsel. In addition, the Appellate Term for the Second, Eleventh and Thirteenth Judicial Districts recently held that partnerships and limited partnerships must also be represented by counsel (*see* Chapter 11).

17. If the Tenants are husband and wife, do they both need to appear in Court?

A party who fails to appear may be held in default where service was properly effectuated. This includes the situation where the Respondents are married. Due to the fact an individual may <u>not</u> bind his or her spouse to a settlement agreement, the Court may instead apply the same terms in the form of a default judgment against the non-appearing spouse. If a settlement is reached where the appearing spouse acknowledges owing rent arrears and is provided an opportunity to pay the arrears over a period of time prior to the issuance of a judgment of possession and warrant of eviction, the Landlord will typically agree <u>not</u> to enforce the default judgment against the non-appearing spouse provided there is compliance with the Stipulation of Settlement. The same rules are applicable where the Tenants are not related (*see* Chapter 12).

18. May the Landlord apply the Tenant's security deposit to the money judgment?

The security deposit is the Tenant's money that is held by the Landlord and is to be applied to make necessary repairs to the premises beyond ordinary wear and tear following the termination of the tenancy. With the consent of the Tenant, the Landlord may choose to apply the security deposit towards unpaid rent and/or a money judgment. It has been held that where the Landlord has regained possession and there are no claims for damages (not including unpaid rent), the security deposit may be used to satisfy the judgment because the security is then considered a liquidated claim. Typically, the Landlord will wait until after the Tenant vacates the premises before deciding whether to utilize or return the security deposit (*see* Chapter 14).

JUDGE'S CHECKLIST— THINGS TO CONSIDER

The Court should pay particular attention to the following common occurrences frequently encountered in the Housing Parts. The list is <u>not</u> exhaustive.

1.   Is the subject premises located within the geographical jurisdiction of the Court?

2.   What type of proceeding was commenced: non-payment or holdover? Or is it a special proceeding to be restored to the subject premises or other type of permitted action?

3.   What is the identifiable Landlord and Tenant relationship?

4.   Is there a written rental agreement? If yes, was it provided to the Court?

5.   How many times has the case appeared on the Calendar? Has there been a "final marking" against either party?

6.   Are all parties present?

7.   Were all "proper" and "necessary" parties named in the proceeding?

8.   If required, was the appropriate predicate notice served in a timely fashion? A lease provision imposing more stringent service requirements than those set forth by statute will generally be enforced.

9. If the subject premises is Section 8 or regulated pursuant to another government funded residency program, was the predicate notice simultaneously served on both the Tenant and the governing agency?

10. Was the Tenant/Occupant in possession of the subject premises at the time the summary proceeding was commenced?

11. Does the Petition include (1) a description of the premises; (2) the Petitioner's interest in the premises; (3) the Respondent's interest in the premises; (4) the relationship between the parties; (5) the facts upon which the proceeding is based; and (6) the relief sought? If the subject premises is Section 8 or pursuant to another government funded residency program, is this fact alleged in the Petition?

12. Is the Petition verified? Counsel may verify the Petition even if located within the same county as the Petitioner.

13. Is it alleged that the Notice of Petition and Petition were properly served and was service completed in a timely manner? Review the affidavit of service.

14. Is the Tenant/Occupant challenging service? If yes, is the Petitioner's process server available to testify at either a traverse hearing or a hearing on the merits?

15. Was an Answer required, and, if so, was an Answer provided? A request by a *pro se* litigant for an adjournment for the purpose of seeking counsel extends the time to answer.

16. What affirmative defenses have been asserted and are they applicable? (e.g., the warranty of habitability only applies to residential non-payment proceedings).

17. Are counterclaims asserted, and, if so, is there a lease provision barring counterclaims? A lease provision barring counterclaims is generally enforceable except where the counterclaims are "inextricably intertwined" with the Petitioner's underlying claims.

18. Is there a timely demand for a jury trial and the appropriate jury trial fee paid? If yes, is there a lease provision barring a jury trial? Jury waiver provisions are generally enforceable.

19. Does Petitioner seek to amend the Petition to include rent or use and occupancy that accrued following commencement of the summary proceeding, insert a proper name of a "John/Jane Doe" and/or correct the property address/description of the premises?

20. Is this a case where there is a potential for money judgments in different amounts (e.g., multiple Tenants but only some appear and Petitioner amends the Petition for a new month's rent that has since become due)?

21. Have the parties discussed an amicable resolution?

22. Does counsel have authority to settle on behalf of all or some of the Tenants?

23. What are the priorities/main objectives of each party?

24. Are the parties and witnesses available for a hearing?

25. Have the parties discussed a possible resolution and how is their relationship? (contentious?, cordial?, respectful?).

26. Are any of the litigants unrepresented (*pro se*)?

27. If a settlement is reached, has the Court explained the terms of the agreement to *pro se* litigants (RPAPL § 746)?

28. Are the settlement terms fair, reasonable and just?

29. If a settlement is reached, did all parties get something?

30. Is there an adequate record of the proceedings?

PRACTITIONER'S CHECKLIST— THINGS TO CONSIDER

Practitioners should pay particular attention to the following common occurrences frequently encountered in the Housing Parts. The list is <u>not</u> exhaustive. Although not identical, there is significant overlap with the Judge's Checklist in Appendix B.

1. Is the subject premises located within the geographical jurisdiction of the Court?

2. What type of proceeding was commenced: non-payment or holdover? Or is it a special proceeding to be restored to the subject premises or other type of permitted action?

3. What is the identifiable Landlord and Tenant relationship?

4. Is there a written rental agreement? If yes, was a copy submitted to the Court?

5. How many times has the case appeared on the Calendar? Has there been a "final marking" against either party?

6. Are all parties present?

7. Were all "proper" and "necessary" parties named in the proceeding?

8. If required, was the appropriate predicate notice served in a timely fashion? A lease provision imposing more stringent service requirements than those set forth by statute will generally be enforced.

9. If the subject premises is Section 8 or regulated pursuant to another government funded residency program, was the predicate notice simultaneously served on both the Tenant and the governing agency?

10. Was the Tenant/Occupant in possession of the subject premises at the time the summary proceeding was commenced?

11. Does the Petition include (1) a description of the premises; (2) the Petitioner's interest in the premises; (3) the Respondent's interest in the premises; (4) the relationship between the parties; (5) the facts upon which the proceeding is based; and (6) the relief sought? If the subject premises is Section 8 or pursuant to another government funded residency program, is this fact alleged in the Petition?

12. Is the Petition verified? Counsel may verify the Petition even if located within the same county as the Petitioner.

13. Is it alleged that the Notice of Petition and Petition were properly served and was service completed in a timely manner? Review the affidavit of service.

14. Is the Tenant/Occupant challenging service? If yes, is the Petitioner's process server available to testify at either a traverse hearing or a hearing on the merits?

15. Was an Answer required, and, if so, was an Answer provided? A request by a *pro se* litigant for an adjournment for the purpose of seeking counsel extends the time to answer.

16. What affirmative defenses have been asserted and are they applicable? (e.g., the warranty of habitability only applies to residential non-payment proceedings).

17. Are counterclaims asserted, and, if so, is there a lease provision barring counterclaims? A lease provision barring counterclaims is generally enforceable unless the counterclaims are "inextricably intertwined" with the Petitioner's underlying claims.

18. Is there a timely demand for a jury trial and the appropriate jury trial fee paid? If yes, is there a lease provision barring a jury trial? Jury waiver provisions are generally enforceable.

19. Does Petitioner seek to amend the Petition to include rent or use and occupancy that accrued following commencement of the summary proceeding, insert a proper name of a "John/Jane Doe" and/or correct the property address/description of the premises?

20. Is there a potential for money judgments in different amounts (e.g., multiple Tenants but only some appear and Petitioner amends the Petition for a new month's rent that has since become due)?

21. Did you assess the strengths and weaknesses of both sides' cases?

22. Have you had a conversation with your client regarding your assessment in Question 21?

23. Have the parties discussed an amicable resolution?

24. What does your client seek to accomplish, and what is his/her main objective/priority?

25. Are any of the litigants unrepresented (*pro se*)?

26. If a settlement is reached, are the terms fair, reasonable and just?

27. If the case is <u>not</u> settled, do you have all of the documents (plus courtesy copies) that you want to introduce at the hearing?

28. Is your client available for a hearing? Are your witnesses available for a hearing? Is the Court available for a hearing?

29. Are you familiar with the Judge's hearing procedures and protocols?

30. Did you prepare your client for the hearing?

APPENDIX D

STATUTORY REFERENCES

I. Real Property Actions and Proceedings Law Article 7 ("RPAPL")

Section

711	Grounds for Summary Proceeding	
711(1)	Holdover Proceeding	Chs. 2, 3, 8
711(2)	Non-payment Proceeding	Chs. 1, 2, 3, 9
711(5)	Premises Used as Bawdy-House/Illegal Business	Ch. 3
713	Additional Grounds for Holdover Proceeding	Ch. 2
713(3)	Squatter	Ch. 3
713(5)	Post-foreclosure	Ch. 3
713(7)	Licensee	Chs. 3, 4
713(9)	Vendee Defaults on Purchase	Ch. 9
713(10)	Unlawful Entry	Ch. 8
713-a	Adult Home Operators (*see also* Social Services Law §§ 461-h, 461-g)	Ch. 10
715	Law Enforcement/Tenants Commence Summary Proceeding (Illegal Business)	Ch. 3
721	Who May Maintain a Summary Proceeding	Chs. 5, 8
731	Notice of Petition Requirements	Ch. 5
	* excluding non-payment proceedings in NYC (*see* RPAPL § 732)	
732	Notice of Petition Requirements (Non-payment Proceedings (NYC))	Chs. 5, 6, 7, 11
733	Service of Notice of Petition/Petition	Ch. 6
	* for non-payment proceedings in NYC, *see* RPAPL § 732	

II. Real Property Law ("RPL")

III. Civil Practice Law and Rules ("CPLR")

IV. General Obligations Law ("GOL")

V. Rent Stabilization Code (NYC)

[9 N.Y.C.R.R.] 2524.2	Predicate Notice	Ch. 3
[9 N.Y.C.R.R.] 2524.3(b)	Nuisance	Ch. 3
[9 N.Y.C.R.R.] 2524.4	Primary Residence	Ch. 3
[9 N.Y.C.R.R.] 2525.4	Security Deposit	Ch. 14
[9 N.Y.C.R.R.] 2525.6	Subletting	Ch. 4

VI. Uniform District Court Act ("UDCA")

Section		
204	Jurisdiction	Chs. 1, 7
208	Counterclaims	Ch. 7
303	Venue	Chs. 1, 5
1303	Jury Trials (*see also* RPAPL § 745)	Ch. 7
1701	Appeals	Ch. 11
1906-a, 1908	Costs and Disbursements	Ch. 1

VII. New York City Civil Court Act ("NYCCCA")

Section		
110	Creation of the Housing Part	Ch. 1
203(j)	Ejectment Proceeding (value $25,000 or less)	Ch. 2
204	Jurisdiction	Chs. 1, 7
208	Counterclaims	Ch. 7
303	Venue	Chs. 1, 5
401[c]	Notice of Petition may only be issued by a Judge or the Clerk of the Court notwithstanding RPAPL § 731	Ch. 5
1303	Jury Trials (*see also* RPAPL § 745)	Ch. 7
1701	Appeals	Ch. 11
1906-a, 1908	Costs and Disbursements	Ch. 1

VIII. Uniform City Court Act ("UCCA")

Section		
204	Jurisdiction/Venue	Chs. 1, 5, 7
208	Counterclaims	Ch. 7
1303	Jury Trials (*see also* RPAPL § 745)	Ch. 7
1701	Appeals	Ch. 11
1906-a, 1908	Costs and Disbursements	Ch. 1

IX. Uniform Justice Court Act ("UJCA")

Section		
204	Jurisdiction/Venue	Chs. 5, 7
208	Counterclaims ($3,000 maximum dollar limit)	Ch. 7
1303	Jury Trials (*see also* RPAPL § 745)	Ch. 7
1701	Appeals	Ch. 11
1903(d),(m), 1908	Costs and Disbursements	Ch. 1

APPENDIX E

SAMPLE SETTLEMENT CONFERENCE

The following is the transcript of a hypothetical settlement conference in a non-payment proceeding involving residential property. Although multiple Tenants were named in the Petition, only one (1) of the Tenants appeared in Court. The Landlord is represented by counsel, and the appearing Tenant is *pro se*. Below is an illustration of the various types of questions and issues that frequently arise. The text is neither all encompassing nor case specific.

SETTLEMENT CONFERENCE

Clerk:	Case # ____. _____ v. _____.
Petitioner's counsel:	Petitioner.
Tenant #1:	Tenant.
Court:	Is Tenant #2 here?
Tenant#1:	No, Your Honor. Tenant #2 is my wife, and she is at work today.
Court:	Are you expecting her?
Tenant #1:	No, Your Honor. She is working for a few hours and then picking up our son at my mother-in-law's home.
Court:	What about the "Jon Doe"? Is there anyone else here for this case?
Petitioner's counsel:	I don't think so.
Tenant #1:	No, Your Honor.
Court:	I want you both to go into the lobby and try to work

out an agreement that is satisfactory. If you reach
an agreement—you will then come back into the
courtroom so we can discuss the details. If, however,
you cannot reach an agreement, that is fine, too.
You will still come back into the courtroom and let
me know. I note this case was previously marked
"final" against the Respondents. If a resolution is
not reached, are both sides ready for a hearing this
afternoon?

Petitioner's counsel: Yes, we are ready.

Tenant #1: I don't think we are ready. My wife should probably
be here if we are going to trial. I want another
adjournment?

Court: Have a discussion with Petitioner's counsel,
first. After your discussion, we will then address
scheduling.

Tenant #1: Ok.

*(The parties leave the courtroom to have a discussion in the lobby.
The Clerk continues to call the First Call of the Calendar.)*

* * *

Court Officer: *(calling into the lobby)* Second Call is beginning.

Clerk: Are there any settlements?

Petitioner's counsel: *(holding up Stipulation Form)* Yes!

Court: *(to the Clerk)* Please call the case.

Clerk: Case # ____. _____ v. _____.

Court: Counsel, your appearance.

Petitioner's counsel: _____, Esq., counsel for the Petitioner.
I am joined by my client _____ (Landlord).
Good morning, Judge.

Court:	Good morning to you both. (*turning towards Tenant #1*) Good morning. Your name sir?
Tenant#1:	Good morning, You Honor. My name is _____ .
Court:	And Tenant # 2 is your wife and she is not present, correct?
Tenant #1:	Yes, Your Honor, that is correct.
Court:	Is anyone else connected to this case in Court today?
Tenant #1:	No.
Petitioner's counsel:	Judge, I am happy to inform the Court that we reached a settlement. The Tenant acknowledges owing rent arrears, and my client will give him time to pay. We started to complete the Court's Stipulation Form, but Tenant #1 had some questions that I could not answer so we stopped.
Court:	Before we get to the form, counsel please give me an overview as to what was agreed.
Petitioner's counsel:	The Tenants are three (3) months in arrears of the rental agreement which is not due to expire until early next year. The monthly rent is $1,000 and the full $3,000 is past due. They have been my client's Tenants for a few years, and, unfortunately, Tenant #1 was recently terminated from his job. His wife, Tenant #2, picked up a second job, but they are still struggling to get back on their feet. Judge, my client is trying to work with them as best she can.
Court:	Do the arrears include this month's rent?
Petitioner's counsel:	No, not yet, Your Honor. This month's rent was due on the 1st, and we still have not been paid. As a result, the Tenants are actually four (4) months behind in their rent. I would like to amend the Petition to include this month's rent for an additional $1,000.

Court:	Tenant #1, the Petitioner is requesting to make this month's rent part of the proceeding. Is there anything that you would like to say regarding the application to include this month's rent in the proceeding?
Tenant #1:	No. We owe the rent.
Court:	The application to amend the Petition with regard to the appearing Tenant is granted. How much time did you agree for the Tenants to pay the arrears?
Petitioner's counsel:	We agreed to eight (8) months—$500 per month for the next eight (8) months.
Court:	Is that acceptable Tenant #1?
Tenant #1:	Yes. I do have a question, however?
Court:	Yes?
Tenant #1:	Do we also have to pay the rent for the next eight (8) months?
Court:	That depends on what you and counsel agreed.
Petitioner's counsel:	Absolutely. I told Tenant #1 that my client was being very generous, but she needs the rent to pay her expenses.
Tenant #1:	That is fair.
Court:	Are these terms reflected in the stipulation?
Petitioner's counsel:	No, we did not get that far.
Court:	Now might be a good time for you to give the stipulation to the Court Officer so I may review it with you both.
Petitioner's counsel:	Yes, Your Honor.
Court:	Tenant #1, did you sign this Stipulation?

Tenant #1:	Yes.
Court:	(*reviewing Stipulation*) The Stipulation states that Tenant #1 acknowledges owing $4,000 in rent arrears that will be paid in eight (8) monthly installments, each in the amount of $500. The $500 arrears is to be paid on or before the 15th day of each month beginning next month. There is an address where each payment should be mailed.
Tenant #1:	Can we make the payment due the 20th of each month?
Court:	Is that acceptable?
Petitioner's counsel:	Yes, that is fine.
Court:	Ok. Counsel please make the change, and, at the end, you will both need to initial the change.
Petitioner's counsel:	Yes, Your Honor.
Court:	The stipulation further states that in the event the Tenants fail to pay the arrears according to the agreed schedule, the Petitioner is entitled to the immediate issuance of a judgment of possession and a warrant of eviction, in addition to a money judgment for the remaining arrears, less credit for any partial payments. The form further states that in the event of a default, Petitioner would then be entitled to an additional $750 in attorney's fees. Did both sides agree to this as well?
Petitioner's counsel:	Yes.
Tenant #1:	Yes, Judge.
Court:	Counsel, do you have a copy of the rental agreement?
Petitioner's counsel:	Yes.

Court:	Please identify the lease provision that states the prevailing party is entitled to attorney's fees. In addition, are the attorney's fees listed in the lease as "additional" or "added" rent?
Petitioner's counsel:	I know there is a provision regarding attorney's fees (*reviewing lease*). It is paragraph 16 which provides for attorney's fees, but the lease does not state the fees are "additional" rent.
Court:	Thank you. The attorney's fees, therefore, may <u>not</u> be included within a money judgment. Perhaps the fees may be recovered in a separate plenary action for damages. Please strike the attorney's fees from the stipulation.
Petitioner's counsel:	Ok. Should we initial?
Court:	Yes, if both sides still wish to settle the case.
Petitioner's counsel:	Yes, we agree.
Tenant #1:	I agree as well.
Court:	Not that a default is anticipated, but Tenant #1 should be aware that the stipulation only applies to Tenant #1.
Petitioner's counsel:	Excuse me?
Court:	Since Tenant #2 is not present, she has not consented to this agreement.
Tenant #1:	She will go along with these terms. We talked about it before I came to Court. I sign her name all the time—she is ok with that, too.
Court:	Sorry, sir, but a spouse is not permitted to bind a non-appearing spouse. You may agree to the terms, but your wife is not present, and, as a result, the stipulation is not applicable to her. Instead, if service is proper and if the Petition is properly verified,

	then Petitioner will be entitled to a default judgment against Tenant #2.
Tenant #1:	Would the judgment be the same?
Court:	To the extent possible, the judgment would mirror the stipulation. However, the money judgment against Tenant #2 is limited to the amount set forth in the Petition because the Landlord may not amend the Petition against a non-appearing party.
Tenant #1:	I understand.
Court:	According to the proposed stipulation, if there is noncompliance with the payment of the arrears, Petitioner may obtain a judgment and warrant against Tenant #1 by submitting with the Clerk of the Court an affidavit of noncompliance. The affidavit may be submitted without notice to Tenants. Do both sides agree to these terms as well?
Petitioner's counsel:	Yes.
Tenant #1:	Yes.
Court:	There is an additional provision that states "All payments shall first be applied towards the current month's rent, with any remainder towards the arrears". Counsel, did you add that language?
Petitioner's counsel:	Yes, I did. I tried to explain what that means to Tenant #1.
Court:	Tenant #1, this last provision states that for you to be in compliance with the stipulation, you must be current on the rent going forward. This is because the first $1,000 that you pay each month will be applied towards the current month's rent, as opposed to the arrears. Thus, you must pay the rent plus an additional $500 in arrears, for a total of $1,500 on or

	before the 20th of each month until the arrears are paid. This is significant. Do you understand this provision?
Tenant #1:	Yes.
Court:	Do you further agree to that requirement?
Tenant #1:	Yes.
Court:	Do you have any questions at this time?
Tenant #1:	No, Your Honor.
Court:	Just so you are aware, there is no prepayment penalty for the arrears. Thus, if you are able to pay the arrears early, the proceeding will be terminated that much sooner. Anything else?
Petitioner's counsel:	A default application against Tenant #2 and "John Doe".
Court:	We'll get to that shortly. Tenant #1, do you have any questions?
Tenant #1:	No, thank you.
Court:	Do you wish to be bound by this agreement?
Tenant #1:	Yes.
Court:	Are you entering this agreement voluntarily and of your own free-will?
Tenant #1:	Yes.
Court:	Are you capable of complying with the arrears payment schedule?
Tenant #1:	Yes.
Court:	Did anyone place any undue influence or pressure upon you to resolve the proceeding?

Tenant #1:	No, of course not.
Court:	And, once again, are you agreeing that you owe $4,000 in rent arrears and that you will pay the arrears at a rate of $500 per month for eight (8) consecutive months beginning next month?
Tenant #1:	Yes.
Court:	And, do you understand that the failure to pay the arrears may result in a final possessory judgment, money judgment and warrant of eviction against you?
Tenant #1:	Yes.
Court:	And do you further understand that in the event you fail to comply with the stipulated terms, then Petitioner may have you, Tenant #2 and "John Doe" evicted?
Tenant #1:	I understand.
Court:	Do you have any questions?
Tenant #1:	No, thank you.
Court:	(*to counsel*) Did you explain to your client the rights and obligations of entering this stipulation?
Petitioner's counsel:	Yes.
Court:	The Court accepts the stipulation between Landlord and Tenant #1. Please wait for your copy.
Petitioner's counsel:	Petitioner further seeks a default judgment and a warrant of eviction against Tenant #2 and "John Doe". Against Tenant #2, Petitioner also requests a money judgment for the Petition amount, which is $3,000. No money judgment is sought against the "John Doe".

Court:	(*to the Clerk*) Is proper service alleged against the non-appearing Respondents?
Clerk:	Yes, Judge. Service was allegedly performed in a timely manner by conspicuous place service. Here is the affidavit of service.
Court:	Does the Court's file include a non-military affidavit of service?
Clerk:	Yes. Here is what was filed.
Court:	(*to Petitioner's counsel*) Since the Petition is verified by yourself, and not your client, the Court does not have a sworn statement from an individual with firsthand knowledge. Before proceeding with the default judgment application against the non-appearing Respondents, the Court requires such sworn testimony. Do you have a person available to provide sworn testimony or do you need an adjournment for the purpose of bringing in such a person?
Petitioner's counsel:	My client is here, and she is prepared to testify under oath that the facts alleged in the Petition are truthful and accurate.
Court:	Would the Clerk please swear-in the Petitioner?
	(*The Petitioner is sworn-in.*)
Petitioner's counsel:	May I inquire of my client, Your Honor?
Court:	Yes.
Petitioner's counsel:	Can we have the Petition marked as Petitioner's Exhibit 1 for identification and shown to the witness?
Clerk:	Petitioner's Exhibit 1 marked for identification.
Petitioner's counsel:	Petitioner, good morning. I am going to ask you a few questions, if I say anything that you do not

understand, please let me know so I can re-phrase the question.

Petitioner: Ok.

Petitioner's counsel: Please review the Petition which was filed in this action on your behalf and look up when you have completed reviewing the document, which is marked as Petitioner's 1 for identification purposes.

Petitioner: Ok.

Petitioner's counsel: Have you seen that document prior to today?

Petitioner: Yes.

Petitioner's counsel: When was that?

Petitioner: Several weeks ago. We met in your office and you asked me to look at the document and to review it for accuracy before it was filed with the Court.

Petitioner's counsel: And were all of the facts stated in the Petition truthful and accurate when you reviewed them in my office prior to the commencement of the summary proceeding?

Petitioner: Yes.

Petitioner's counsel: And are those facts still truthful and accurate today?

Petitioner: Yes, with the exception that the Tenants owe an additional $1,000 in rent that became due after we commenced this case.

Petitioner's counsel: Have the Tenants paid this month's rent?

Petitioner: No. It is still owed.

Petitioner's counsel: Any other changes in the facts?

Petitioner: No.

Petitioner's counsel: Your Honor, I re-new my request on behalf of my client for a default judgment against Tenant #2 and "John Doe".

Court: Does your client agree not to enforce a default judgment against any of the Respondents provided Tenant #1 complies with the Stipulation of Settlement?

Petitioner's counsel: Yes.

Court: Noting the non-appearance of Tenant #2, the Court grants a judgment of possession in favor of the Petitioner against Tenant #2, plus a money judgment in the sum of $3,000, and a warrant of eviction with a stay on execution until _____, __, 20__ (*date the first payment of arrears is due*). Against the "Doe", the Court grants a judgment of possession and warrant of eviction with a similar stay date of _____, __, 20__. No money judgment is awarded against "John Doe".

Petitioner's counsel: Thank you.

Court: Counsel, submit judgment.

APPENDIX F

SAMPLE FORMS

FORMS—TABLE OF CONTENTS[901]

---

901 The forms provided are neither all encompassing nor necessarily applicable to your particular situation. The reader should refer to the local and other laws regarding a specific matter, including, but not limited to, rent control and rent stabilization laws where applicable.

THREE-DAY RENT DEMAND

TO: SEAN JONES, FRANK "DOE"
JOHN DOE #1-3 and JANE DOE # 1-3, being fictitious
persons, intended to be any other occupants or subtenants or
undertenants in the premises known as_____
Street,_____, New York ____, Apt. ____
(the "Subject Premises")

          Re: Rental Agreement, dated _____, between
the Landlord,_____ and Tenant,
_____, regarding the Subject
Premises, a residential property

PLEASE TAKE NOTICE, that you have failed to make the payment of rent and added rent as obligated under your rental agreement for the Subject Premises, and, that, as a result, the following arrears are due and owing the Landlord:

January, ____, rent	$ _____
January, ____, utilities	$ _____
February, ____, rent	$ _____
Total due: $_____	

PLEASE TAKE FURTHER NOTICE, that you are required to pay the above total on or before_____, three (3) days from the date of service upon you of the herein rent demand, or, alternatively, you must vacate and surrender possession of the Subject Premises to the Landlord. The failure to pay the aforementioned amount by_____ will result in a summary proceeding being commenced to recover possession of the Subject Premises and all rent and added rent, with interest, the Landlord is entitled pursuant to the rental agreement, plus attorney's fees, costs and disbursements.

Dated:

_____

Owner/Landlord or authorized individual on behalf of the Owner/Landlord

TEN-DAY NOTICE TO QUIT

TO: **SEAN JONES, FRANK "DOE"**
JOHN DOE #1-3 and JANE DOE # 1-3, being fictitious
persons, intended to be any other occupants or subtenants
or undertenants in the premises known as __ _____
Street, _____, New York ____, Apt. ____ (the "Subject
Premises")

    Re: **License Agreement, dated _____, between**
            the Owner/Licensor, _____ and Occupant,
            _____, regarding the Subject
            Premises, a residential property

PLEASE TAKE NOTICE, that you and all other persons occupying the Subject Premises must quit and vacate the Subject Premises on or before _____, a date no less than ten (10) days from the date the herein Ten-Day Notice was served upon you, on the grounds that your license to possess the Subject Premises has been revoked. [*Modify accordingly if the Occupant is a squatter or the Subject Premises had been foreclosed upon and the Occupant is not a bona fide Tenant*].

PLEASE TAKE FURTHER NOTICE, that the failure to quit and vacate the Subject Premises by the above date will result in a summary proceeding being commenced to recover possession of the Subject Premises, together with a money judgment and further all other reasonable relief the Owner/Licensor is entitled.

Dated:

_____

Owner/Licensor or other authorized individual

ONE MONTH NOTICE OF TERMINATION[902]

TO: **SEAN JONES, FRANK "DOE"**
             JOHN DOE #1-3 and JANE DOE # 1-3, being fictitious persons, intended to be any other occupants or subtenants or undertenants in the premises known as __ _____ Street, _____, New York ____, Apt. ____ (the "Subject Premises")

            Re: **Rental Agreement, dated _____, between the Landlord, _____ and Tenant, _____, regarding the Subject Premises, a residential property**

PLEASE TAKE NOTICE, that the undersigned Landlord and owner of the Subject Premises elects to terminate your tenancy of the Subject Premises, which is presently being held by you pursuant to a month-to-month tenancy.

PLEASE TAKE FURTHER NOTICE, that you and all other persons occupying the Subject Premises must vacate and surrender the Subject Premises on or before _____, a date no less than one (1) month from the date the herein One Month Notice of Termination was served upon you.

PLEASE TAKE FURTHER NOTICE, that the failure to quit and vacate the Subject Premises by the above date will result in the Landlord commencing a summary proceeding to have you evicted from the Subject Premises for holding over past the termination of your tenancy and for a money judgment for all monetary relief, including unpaid rent and additional rent during the rental agreement and use and occupancy of the Subject Premises during the holding over, with interest, plus attorney's fees, costs and disbursements, together with all other reasonable relief the Owner/Landlord is entitled.

Dated:

_____

Owner/Landlord or authorized individual on behalf of the Owner/Landlord

---

902   Thirty (30) Days Notice, as opposed to one (1) month, is required to terminate a month-to-month tenancy within New York City. *See* RPL § 232-a.

NOTICE TO QUIT POSSESSION—90-DAY NOTICE

TO: SEAN JONES, FRANK "DOE"
JOHN DOE #1-3 and JANE DOE # 1-3, being fictitious persons, intended to be any other occupants or subtenants or undertenants in the premises known as __ _____Street, _____, New York ____, Apt. ____ (the "Subject Premises")

Re: Post-foreclosure of the Subject Premises - Notice to Quit Possession and Vacate the Subject Premises, a residential property

PLEASE TAKE NOTICE, that the Subject Premises described in Schedule "A" annexed hereto has been sold to BANK _____, pursuant to a Judgment of Foreclosure and Sale, dated _____, that was duly entered in the Clerk's Office of Suffolk County on _____, relating to a foreclosure action entitled _____v. _____, Index No. __-_____. Pursuant to the aforementioned Judgment, a sale was held on _____, and the referee duly delivered a deed to Bank _____. **A certified copy of the Referee's Deed is attached hereto and is now exhibited to you.** The Judgment of Foreclosure and Sale states, *inter alia*, that the subsequent purchaser at said sale shall be let into full possession of the entire Subject Premises.

PLEASE TAKE FURTHER NOTICE, that pursuant to the Protecting Tenants at Foreclosure Act of 2009, Pub. Law No. 111-22, §§ 701-04, 123 Stat. 1660 (2009) ("PTFA"), and pursuant to §§ 221, 713 and 1303 of the New York State Real Property Actions and Proceedings Law ("RPAPL"), if you are occupying the Subject Premises as a bona fide tenant, then you have until _____, that being a date not less than ninety (90) days from the date a copy of this Notice to Quit Possession was served upon you, to quit and vacate the Subject Premises.

PLEASE TAKE FURTHER NOTICE, that if you are a bona fide Tenant or your lease qualifies under New York State Law, and your lease term expires <u>after</u> the above date, you may have the right to continue to occupy the Subject Premises for the greater of the remainder of the lease term or a period of ninety (90) days, under the same terms and conditions that were in effect at the time of entry of the Judgement of Foreclosure and Sale or if no such Judgment was entered, upon the terms and conditions that were in effect at the time of the transfer of ownership of such property.

The PTFA defines a bona fide Tenant as one who: (a) entered into the rental agreement with the former owner before the Notice of Foreclosure; and (b) is not the former owner or the child, spouse or parent of the former owner; and [c] the rental agreement was the result of an arms-length transaction; and (d) the rent is not substantially less than the fair market rent for the property or your rent is reduced or subsidized due to a Federal, State or local subsidy.

According to RPAPL § 1305, for a lease to qualify for the ninety (90) day Notice period: (a) you must not be the owner of the Subject Premises and (b) the rent must not be substantially less than the fair market rent for the Subject Premises unless the Subject Premises is subject to a Federal or State statutory system of subsidy or other federal or state statutory scheme.

The name and address of a new owner, any person or entity which becomes a successor-in-interest after the issuance of the Ninety-Day Notice provided for in this subdivision shall notify all Tenants of its name and address and shall assume such interest subject to the right of the Tenant to maintain possession as provided herein. Please contact us upon receipt of this Notice to discuss your lease and rent obligations.

If you do not contact us, then you must vacate the Subject Premises by the above date. Bank _____ hereby demands that all occupants and all persons occupying the Subject Premises under you, including all family members, lessees, licensees, etc., to quit and surrender possession of the Subject Premises to Bank _____ on or before the above vacate date. The Subject Premises is to be left in broom clean condition. You are not to remove anything attached to or used in connection with the Subject Premises or covered by the mortgage that has been foreclosed.

PLEASE TAKE FURTHER NOTICE, that unless each person occupying the Subject Premises quits and vacates the Subject Premises on or before the above date, Bank _____ will commence a summary proceeding to have you evicted from the Subject Premises and further seek all monetary relief, including, but not limited to, use and occupancy of the Subject Premises, that the Bank may be entitled.

Dated: _____

Attorneys for BANK _____

The undersigned, an attorney duly licensed to practice law within the State of New York hereby certifies pursuant to CPLR § 2105 that I have compared the accompanying deed to the original of same referred to within this Notice to Quit Possession—90-Day Notice and have found same to be a true and complete copy.

Dated: _____

NOTICE TO CURE

TO: COMPANY XYZ
JOHN DOE #1-3 and JANE DOE # 1-3, being fictitious
persons, intended to be any other occupants or subtenants or
undertenants in the premises known as __ _____ Street,
_____, New York ____, Suite ____ (the "Subject
Premises")

      Re: Rental Agreement, dated _____, between
the Landlord, _____ and Tenant,
_____, regarding the Subject
Premises, a commercial property

PLEASE TAKE NOTICE, that pursuant to Paragraph ___ of your rental agreement for the Subject Premises duly executed on _____ __, 20__, and further applicable law, Notice is hereby given that you have materially violated said rental agreement in that you violated Paragraph __ of the rental agreement in that you [*specify the breach*].

PLEASE TAKE FURTHER NOTICE, that the following includes an accurate description of the facts establishing the breach: [*state the factual allegations resulting in the breach*]. The breach is on-going, and the Landlord continues to incur damages as a result.

PLEASE TAKE FURTHER NOTICE, that you must cure this breach on or before_____, as specified within the rental agreement, and, the failure to cure the breach by this date will result in the rental agreement terminating and the Landlord commencing a summary proceeding to have you evicted from the Subject Premises.

PLEASE TAKE FURTHER NOTICE, that pursuant to Paragraph __ of the rental agreement, you are responsible for all costs, including attorney's fees, incurred by the Landlord as a result of your breach and such monies, as well as all other relief the Landlord may be entitled, will be sought in a summary proceeding if the breach is not cured by the above date.

Dated:

_____

Attorneys for Landlord

TENANT'S NOTICE OF SURRENDER OF THE PREMISES

TO: **COMPANY XYZ**
          Landlord

      Re: **Surrender of Premises located at
           _____, _____, New York (a
           commercial property)**

Dear_____,

As of this date, the __th day of _____, 20__, Tenant ____ hereby surrenders the above premises and returns same to the Landlord, _____. As per
our discussion, Tenant's possessions have been removed from the premises.
Enclosed please find all sets of the keys that were in our possession for the
subject premises. The premises have been returned in broom-swept condition. Kindly return my client's security deposit upon receipt.

Very truly yours,

Counsel for Tenant _____

LANDLORD COMPANY XYZ

ACKNOWLEDGED RECEIPT AND KEYS RECEIVED

By: _____

Name: _____

Position:_____

Date and Time: _____

SUFFOLK COUNTY SIXTH DISTRICT COURT

PATCHOGUE, NEW YORK

_____

Petitioner,

- against -

Respondent.

_____

Index No. BRLT __-_____

NOTICE OF PETITION

(Non-Payment Proceeding)

To the Respondent: [name(s) and address(es) of each Respondent]

PLEASE TAKE NOTICE, that a hearing at which you must appear and answer will be held at the Suffolk County Sixth District Court, 150 West Main Street, Patchogue, New York, on _____ at 9:30 a.m., and each and every adjourned to date thereafter, upon the annexed Petition, which requests a final judgment to evict you from and award the Petitioner the possession of the subject premises located at _____, New York _____ County of Suffolk, and, more specifically, [*description as appropriate—* Apartment No. ___; the _____ rooms on the ____ floor, first floor, second floor, etc.], and such other and further relief as requested in the Petition and/ or the Court deems proper and appropriate.

PLEASE TAKE FURTHER NOTICE, that Petitioner also seeks, as set forth in the Petition, a money judgment against you for unpaid rent and continued use and occupancy in an amount to be determined at the hearing but believed not to be less than $_____, with interest thereon from [*first day unpaid rent was due*], plus reasonable attorney's fees, costs and disbursements.

PLEASE TAKE FURTHER NOTICE, that your answer to the Petition may set forth any applicable defense(s) and further assert a counterclaim(s) against the Petitioner, but if you fail to interpose such an answer in a timely manner, you may be precluded from asserting such defenses and claims that you may have or ever had in this and any other proceeding or action.

PLEASE TAKE FURTHER NOTICE, that the failure to appear on the date indicated above, and each adjourned to date thereafter, may result in the entry of a default judgment against you for the relief sought in the Petition.

DATED: _____

_____

Issuing Judge/Clerk/Attorney

SUFFOLK COUNTY SIXTH DISTRICT COURT

PATCHOGUE, NEW YORK

Petitioner,	Index No. BRLT __-_____
- against -	**PETITION**
Respondent.	**(Non-Payment Proceeding)**

Petitioner, _____ ("Petitioner" or "Landlord"), by his/her/its attorneys _____, LLP, asserts and alleges the following:

1. Petitioner is the owner and Landlord of the parcel of residential real property located at _____, New York _____, County of Suffolk, and, more specifically, [*description as appropriate*—Apartment No. ___; the _____ rooms on the ____ floor, first floor, second floor, etc.] (the "Subject Premises").

2. Respondent [*list every Tenant's name(s)*] ("Respondent" or "Tenant") is the Tenant of the Subject Premises, having entered into possession of the Subject Premises pursuant to an [*oral or written*] rental agreement, dated on or about _____ (the "Lease") between Petitioner and Respondent.

3. The Lease is for a period of ___ years, commencing _____.

4. Within the aforementioned Lease, Respondent promised to pay Landlord as rent the sum of $_____ each [*month or weekly or other arrangement*] on or before the __th day of each month for the duration of the Lease (the "Rent").

5. Respondent is presently in possession of the Subject Premises, and has been in possession since _____.

6. Pursuant to the Lease, Petitioner is entitled to but Respondent has failed and/or refuses to pay the Rent due and owing Petitioner for each of the following periods:

    (Month) _____, 20___ (Amount) $_____

    (Month) _____, 20___ (Amount) $_____

    (Month) _____, 20___ (Amount) $_____ etc.

7. Further pursuant to the Lease, Petitioner is entitled to a late fee as "additional" rent in the amount of $_____ for each month specified above due to the Rent not having been paid in those months on or before the __th day of each month.

8. Further pursuant to the Lease, Petitioner is entitled to an award of reasonable attorney's fees as "additional" rent in an amount to be determined at the hearing but believed to be not less than $_____, due to the Respondent's failure to pay rent as agreed.

9. Respondent has defaulted in his obligations pursuant to the Lease as set forth above and the total now due and owing Petitioner is an amount to be determined at the hearing but believed not to be less than $[add paragraphs 6, 7 and 8].

10. Petitioner has demanded that Respondent pay the unpaid Rent for each month indicated above since same has become due in the following manner: [Orally by the Petitioner prior to commencing this summary proceeding or By the attached written Three-Day Demand for the Rent that was served on the Respondent in the manner set forth in the accompanying Affidavit of Service].

11. Respondent continues to remain in possession of the Subject Premises without the consent or permission of the Landlord due to the above described default.

12. The Subject Premises is not subject to rent control because [insert that which is applicable—the Subject Premises is located in a community which has not adopted the Emergency Tenant Protection Act of 1974 ("ETPA"); the building in which the Subject Premises is located was constructed after December 31, 1973; or the building in which the Subject Premises is located has fewer than six (6) units].

or

12. Petitioner is in full compliance with the Emergency Tenant Protection Act of 1974 ("ETPA"), as amended, and [insert that which is applicable—the Rent demanded herein is not greater than the maximum rent permitted by law; the Subject Premises is subject to rent control and the Rent demanded herein does not exceed the maximum rent prescribed by the New York State Divisions of Housing and Community Renewal (DHCR) and/or Homes and Community Renewal (HCR); or the Subject Premises is presently subject to the Emergency Tenant Protection Act of 1974 (ETPA), as amended, because _____ and the Petitioner/Owner of the Subject Premises

235

has registered the Rent and services with the DHCR and/or HCR pursuant to ETPA and the Tenant Protection Regulations thereunder; is in compliance with ETPA; and the Rent demanded herein does not exceed the legal regulated rent permitted the Petitioner under said Law, Regulations and appropriate Rent Guidelines Board Orders].

13. [*If applicable*] Petitioner lacks written information or notice of any address where the Tenant resides, is employed, or has a place of business in New York other than the Subject Premises sought herein [*list any additional known addresses*].

WHEREFORE, Petitioner requests (1) a final judgment of possession in Petitioner's favor; (2) a money judgment in the sum of $_____, with interest from [*the first date that the unpaid rent was due*], plus late fees and reasonable attorney's fees; (3) issuance of a warrant of eviction; and (4) costs and disbursements, together with such other and further relief that the Court deems just and proper.

Dated:_____

ATTORNEY'S FIRM NAME

_____
Attorneys for Petitioner _____
By:_____
Address
City, State Zip Code
Telephone Number
Facsimile Number

STATE OF NEW YORK)
ss:
COUNTY OF _____)

[*Petitioner or duly authorized Agent for Petitioner*], being duly sworn, states that deponent has read the foregoing Petition, and that the contents of the Petition are true to deponent's own knowledge except as to those matters that are alleged upon information and belief, and as to those matters, deponent believes them to be true.

_____
Petitioner (signature)
Print Name/Title

Sworn to before me this ___th day
of _____, 20___

_____
Notary Public

SUFFOLK COUNTY SIXTH DISTRICT COURT

PATCHOGUE, NEW YORK

Petitioner,	Index No. BRLT __-_____
- against -	**NOTICE OF PETITION**
Respondent.	**(Holdover Proceeding)**

To the Respondent: [name(s) and address(es) of each Respondent]

PLEASE TAKE NOTICE, that a hearing at which you must appear and answer will be held at the Suffolk County Sixth District Court, 150 West Main Street, Patchogue, New York, on _____ at 9:30 a.m., and each and every adjourned to date thereafter, upon the annexed Petition, which requests a final judgment to evict you from and award the Petitioner the possession of the subject premises located at _____, New York _____ County of Suffolk, and, more specifically, [*description as appropriate—* Apartment No. ___; the _____ rooms on the ____ floor, first floor, second floor, etc.], and such other and further relief as requested in the Petition and/ or the Court deems proper and appropriate.

PLEASE TAKE FURTHER NOTICE, that Petitioner also seeks, as set forth in the Petition, a money judgment against you for unpaid rent and continued use and occupancy in an amount to be determined at the hearing but believed not to be less than $_____, with interest thereon from [*first day unpaid rent was due*], plus reasonable attorney's fees, costs and disbursements.

PLEASE TAKE FURTHER NOTICE, that your answer to the Petition may set forth any applicable defense(s) and further assert a counterclaim(s) against the Petitioner, but if you fail to interpose such an answer in a timely manner, you may be precluded from asserting such defenses and claims that you may have or ever had in this and any other proceeding or action.

PLEASE TAKE FURTHER NOTICE, that the failure to appear on the date indicated above, and each adjourned to date thereafter, may result in the entry of a default judgment against you for the relief sought in the Petition.

DATED:_____

_____
Issuing Judge/Clerk/Attorney

SUFFOLK COUNTY SIXTH DISTRICT COURT

PATCHOGUE, NEW YORK

Petitioner,

\- against -

Respondent.

Index No. BRLT __-_____

PETITION

(Holdover Proceeding)

Petitioner, _____ ("Petitioner" or "Landlord"), by his/her/its attorneys _____, LLP, asserts and alleges the following:

1. Petitioner is the owner and Landlord of the parcel of residential real property located at _____, New York _____, County of Suffolk, and, more specifically, [*description as appropriate*—Apartment No. ___; the _____ rooms on the ____ floor, first floor, second floor, etc.] (the "Subject Premises").

2. Respondent [*list every Tenant's name(s)*] ("Respondent" or "Tenant") is the Tenant of the Subject Premises, having entered into possession of the Subject Premises pursuant to an [*oral or written*] rental agreement, dated on or about _____ (the "Lease") between Petitioner and Respondent. [*To the extent Respondent may be a licensee, tenant-at-will, squatter, etc., add the applicable information*].

3. The Lease, which was for a period of ___ years commencing _____, expired by its own terms on _____.

4. Within the aforementioned Lease, Respondent promised to pay Landlord as rent the sum of $_____ each [*month or weekly or other arrangement*] on or before the __th day of each month for the duration of the Lease (the "Rent").

5. At the time of the expiration of the Lease, Respondent owed Petitioner rental arrears in the sum of $_____, representing the final month's Rent pursuant to the Lease that was duly demanded but not paid by Respondent.

6. Respondent has been and continues to remain in possession of the Subject Premises since the expiration of the Lease without the permission of Petitioner.

7. Respondent has not tendered and Petitioner has not received any use and occupancy for the period of time Respondent has been in possession of the Subject Premises since the Lease expired.

8. Pursuant to the now-expired Lease, Petitioner is entitled to an award of reasonable attorney's fees as "additional" rent in an amount to be determined at the hearing but believed to be not less than $_____ for commencing this action due to the Respondent's failure to vacate the Subject Premises at the expiration of the Lease.

9. The Subject Premises is not subject to rent control because [*insert that which is applicable*—the Subject Premises is located in a community which has not adopted the Emergency Tenant Protection Act of 1974 ("ETPA"); the building in which the Subject Premises is located was constructed after December 31, 1973; or the building in which the Subject Premises is located has fewer than six (6) units].

or

9. Petitioner is in full compliance with the Emergency Tenant Protection Act of 1974 ("ETPA"), as amended, and [*insert that which is applicable*—the Rent demanded herein is not greater than the maximum rent permitted by law; the Subject Premises is subject to rent control and the Rent demanded herein does not exceed the maximum rent prescribed by the New York State Divisions of Housing and Community Renewal (DHCR) and/or Homes and Community Renewal (HCR); or the Subject Premises is presently subject to the Emergency Tenant Protection Act of 1974 (ETPA), as amended, because _____ and the Petitioner/Owner of the Subject Premises has registered the Rent and services with the DHCR and/or HCR pursuant to ETPA and the Tenant Protection Regulations thereunder; is in compliance with ETPA; and the Rent demanded herein does not exceed the legal regulated rent permitted the Petitioner under said Law, Regulations and appropriate Rent Guidelines Board Orders].

10. [*If applicable*] Petitioner lacks written information or notice of any address where the Tenant resides, is employed, or has a place of business in New York other than the Subject Premises sought herein [*list any additional known addresses*].

11. Petitioner is entitled to an award for the unpaid Rent for the final month during the tenancy plus use and occupancy through at least the hearing date at a monthly rate to be determined by the Court but believed to be not less than $_____.

239

WHEREFORE, Petitioner requests (1) a final judgment of possession in Petitioner's favor; (2) a money judgment in the sum of $_____, representing rent arrears; (3) a money judgment for the fair value of use and occupancy in an amount to be determined at the hearing but believed to be not less than $_____, for the period from _____ to at least the date of the hearing; (4) a money judgment for reasonable attorney's fees: (5) issuance of a warrant of eviction; together (6) with interest and costs and disbursements, and (7) such other and further relief that the Court deems just and proper.

Dated:_____

ATTORNEY'S FIRM NAME
_____

Attorneys for Petitioner _____
By: _____
Address
City, State Zip Code
Telephone Number
Facsimile Number

STATE OF NEW YORK)

ss:

COUNTY OF _____)

[*Petitioner or duly authorized Agent for Petitioner*], being duly sworn, states that deponent has read the foregoing Petition, and that the contents of the Petition are true to deponent's own knowledge except as to those matters that are alleged upon information and belief, and as to those matters, deponent believes them to be true.

_____
Petitioner (signature)

Print Name/Title

Sworn to before me this ___th day

of _____, 20___

_____

Notary Public

SUFFOLK COUNTY SIXTH DISTRICT COURT

PATCHOGUE, NEW YORK

Petitioner,	Index No. BRLT __-_____
- against -	**VERIFIED ANSWER**
	WITH COUNTERCLAIMS
Respondent.	**(Non-payment Proceeding)**

Respondent, _____ ("Respondent"), by his/her/its attorneys, _____, P.C., hereby interposes in response to Petitioner's Petition the following Answer with Counterclaims.

1. Respondent denies knowledge and information sufficient to form a belief as to the truth of the allegations set forth in paragraphs 1, 12 and 13 of the Petition.

2. With respect to the allegations set forth in paragraph 2 of the Petition, Respondent admits occupying the Subject Premises pursuant to a rental agreement with Petitioner. Respondent denies the remaining allegations set forth in that paragraph of the Petition.

3. Respondent denies the allegations set forth in paragraphs 3, 4, 5, 6, 9, 10 and 11 of the Petition.

4. With respect to paragraphs 7 and 8 of the Petition, Respondent respectfully refers all conclusions of law to the Court for determination, and, further to the extent that a response is required, the allegations are denied.

AS AND FOR A FIRST AFFIRMATIVE DEFENSE

5. Respondent hereby repeats and reiterates each and every allegation contained in paragraphs 1 through 4 as if fully set forth herein.

6. Petitioner failed to properly serve Respondent with the Notice of Petition and Petition pursuant to Real Property Actions and Proceedings Law § 735, and, as a result, the Court lacks jurisdiction over Respondent.

7. Alternatively, Respondent respectfully requests a traverse hearing.

AS AND FOR A SECOND AFFIRMATIVE DEFENSE

8. Respondent hereby repeats and reiterates each and every allegation contained in paragraphs 1 through 7 as if fully set forth herein.

9. Petitioner failed to make a proper rent demand prior to the commencement of this summary proceeding.

AS AND FOR A THIRD AFFIRMATIVE DEFENSE

10. Respondent hereby repeats and reiterates each and every allegation contained in paragraphs 1 through 9 as if fully set forth herein.

11. Respondent tendered the Rent claimed due herein to Petitioner but Petitioner refused to accept same by rejecting and/or returning the payments to Respondent.

AS AND FOR A FOURTH AFFIRMATIVE DEFENSE

12. Respondent hereby repeats and reiterates each and every allegation contained in paragraphs 1 through 11 as if fully set forth herein.

13. The late fee and attorney's fees provisions within the Lease are excessive and unconscionable, and otherwise unenforceable.

AS AND FOR A FIFTH AFFIRMATIVE DEFENSE AND FIRST COUNTERCLAIM

14. Respondent hereby repeats and reiterates each and every allegation contained in paragraphs 1 through 13 as if fully set forth herein.

15. The conditions of the Subject Premises are dangerous, hazardous and detrimental to the safety of Respondent and all others entering same.

16. The aforementioned conditions include: [list the dangerous conditions].

17. The aforementioned conditions have been ongoing and continuous since _____.

18. Petitioner was provided ample notice of the defective conditions yet Petitioner failed to remedy the conditions thereby breaching the warranty of habitability.

19. Based upon the foregoing, Respondent is entitled to an abatement of the rent plus a a money judgment for damages sustained due to Landlord's breach.

AS AND FOR A SECOND COUNTERCLAIM

20. Respondent hereby repeats and reiterates each and every allegation contained in paragraphs 1 through 19 as if fully set forth herein.

21. The applicable Lease includes a provision awarding a prevailing Petitioner reasonable attorney's fees.

22. Respondent is thus entitled to the same consideration pursuant to Real Property Law § 234.

23. Based on the foregoing, Respondent requests an award of reasonable attorney's fees in an amount to be determined by the Court.

WHEREFORE, Respondent respectfully requests judgment against Petitioner (1) dismissing the Petition or, alternatively, granting a traverse hearing on the issue of service; (2) in the event the Court is not inclined to dismiss the Petition, Respondent seeks an abatement of the alleged unpaid rent; (3) plus a money judgment in an amount to be determined by the Court on the first and second counterclaims; and (4) and such other and further relief as the Court deems just and proper.

Dated:_____

ATTORNEY'S FIRM NAME

_____

Attorneys for Respondent _____
By: _____
Address
City, State Zip Code
Telephone Number
Facsimile Number

STATE OF NEW YORK)

ss:

COUNTY OF _____)

[*Respondent*], being duly sworn, states that deponent has read the foregoing Answer with Counterclaims, and that the contents of the Answer with Counterclaims are true to deponent's own knowledge except as to those matters that are alleged upon information and belief, and as to those matters, deponent believes them to be true.

_____
Respondent (signature)
Print Name/Title

Sworn to before me this __th day

of _____, 20__

_____
Notary Public

SUFFOLK COUNTY SIXTH DISTRICT COURT

PATCHOGUE, NEW YORK

_____ Petitioner, - against - Respondent. _____	Index No. BRLT __-_____ **VERIFIED ANSWER** **WITH COUNTERCLAIM** **(Holdover Proceeding)**

Respondent, _____ ("Respondent"), by his/her/its attorneys, _____, P.C., hereby interposes in response to Petitioner's Petition the following Answer with Counterclaim.

1. Respondent denies knowledge and information sufficient to form a belief as to the truth of the allegations set forth in paragraphs 1, 9 and 10 of the Petition.

2. With respect to the allegations set forth in paragraph 2 of the Petition, Respondent admits to formerly occupying the Subject Premises pursuant to a rental agreement with Petitioner. Respondent denies the remaining allegations set forth in that paragraph of the Petition.

3. Respondent denies the allegations set forth in paragraphs 3, 5, 6, 7 and 11 of the Petition.

4. With respect to paragraphs 4 and 8 of the Petition, Respondent respectfully refers all conclusions of law to the Court for determination, and, further to the extent that a response is required, the allegations are denied.

AS AND FOR A FIRST AFFIRMATIVE DEFENSE

5. Respondent hereby repeats and reiterates each and every allegation contained in paragraphs 1 through 4 as if fully set forth herein.

6. Respondent surrendered possession of the Subject Premises prior to the commencement of the herein summary proceeding.

7. Based on the foregoing, the action must be dismissed.

AS AND FOR A SECOND AFFIRMATIVE DEFENSE

8. Respondent hereby repeats and reiterates each and every allegation contained in paragraphs 1 through 7 as if fully set forth herein.

9. To the extent a Landlord and Tenant relationship existed between Petitioner and Respondent, since Respondent tendered payment for use and occupancy following the alleged expiration of the Lease, the tenancy was on a month-to-month basis, thereby requiring Petitioner to cause to be served upon Respondent a one month notice prior to the commencement of the herein summary proceeding.

10. Petitioner failed to cause to be served upon Respondent a one month notice pursuant to Real Property Law § 232-b [*thirty (30) day's notice within New York City, Real Property Law § 232-a*] prior to commencing this proceeding.

11. The failure to serve such notice requires dismissal of the action.

12. Alternatively, in the event Petitioner claims there was service of a predicate notice, Respondent respectfully requests a traverse hearing.

AS AND FOR A THIRD AFFIRMATIVE DEFENSE

13. Respondent hereby repeats and reiterates each and every allegation contained in paragraphs 1 through 12 as if fully set forth herein.

14. Petitioner commenced this summary proceeding in retaliation for Respondent filing a complaint with the local Code Enforcement agency regarding dangerous conditions within the Subject Premises that are in violation of the local Town Code.

15. Respondent made the aforementioned complaint on _____, two (2) months prior to the commencement of this summary proceeding.

16. The Subject Premises is not an owner-occupied property with fewer than four (4) units.

17. The stated reasons for the commencement of this summary proceeding are a pretext for the true reason which is contrary to law and in violation of the exercise of Respondent's lawful rights.

18. Accordingly, the Petition must be dismissed.

AS AND FOR A FIRST COUNTERCLAIM

19. Respondent hereby repeats and reiterates each and every allegation contained in paragraphs 1 through 18 as if fully set forth herein.

20. The relevant Lease includes a provision awarding a prevailing Petitioner reasonable attorney's fees.

21. Respondent is thus entitled to the same consideration pursuant to Real Property Law § 234.

22. Based on the foregoing, Respondent requests an award of reasonable attorney's fees in an amount to be determined by the Court.

WHEREFORE, Respondent respectfully requests judgment against Petitioner (1) dismissing the Petition or, alternatively, granting a traverse hearing; (2) a money judgment in an amount to be determined by the Court on the counterclaim; and (3) such other and further relief as the Court deems just and proper.

Dated:_____

ATTORNEY'S FIRM NAME

_____

Attorneys for Respondent _____

By: _____

Address

City, State Zip Code

Telephone Number

Facsimile Number

STATE OF NEW YORK)

ss:

COUNTY OF _____)

[*Respondent or Respondent's Attorney*], being duly sworn, states that deponent has read the foregoing Answer with Counterclaim, and that the contents of the Answer with Counterclaim are true to deponent's own knowledge except as to those matters that are alleged upon information and belief, and as to those matters, deponent believes them to be true.

_____

Respondent (signature)

Print Name/Title

Sworn to before me this __th day

of _____, 20__

_____

Notary Public

SUFFOLK COUNTY SIXTH DISTRICT COURT

PATCHOGUE, NEW YORK

Petitioner,	Index No. BRLT __-_____
- against -	**STIPULATION OF**
Respondent.	**SETTLEMENT**
"John Doe".	

It is hereby stipulated and agreed by and between the undersigned parties that the above-captioned action is settled as follows:

1. The Petition is amended to include the current month's rent of _____ in the amount of $_____ which became due following the commencement of this summary proceeding.

2. Respondent consents to the jurisdiction of the Court, waives any and all jurisdictional defenses and withdraws the counterclaims.

3. Subtenant _____, having consented to the jurisdiction of the Court, further consents that his proper name shall be substituted for the "John Doe" named in the Notice of Petition and Petition.

4. Respondent _____ and Subtenant _____ consent to the immediate entry of a judgment of possession in favor of the Petitioner and the issuance of a warrant of eviction. The execution of the warrant of eviction shall be stayed until _____. Tenant _____ further consents to entry of a money judgment against him in the amount of $ _____.

or

Respondent _____ and Subtenant _____ are currently in possession of the subject premises, and Tenant _____ acknowledges owing Petitioner rent arrears in the sum of $_____, and further agrees to pay such arrears on or before _____. Payments are to be made in the following manner: [*payment schedule - dates, amount and form of payment*]. In the event Tenant _____ fails to pay the rental arrears as agreed above, then the Petitioner, upon submission of an affidavit of non-compliance, will be entitled to a judgment of possession and issuance of a warrant of eviction against Tenant _____ and Subtenant _____, plus a money judgment against Tenant _____ only, in the amount of $ _____ [*amount in the Petition as amended on the record, the Petition amount or a lower amount*], with credit given for any partial payments made. The parties further agree that all monies received from this date forward will first be applied to the current month's rent with the remainder towards the arrears. It is expressly agreed that the failure on the part of the Tenant to pay future rent may <u>not</u> be a basis for default under the terms of this Stipulation of Settlement nor may future rent be included in a monetary judgment.

5. Tenant _____ further waives his right to the return of the security deposit in the amount of $ _____.

Date: _____

_____   _____
Petitioner   Attorney for Petitioner

_____   _____
Respondent   Attorney for Respondent

_____   _____
Subtenant   Attorney for Subtenant

SUFFOLK COUNTY DISTRICT COURT

JUDGMENT OF POSSESSION

_____

Petitioner,
- against -
Respondent.

Index No. BRLT ___-_____

_____

WHEREAS a Notice of Petition and Non-Payment Petition duly verified and proof of service having been filed with this court and the issue having been decided by the Hon. _____, District Court Judge on September __, 20__, a final order is made, after a hearing in favor of Petitioner.

WHEREAS Petitioner _____ has an address at _____ Rd., _____, NY _____.

WHEREAS Respondent _____ has an address at _____ St., _____, NY _____.

NOW, upon the motion Petitioner's counsel, _____, Esq., _____ Rd., _____, NY _____,

IT IS HEREBY ADJUDGED that possession of the premises, described in the Petition located at __ _____ Street, _____, NY _____, said property is further described as: Apartment located on the second floor, be awarded to the Petitioner, along with a monetary judgment in the amount of $2,500.00 for a total judgment of $2,500.00.

AND IT IS FURTHER ORDERED that a warrant of eviction shall issue removing all named Respondents from the described premises. The execution of the warrant is stayed to and including 9/__/20__.

Date of Decision: 9/__/20__

_____
J.D.C.

Judgment entered at Suffolk County District Court - 6th District, 150 West Main Street, Patchogue, NY 11772, in the State of New York in the total amount of $2,500.00 on September __, 20__ at 2:06 pm.

_____
Clerk of the Court

SUFFOLK COUNTY DISTRICT COURT
WARRANT OF EVICTION

Petitioner, - against - Respondent.	Index No. BRLT __-_____ Original Issuance **WARRANT OF EVICTION** Non-Payment

TO THE SHERIFF OF SUFFOLK COUNTY

Final decision in favor of the Petitioner has been granted based on the judgment of possession entered in the Suffolk County District Court—6th District on 9/__/20__, which awarded Petitioner the delivery of the premises:

Therefore, you are commanded to remove the Respondent(s) listed below:

(1) Respondent

And all other persons from the following described premises, located in the County of Suffolk and to put said Petitioner in full possession thereof:

(1) Property Address

Said property is further described as: Apartment located on the second floor

Witness,

Hon. _____
District Court Judge
Dated: 9/__/20__

J.D.C.
Sequence 1A

Warrant Issued With Stay Until 9/__/20__

HON. _____, JUDGE
OF THE SUFFOLK COUNTY DISTRICT COURT

At a Motion Term of the District Court of the State of New York, County of Suffolk

---

Petitioner,	Index No. BRLT __-_____
- against -	**ORDER TO SHOW CAUSE**
Respondent.	**TO VACATE DEFAULT**

Upon the affidavit of Respondent _____, sworn to on _____, and upon all prior papers and proceedings,

Let the Petitioner show cause at a Motion Term of this Court to be held at the Courthouse located at _____, _____, New York, on the __th day of _____, 20__, at 9:30 am, or as soon thereafter as the parties can be heard, why an order should not be entered vacating the default and/or the judgment granted in favor of the Petitioner and dismissing the proceeding, or setting the matter down for a hearing, and why the Respondent should not be awarded such other and further relief as may be just and proper.

Sufficient reason being presented for the relief requested, it is,

ORDERED, that pending the hearing and determination of this motion, the Sheriff and Petitioner and all of his/her agents are stayed from conducting any proceedings to enforce the judgment, and further it is

ORDERED, that Respondent serve a copy of this Order, and the papers upon which it is based, on Petitioner *pro se* at _____, _____, New York __, and the Sheriff of _____ County at _____, _____, New York _____, by personal delivery by the __th day of _____, 20__.

All papers the Petitioner wishes to submit in opposition to the Respondent's motion must be forwarded to the Court and Respondent's counsel prior to the hearing date. Personal appearance is required and oral statements will be considered on the return date of the motion.

Order signed at _____, New York
Date:_____

Enter,

J.D.C.

SUFFOLK COUNTY SIXTH DISTRICT COURT

PATCHOGUE, NEW YORK

Petitioner,

- against -

Respondent.

Index No. BRLT __-_____

**MOTION TO VACATE
DEFAULT JUDGMENT**

_____ being duly sworn, deposes and says:

1. I am the Respondent in the above-captioned summary proceeding wherein Petitioner seeks a final judgment of possession, a money judgment for alleged unpaid rent and a warrant to evict me from the subject premises.

2. Your deponent resides at the subject premises, located at _____, _____, New York _____. Together with my family, including my spouse and two (2) minor children, we have lived at this address for the past five (5) years.

3. This is an action for the non-payment of rent pursuant to a lease agreement my spouse and I entered into with the Petitioner-Landlord.

4. On _____, __, 20__, a default judgment, including a judgment of possession, a money judgment in the amount of $8,000 and a warrant of eviction, without stay, was entered by this Court.

5. I did not appear [*must state a reasonable explanation for not appearing*—e.g., because I was never served with the Notice of Petition and Petition. I first learned of this action when I called the Landlord last evening to complain that the heat was not working again. The Landlord told me that my family and I had to leave because the Petitioner prevailed in Court. When I explained that I did not receive any notices, the Landlord again stated we had to leave. I have since reviewed the Court's file, and note that the affidavit of service alleges that I was personally served with the Notice of Petition and Petition on _____, __, 20__ at 4:15 pm at the property address. The process server is mistaken as I was at work on that date at that time. I do not arrive home until about 6:30 pm in the evening. Moreover, the description indicates that a male approximately 35

253

years of age weighing about 250 pounds and standing 6' tall was served. As you will discover if the relief sought is granted and I am given the opportunity to defend myself, I am 48 years of age, 5'8" tall and weigh about 170 pounds. My son does not meet the description either and my other child is a female. In addition, the documents were not mailed to my address. At minimum, I am requesting a traverse hearing because I was not served and am disputing the allegations set forth in the affidavit of service].

6. In addition, your Deponent has a meritorious defense to the action. [*must state the possibility of a meritorious defense*—e.g., The rent is paid in full. I have attached a copy of the cancelled checks demonstrating that we are current on the rent including this month. In addition, the Petitioner did not name my wife as a party in the action even though she co-signed the lease with me and we are both listed as Tenants. Accordingly, my wife is a necessary party, and the failure to name her requires dismissal of the proceeding].

7. No previous application for this relief has been made.

WHEREFORE, deponent respectfully requests an order vacating the judgment entered on the __th day of _____, 20__, and dismissing the proceeding, or such other relief as may be just and proper.

Dated:

_____

Respondent

Sworn to before me this __th day

of _____, 20__

_____

Notary Public/Clerk

CLERK'S DEPARTMENT OF SOCIAL SERVICES EMERGENCY LETTER

(to assist Respondent in finding an alternative place to reside)

**Suffolk County District Court—
Sixth District
150 West Main Street
Patchogue, New York 11772**

Date: _____

TO: Department of Social Services

        Address

Re: _____ **v.** _____ **(Index No. __-BRLT_____)**

Sir/Madam:

Please be advised that the above-referenced matter was heard in this Court on the above date and disposition was as follows:

Judgment has been granted in favor of the Landlord against the Tenant for possession of the subject premises and a money judgment in the amount of $_____. In addition, a warrant of eviction is to be issued [without stay *or* with a stay on execution until _____, __th, 20__].

_____
CLERK OF THE COURT

Notes:

The Bench Guide to Landlord and Tenant Disputes in New York©
(Third Edition)

Notes:

The Bench Guide to Landlord and Tenant Disputes in New York©

(Third Edition)

Notes: